# Make More Money with Your Book

**From Getting Started to Creating Additional Materials, Online Campaigns, Podcasts, Blogs, Videos, Advertising, PR, and the Social Media**

## by Gini Graham Scott, Ph.D.

**MAKE MORE MONEY WITH YOUR BOOK**

# Table of Contents

7

# PART I: GETTING STARTED

# INTRODUCTION

The world of book publishing and sales has gone through a major transformation in the last decade, so if you aren't already famous, major book publishers and agents will generally not be interested in your book. The one exception is the very well-written novel that captivates an editor at a major publisher. So mostly, writers have to do their own marketing and PR, whether their book is published by a traditional publisher (usually one of the smaller or medium sized niche publishers) or self-published.

Since there are over 1 million new books published each year, the vast majority self-published, you have to do something to stand out. Otherwise, the average self-published book sells around 150 copies and most other books with traditional publishers sell in the low thousands or even less. If you are making about $2-5 per self-published book or .75-$1.00 in royalties on each traditional book, that isn't very much.

If you want your book to do well, you have to do more. You have to develop your own marketing and promotion campaign, and do it yourself or bring in assistants and affiliates to help you sell your book.

Here are 10 ways to help you make more money from your book, not just by selling it, but by developing related books and programs, getting more attention from the social and traditional media, and by marketing these materials effectively. This list will give you a general idea of the many things you can do to make more money. Then, choose among them for what you want to do and prioritize which ones you want to do first. *Monetizing Your Book* provides even more suggestions and describes how to implement these ideas to increase your income from your book and programs.

1) Create additional programs and products based on your book, such as workshops, seminars, webinars, CD and DVD packages, and consulting packages, which you can use to promote your book as well as gain additional sales.

2) Put on programs for local groups and contact the local press, and gradually develop a track record and video of what you are doing, so you can gain interest from speaking bureaus, meeting planners.

3) Get reviews from book reviewers on Amazon, independent book reviewers and bloggers, and book reviewers for magazines, newspapers, and Internet publications. Then, use the good reviews in your promotional and marketing copy.

4) Create short videos to promote your book and programs, as well as create a program on video which you can sell.

5) Create a website to feature your book and blogs. Put your blogs on your website, so when people are drawn to your blog, they also see your website. Create blogs of about 500-700 words at least once a week, but instead of talking about your book, talk about a related subject where you give people valuable information that can help them in their daily life. For example, if your book deals with education, write about trends in education; if your book deals with health, comment on new developments in health.

6) Develop an online sales and marketing program to promote and sell your books and other programs. While you can use your website for this purpose, another effective approach is to create an online sales campaign which includes a squeeze or landing page, a free gift, such as a book chapter, article, or report, and a sales page, where you present your offer. Other pages might promote a webinar or other materials based on your book.

7) Publish your book on multiple platforms, including ebooks on different formats, such as Kindle, and Smashwords. Plus you can make it available through many platforms, such as Scribd and GoodReads.

8) Actively promote your book and market your book on the social media, including Facebook, LinkedIn, and Twitter. Create frequent posts about your book or related activities, such as announcing when you are presenting a webinar. You can also post sales pages and promotional videos on Facebook, as well as links to your squeeze page. Join groups of individuals who might be interested in the topic of your book and post there, though provide information and advice in your posts, not just promotional and marketing information. That way, you become part of the conversation and establish your credibility, which will help people become interested in your book.

9) Contact reporters who are doing stories on your topic to present yourself as an expert who they might quote in a story in return for mentioning your book or website. You can work with various services that connect reporters to experts on a particular subject.

10) Contact the traditional media about your book if you can tie what you are writing to something in the news; then you become an authority who has written about that topic, and the media might want to include you in the story.

11) Go to business referral, networking, and Meetup groups in your area that have an interest in your topic. Typically, you briefly describe what you are doing and what you are looking for, and you can make a presentation of about 7-10 minutes to these groups after you are a member for a while.

Plus there are still other things you can do. You will see more information on these different strategies in *Monetizing Your Book,* along with other ways to make money from your book and any programs you develop based on it.

# CHAPTER 1: SETTING YOUR GOALS FOR MAKING MORE MONEY

Today, unless you are already famous, you have to take additional steps to increase book sales or use your book to obtain other income. These steps will also help you build your platform which will help you better sell your next book to a publisher or the general public.

You can use these tools wherever you are in the publishing process and whether you are published by a traditional publisher or self-publishing. Or in some cases, you may start with self-publishing and later find a traditional publisher for this or a follow-up book.

As a first step, assess where you are now.
1) You have a book or series of books to be published by a traditional publisher.
2) You have a completed manuscript(s) and are searching for a traditional publisher.
3) You have a book or series of books to self-publish.
4) You have an already self-published book or series.
5) A combination of the above, since you have one or more books with a traditional publisher, one or more manuscripts where you are seeking a traditional publisher, or one or more self-published books.

Wherever you are in the process, you can to monetize your book. Importantly, have a single goal or focus for each monetizing approach, so you can target the same market and use your marketing and sales materials to support that goal. Otherwise if you have books on different topics, you will scatter your efforts at sales, promotion, workshops, and other activities, and confuse your audience about what you are doing.

So pick one book or book series to start, so you concentrate your efforts on a single goal or target. By aiming all of your shots at a single target, you are more likely to hit it or get closer to a bullseye than if you aim at a second or multiple targets.

Next, determine which goal to focus on. If you have two or more topics you write about, choose one to start. Take into consideration what are you most passionate about and what you think has the most potential for a paying market.

Ideally, both elements will come together, so the money will follow in doing what you love. But sometimes what you love isn't very marketable, unless you can develop a way to market and get money for it.

For example, suppose you love hiking in the mountains, have written a memoir about your journey, and work at a health clinic that offers workshops on new ways to lose weight and get healthy. Maybe you could incorporate tips on losing weight and getting healthy into your memoir, since you have to stay fit for these long hikes. Then, you can combine your passion with health tips.

But suppose your topics don't really go together. Then, think of how you might turn your passion into something with broad appeal – such as incorporating your experiences in hiking with a guide for other hikers on how to have a successful hiking experience or great trails for hiking in the area. If you can't transform your passion into something you can sell to a broad market, choose the book or series that you think has the most potential for a paying market. Unless you are writing books for your own pleasure or for your family and friends, you have to think in terms of what will sell and build your marketing program around that.

To get started, do the following exercise. Ask yourself these questions and write down the answers:

1) What topic am I most passionate about?

2) What have I written about – or want to write about - that has the most potential for a paying market?

3) How can I make what I am most passionate about into a topic that will appeal to a broad market? Can I combine what I am most passionate about with the topic that has the most potential for a paying market?

4) Based on my answers to the previous questions, what is my goal for publishing? What do I want to focus on writing and publishing, which will have the most chances for success in making money?

Once you have your goal, you are ready to start working on turning this into a source of added income, beyond just selling the books.

# CHAPTER 2: BUILDING OTHER INCOME SOURCES FROM YOUR BOOK

No matter where you are in the publishing process, you can start thinking of ways to monetize your book through other sources of income. Or use some of the content in your book to promote it and these other income sources, such as writing articles and blogs. Anything you do will help build your "platform" – your visibility as an author, which will help you sell your book if already published or help you attract a traditional publisher if your book is not yet published.

Thus, even before your book is published, you can start doing things to make money from its content and increase your public persona. In effect, you are developing a branding campaign before or after your book is published, and this will both help book sales and your income from other sources, which will typically be much more than from your book however it is published. At the same time, having a published book can help you attract interest to whatever else you are doing to build your brand and monetize your message. So all these efforts combine together to create a more successful YOU!

As first step to monetizing your book and other spinoff projects, consider all of the different possibilities. You won't have time to do everything – though you can expand your efforts by delegating or outsourcing certain activities, especially the ones that you don't like or take time away from what you most want to do.

Here's a list of the different possibilities to consider. I'll discuss what to do about each of these paths to monetizing your book in subsequent chapters.

Consider the following activities as either ways to promote awareness about you and your subject or help you sell more books or other programs. In this way, you are building and promoting your brand and using it to increase your income, which can come directly from your book or from the related activities made possible by your book. Then, too, whatever you do to increase your income can help promote and build your brand, while promoting and building it can help you earn more, too.

You might think of this relationship as illustrated in the diagram below:

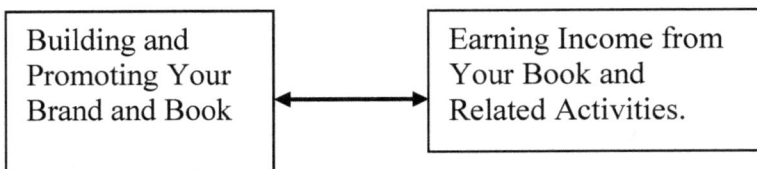

| Building and Promoting Your Brand and Book | ←→ | Earning Income from Your Book and Related Activities. |

Here are some of the related activities you can engage in to promote your brand or book and earn money.

- Creating and publishing articles and blogs
- Creating videos for YouTube, Vimeo, or other platforms
- Putting on webinars or teleseminars
- Creating and broadcasting podcasts
- Putting on workshops and seminars
- Engaging in joint ventures with individuals with related or complementary books, products, services, or programs
- Engaging in interviews or guest appearances on radio or TV shows
- Sending out press releases to the local and national press
- Creating squeeze and sales pages to sell your book or related programs
- Coaching to help others acquire your skills

- Turning your printed book into an ebook – or turning your ebook into a printed book
- Developing products based on your book's content
- Using email blasts or direct mail to promote your book or related activities
- Participating in panels
- Volunteering at trade shows, exhibits, or other events
- Joining and participating in organizations in your field or in business generally, such as in your local Chamber of Commerce.
- And more – whatever else you think of that can help build and promote your brand and book and earn you money.

# CHAPTER 3: POSITIONING YOUR BOOK FOR SUCCESS

Positioning your book effectively is a key to success since it helps to direct your book to your audience.   By doing this, you will do two key things:

1) Sell more books

2) Use your book to sell more related things, from products to services, including you as a speaker, seminar leader, and consultant.

You will be in a better position to sell a follow-up book and use that to sell other things.

If you have written a novel, these guidelines are less relevant, unless your novel is like a fictionalized memoir or in a setting where it might be linked to current conditions.  Otherwise, if it is historical fiction, sci-fi, romance, horror, or other fiction genres, these guidelines might not apply.

Positioning starts with how you write your book.   For example, if you are writing a memoir, think about how you might include take-aways or insights from what you learned for the reader. Or if you are writing about a devastating personal experience, think of how to end the book on a positive, uplifting note to show how you gained in some way from what happened.  Readers like to gain these insights as well as feel some satisfaction at the end of the book.

Another key consideration is the title.  If you have found a mainstream publisher, the publisher will normally choose the title, although you can provide some suggestions.  If you are self-publishing, think carefully about the title and ideally get some input from others, such as a business group or mastermind group, to see what they think.  Don't just get input from family and friends, since they may be more apt to like whatever you show them, since they want to support you, rather than giving you a more objective opinion.

Preferably, keep the title short – up to about 7 words, since it will be more memorable, and use the subtitle, if you have one, to more explicitly indicate what the book is about in up to about 15 words, so it fits in one or two lines on the cover. The trend is to use keyword that help the search engines find your book, rather than something cute and catchy. For instance, if your book is about finding that perfect date and mate, you might call it something like: *How to Find Your Perfect Date and Mate*, which clearly states what your book is about, rather than something like: *From Tinder to Tender*, which may need some explanation, especially for those who weren't heard of using the Tinder app for hook-ups.

Also, consider how you might take short excerpts from your book to use as give-away articles on websites, in blogs, and in ezines with a link to your book to help you both sell books and increase your visibility, so you are better able to get consulting and speaking engagements based on your book.

Once your book is positioned, you can use it to start building your position and monetizing your book, even before the book is published. You can start getting pre-sales even 6 months or more before the book's publication date, and you can use this future pub date to line up different income opportunities, from consulting and speaking to other possibilities. You can also show photos, covers, or prototypes of your future book to add to your credibility as you develop these various opportunities to make money from your book and any spin-off programs.

# CHAPTER 4: WORKING WITH AFFILIATES

Whether your book is published or not, one way to earn money as well as build your credibility and an audience is by finding affiliates you can team up with. Affiliates are someone with a product, service, or program you like, where you can get a commission for promoting what they are selling, when someone you refer to them buys that product, service, or program. An affiliate arrangement can be an ideal approach to use before you have your own products, services, or programs based on your book.

However, while anyone can become an affiliate for anything, when you are promoting a book or yourself, select affiliates with a product, service, or program in your own field. Then, you can tie yourself and your book to your promotion for your affiliate.

Importantly, the affiliate should complement whatever you or your book is about, and not be a direct competitor. Also, affiliates should have an already established platform, so you can build on their success and reputation. Moreover, you should get a large-enough commission for your referral (at least 10%, preferably 20-25%), depending on how much effort you are putting into making referrals. If you are just referring someone by name, 10% is a reasonable amount; but if you are creating a promotional page, commonly known as a "squeeze" page to pitch the affiliate's offering, then 20-25% is a more typical commission.

For example, if you are doing a memoir about experiencing difficult relationships or a self-help book about avoiding or getting out of difficult relationships, you might find an online workshop offered by a well-known relationships guru and market that along with your own book.

One way to do any marketing and sales is to set up a squeeze page, which is a free standing page or a page on your website, where you feature the offer describing why this is such a great product, service, subscription, or program. Sometimes you will get the copy from your affiliate along with a code your referrals can use or which you put on your own site. This way your affiliate knows you are making the referral in order to pay you a commission.

However you set up the offer, design your referral page, so you capture the person's email. Then, you can later pitch your own book or program, and as you add new books or programs, you can let the person with that email know. Another effective online sales approach is to offer the prospect a free gift of your own, such as a book chapter, which can result in sales of your book, as well as capture the person's email. To capture the email, ask the visitors to your site to fill in a form with their email, so you can send them their free gift.

If you are writing copy for what you are offering, use bullet points to highlight the main topics and benefits to the individual. As possible, offer special savings for acting now, and if your own book or program is now available, offer a lower price special for buying it now.

There are some tried and true methods for writing these squeeze pages, so they are very compelling according to online marketing specialists. One method is to use a short page with an image, headline, and short copy highlighting the main benefits of the program and urge the person to sign up now to get a discount or free gift. Another method is to use a longer sales pitch where you repeat the offer several times but in slightly different ways, and after each pitch, you include a buy button, so the prospect can immediately go to a buy page for your book or an affiliate's book or program. Each pitch builds up the appeal and need for the offer followed by the buy button, followed by more and different information making the offer more enticing, so the individual will keep reading and become more and more convinced, until he or she finally buys. The approach is like luring in a fish with a colorful lure, getting it closer and closer with each enticement, until it finally snaps its teeth around the hook – and in this case, instead of being cooked, he or she will enjoy the book or whatever else is being offered.

Meanwhile, whether you sell your own book or not, you are using it as a lure to offer related programs. Then, if the prospect has a good experience with the free gift offered as bait, he or she will be more responsive to your pitch for whatever you are selling, which you can make since you now have gotten that person's e-mail. Plus you have increased your name recognition in the field, because of your association with a more well-known person. Additionally you may sell some of our own books, when offering something else which is related and has a wide appeal, which can increase the appeal of your own book and other materials. After all, by being associated with something that is very popular and powerful, you gain some of the appeal of that offering.

Eventually, it's better to use a marketing approach to attract customers for your own products, services, and programs based on your book. Then you are not just getting a commission for marketing someone else's programs. But before then, an affiliate program is a good way to build your income, reputation, brand, and association with your book, and you can gain some sales, too.

# CHAPTER 5: BUILDING YOUR NICHE

Whether or not you have written and positioned your book, consider what your niche or niches should be, and focus on writing and promoting your books in that arena. This way you will direct your appeal to the target market for that niche, so your efforts will be more effective and efficient than if you try to appeal to everyone.

Preferably, pick one niche to start, and then you can expand to one or two other niches. It's best not to appeal to more than that number, since you will scatter your efforts like a shotgun shooting multiple pellets, rather than using revolver that hits the target more powerfully when you have the correct aim.

To choose your niche, consider what you have already written about or want to write about and look at the niches where it falls – or could fall with some tweaking. There are pre-existing markets for many of these niches, and that can help your marketing efforts if your book or program falls within an already established niche. In the event your book falls in two or more niches, emphasize the features of the book to appeal to that market. For example, if your work deals with going on hikes and hunting, emphasize the hikes to appeal to hikers; emphasize the hunting to appeal to hunters. Pitch your book to whatever niches apply. This promotion of a single book and related programs to multiple niches is different from having different books which appeal to different niches, which scatters your efforts.

For example, suppose you have a memoir in which you talk about how you became successful flipping homes in real estate after going through a program of weight loss and personal development, so you gained more confidence. Your primarily niche might be real estate investing, and then making money. Other niches would be weight loss, diet, and self-improvement. So you can emphasize different aspects of the book and your real estate flipping program, based on gaining the confidence to do this effectively.

By contrast, if you have one book on making money through for selecting winning stocks and another book on fly fishing, since you love relaxing after a hard day of picking stocks, those are two different niches. Start with the one that has the largest market first (i.e. the making money and investing in stocks markets) and build up a stream of income in that first, before you seek to make money from promoting a book to fishing fans or outdoors aficionados.

One advantage of targeting a pre-existing niche for your book and other related programs is that there is already an established audience in this niche that is receptive to buying multiple products and services on the same subject, as long as you show them a different approach. By doing so, you are just selling audience members on buying your book or other programs, not on the concept. They already know the benefits they might expect, because they have gotten other products and services in this niche.

Additionally, think about how to supplement your book with related programs of your own or an affiliate. Ideally, offer your own products, services, or programs for at least $25 and affiliate programs for $50 or more, so you are making enough with each sale. The reason for developing these programs or working with an affiliate is that your book sales, unless in the thousands or more, will not be a major source of income – but your book can be used to market other programs to that same niche.

So think about what else you can do that might be turned into programs that relate to the subject of your book and can be a source of income. Consider the various vehicles that might be used to promote your book and any products or programs, such as a blog, YouTube video, posting on Facebook and Twitter, and interviews with the traditional media. Also, think of what skills or services you can offer. In the long run, it is better to create your own products, services, and programs, rather than looking to affiliates, although you might use affiliate programs in the interim to make money and promote your own book and services.

To start, make a list of what you can do to help other people with whatever your book is about. For example, if your book is about overcoming problems with relationships at work, consider how you might help others deal with co-workers, employees, and bad bosses. Some possibilities might include:
- a workshop or seminar on how to overcome relationship problems at work,
- an online webinar on improving work relationships,
- a training video on how to deal with difficult co-workers, employees, or bad bosses.

If you decide on pitching for an affiliate, obtain or create the promotional materials, so people can sign-up. Highlight your published or forthcoming book in your promotional materials to build your credibility – and possibly sell some books. Initially, you might charge an introductory price for your first or second workshop, seminar, or webinar, or offer a discount for those opting to sign up before a certain date.

Also, develop any workshop, seminar, webinar, or training videos as needed. You can presell these programs to determine if there is a market; then quickly put together the materials you are selling. Or create these materials in advance. You can keep your costs down by creating these materials yourself, using photos from low-cost stock photo houses like the Dollar Photo Club (www.dollarphotoclub.com), and hiring film and video students at local schools to film and edit a simple video of you talking. Or project the slides you have created in a webinar service like GotoMeeting (www.gotomeeting.com) as you talk.

# CHAPTER 6: CREATING YOUR PRODUCTS

Creating your products can help you both sell your original book and the more specialized products for those who want to go deeper. These products can take the form of workshops, seminars, webinars, training videos, subscriptions, consulting packages, or other services you offer. I'll be referring to them collectively as "products," which can take multiple forms, from tangible and physical products to digital merchandise available online.

A first step is deciding what you want to sell in addition to your book, and then how to best package it. For example, rather than charging on an hourly basis for consulting with a client, though you can do this, too, for sales purposes, it is good to create a package which reflects what people commonly ask you about. Figure out how many hours you need to provide that service and put a price on your initial consulting arrangement – possibly charge even less than usual to get a client started in working with you. For example, if you charge $125 an hour and a typical initial consult is for 2 hours, you might have an introductory $195 consulting package and list what it includes (ie: an introductory 1 ½ hour session, two follow-up calls for 30 minutes each, and a recording of your session).

The particular type of product you choose will affect how you market it, such as whether it's a tangible product, like a workbook or DVD; a digital product, like a video or workshop to view online or download; or a seminar or workshop that has to be presented to a live audience.

Moreover, some products can be sold in multiple channels, such as a workshop or seminar based on your book. The first sales venue might be a face-to-face event in a physical location, such as a conference room or private home. Then, if you make an audio recording or videotape the session, you have a product you can sell on CDs, DVDs, or online. Should you do a series of workshops, you could turn this into a subscription program. Still another possibility is to create a workbook to go along with your book. Or perhaps your book lends itself to other products, such as posters, calendars, postcards, and greeting cards, or even a game based on the steps to reach the goal described in your book.

So take some time to consider what types of products best fit your book, and make a list of the products you might create to sell. Also, consider how you might use these products to sell your book (for example, you can sell your book at a workshop or when you offer this program online). At the same time, your book adds to your credentials for marketing these other products.

The next step is to create these products, so they are available once a customer places an order. Since physical products are more expensive to produce and market, I'll focus on programs you can make available online through Internet marketing, along with programs you can personally present and turn into online offerings. Often with such programs, you can repurpose the content, so you can use it in multiple ways.

To this end, some products to start with to develop to monetize your book are these:
1) a workbook, which can be available not only as a physical book, but as a PowerPoint or in a PDF file.
2) a workshop or seminar, which you present live, but then you make an audio or video recording of it to sell in different formats – on a DVD or flash drive; as a file to download available for downloading; as an online program which customers can access online, and as an interactive webinar, where participants can listen and ask questions live or through a chat function, and you can record that for future purchases.
3) an online workshop or seminar, which is available live for

those who want to attend; but then you create an audio or video recording, which subscribers can replay and you sell to them online.

While you can use any of these products to promote and sell your book, you can use the sales materials you develop for your book to sell your own related products or products for affiliates for a commission.

You can develop a growing number of programs for each book – for example, you can turn one or more chapters into a workshop or seminar, so you have a series of products developed from the different chapters in each book. As you write additional books, you can add material from them to your arsenal of products you can sell.

So that these opportunities to monetize your book don't seem daunting, start by picking one or two products to create and sell first. Then, develop your marketing, sales, and promotional system around that. Later, as you achieve success with one or two products, you can expand to add additional products and sell even more.

# CHAPTER 7: CREATING A WORKBOOK

A workbook with worksheets and supplemental materials to accompany your book can be a natural extension, and you can use these materials for a workshop or seminar, too.  In some nonfiction books, worksheets and supplemental, such as resources, are included.  If not, these can be readily developed for a workbook, and you can add to the worksheets and other materials in your book.

Unless you publish your workbook like a regular book, this can be marketed as a specialized product for individuals who want to go into your material in more depth, so you can charge more for it.  For instance, the typical price of a nonfiction book is about $20-30, while you can price your workbook at $35-50.  If you are using this in a workshop you are developing, include the price of the workbook in pricing the workshop.

The kinds of things to put in a workbook include the following:
- a form for people to write down their ideas, when you tell them to create a list or write down anything, such as indicating their goals, describing their favorite activities, or noting what they most like or dislike about something;
- a list of resources with the names of individuals, companies, addresses, contact information, and a short description of what an individual or company does or is looking for;
- a list of the most important tips and techniques to use in a particular situation;
- a list of vendors who provide supplies and services of interest to book writers and publishers, and their contact information;
- a summary of the key take-aways in each of chapter of the book, unless these are already in the book;
- a list of references for additional reading on the subject, unless this is already in the book;

- a list of frequently asked questions and answers posed by people who have read the book or have attended previous workshops;

- an offer with specials on additional products or programs by you or your affiliates;

- a checklist of the steps to follow in participating in a program suggested in your book, so people can check off the steps as they complete them;

- a "measure your progress" chart, in which people can indicate what they have done since using your products or putting your program into practice;

- a form where people can create their own to-do list of plan to do and when; this should also include a column on the tasks completed and when;

- testimonials from people who have read your book or taken your workshops and seminars.

In short, think of the various ways in which you can supplement your book with added tips, charts, lists, or other information that will help people put any tips and techniques described in your book into practice.

# CHAPTER 8: CONDUCTING A WORKSHOP OR SEMINAR

A workshop or seminar based on your book is an excellent tool for monetizing your book. Besides selling your book there, you can make money for the workshop or seminar. You can also record the seminar on an audio recorder or arrange for a videographer to film it, and can use either volunteer or low-cost videographers from local schools or film groups or a professional videographer. While it's great to have a live audience, you can create a workshop or seminar without an audience and market an audio recording or video of it.

If you are a speaker or panelist at a conference or you could use that event to get a short pitch or video trailer for your program, as well as to sell or promote your book at the event. You can use the program for advertising your upcoming workshop or seminar, too.

Skip doing book signings or talks in book stores, since they generally don't sell many books, and often you may only attract a small crowd. If you are celebrity stopping at a book store to sell books, everything changes. Otherwise, if you are a relatively unknown author, book signings commonly draw a half-dozen to a dozen or so attendees, and only a few of them will buy your book.

Assuming you want to create a workshop or seminar where you do a presentation to a live audience, here are the next steps.

- Consider what the program will be about, how long it will be, and how much you want to charge, which is commonly based on the length of the program. One approach is to feature the highlights of the book in a single workshop; then if there is sufficient interest, you might have a follow-up program with either additional information for a broad and hopefully larger crowd or a smaller follow-up program to delve more deeply into the topics you covered. Often you can charge for such a follow-up program. For example, say your book is about building a good relationship with a person you have met online. In the first workshop, you might cover the basic considerations, such as meeting in a public place, getting to know the person, and how and when to become more serious. In a more focused workshop, you might address individual questions about problems that come up in the relationship or how to know if the person you are with is really honest.

- Another approach is to divide your book into a series of programs based on different chapters or different parts of the book. Clearly indicate this in your introductory promotional materials and highlight what you will focus on in each week. Then, as in the first model, if there are questions beyond the time or scope of the first meeting, you can create a follow-up program to address individual questions.

The next step is to develop your materials, based on the length of your program. Some common formats for workshops and seminars are about 1 ½ to 2 ½ hours for a morning, afternoon, or evening program. Allow the first 15 minutes to half hour for networking, light refreshments, and getting everyone settled to listen to the presentation. You might include copies of your book at the check-in desk or at a table in the front of the room, so attendees can look at it and ideally buy a copy before the presentation begins.

Plan for 1 to 1 ½ hours for the presentation, with about 10-15 minutes for questions, and conclude with more networking, along with selling your book. Depending on your style, use a PowerPoint to feature the main points of your presentation or not. If you use a PowerPoint, put short points on your slide, so you can use these as a jumping off point to give more information about that point. Don't try to create sentences or extended explanations like you might in a book. Consider the PowerPoint slides more like a structure or frame to keep your talk focused and on target; then expand upon these major points. This way you continue to engage with your audience, rather than detaching as you read the main points on a series of slides.

Also prepare a handout for your presentation, which includes your contact information and information about getting your book, along with a photo of your book and ideally a photo of yourself, either as a portrait or as a photo of you holding the book. If you already have or soon will have workbooks, audio recordings, or videotapes of your program for purchase or are consulting on the topic, include information about that. Finally, include doing consulting on the topic, a brief description of your program and the main topics covered are on handout. If this is one of a series of programs, indicate the main titles of other programs in the series. Ideally, put all of this information on a single one-sheet, or at most two pages back-to-back.

If you are skilled at writing and putting together a basic handout or flyer, you can create this in Word and insert one or two photos. Then, print your handout or flyer as needed. If you send this information to anyone as an attachment, turn your Word document into a PDF and send that. Or if someone else will be adapting the flyer to include their contact or other information, send a Word document, so he or she can edit that. If you want a more polished one-sheet and have the budget for this, hire a graphic designer to put together these materials for you.

Adjust your program for different groups, based on the interests of the audience and the time allotted. For instance, if you are on a panel, you typically have 5 to 10 minutes to introduce yourself and your program; if you are a keynote speaker, you usually have 15 to 30 minutes; and if you are doing a workshop, you have 1 to 2 hours, allowing for some networking and refreshments before and after the program.

So now, with your program and handouts prepared, you are ready for the next step – finding an organization to work with to present your program or setting up your program and promoting it yourself.

# CHAPTER 9: PUTTING ON PROGRAMS FOR LOCAL GROUPS

Once you have developed your talk or workshop and have a one-sheet to describe it, the next step is to put on some local programs. One approach is to go through already established organizations. The other is to organize your own program and invite attendees, possibly by using a platform like Meetup to spread the word.

In either case, when you start doing this, you may not be able to charge for the programs or only charge a small amount. But figure on putting on these first programs as a way to build up a track record and get testimonials for future programs. You can use these programs to sell more books and set up individual consultations with attendees.

Ideally, get testimonials from attendees which you can use in announcing and promoting future programs. You can ask attendees to write up something after the program, or print up a testimonial sheet which you hand out. Ask attendees to include their company name, if they have one, and their city and state.

You can also arrange to record these programs, using a digital recorder or smart phone for an audio recording. Or have a videographer come, record, and edit the program, showing not only you but the audience in attendance. You can later use these recordings or videos to promote future programs as well as sell these materials, just as you might promote an online webinar.

# Setting Up Programs with Already Established Groups

The easiest way to get started is to contact established groups who might be interested in a talk, seminar, or workshop on your topic. Then, you simply present your program and the group members and guests attend, though you might increase the number of attendees by announcing the event to our own email and social media contacts.

The subject of your book will affect which groups you contact. When you make this contact, ask for who in the organization makes arrangements for speakers. Then, call or send that person an email, send an email and follow-up with a phone call, or call first and send an email with further details.

For any subject, local writer groups may be one source, especially if your book can help writers do something better, though many writers will be interested in other topics that appeal to them. So look for writer groups and chapters of groups in your area, such as the California Writers Club (http://calwriters.org) or Nonfiction Authors Association (http://nonfictionauthorsassociation.com). Check in Google search to find local groups by putting in terms like "writers," "authors," and "book clubs," plus your city or zip code.

Other groups which are always looking for speakers are church groups, civic groups like the Rotary, library groups, and community groups. Check your local directories or search online for local groups to find contact information.

Additionally, check for groups in your industry in your city, county, and neighboring city and counties.

Another source of leads is each city's Chamber of Commerce. Many have a printed or online directory, and most Chambers have after-work mixers which you can attend. When you call or meet people at mixers, just mention that you are looking for speaking engagements to talk about certain topics based on your book and follow-up from there.

When you reach someone who is interested, follow-up with your one sheet about your book and topics of your talks. If you later have a one-on-one meeting, be sure to bring your book.

Once you set up a program, follow the organization's guidelines on what to do next. Work out the details for what you will bring for your event, such as a DVD or flash drive for the organization's projector or your own laptop, if you have a PowerPoint or video to present. Plan to arrive about 15-30 minutes early to test out any equipment and hook-ups, so your presentation is ready to go. Bring flyers to pass out with information on ordering your book, arranging for consultations, or obtaining any other products or services from you. Find out how many people to expect, so you can have enough flyers to distribute, and bring some books, so people can buy now if they want, while others can order from your flyer.

Usually, the organizers will have their own format for introducing you, so give them the information they need from you to do that.

If you can, get business cards from attendees, so you can add them to your mailing list to send them more information about your book and online products. One way to get their email is to offer a free gift, such as a report delivered via email with a more in-depth look at your topic if they give you a business card after the meeting.

# Organizing Your Own Programs

In organizing your own programs, you are putting on the same program as for another group. The big difference is that you are making the arrangements about where to have the program and have to get the attendees yourself.

In selecting the location, you might be able to get a free venue, such as a room in a local restaurant or coffee shop. Often these companies may give you the room for free, in return for you promoting their company to others in your network or getting attendees to purchase food or beverages. Other sources of rooms are your local library, community center, or bank. Another possibility is your own house if your place is large enough or relatively close and accessible. For example, I have used my living room, which seats up to about 15 people, and its in an ideal location, since I am about a half-mile from the BART (Bay Area Rapid Transit) stop for my city, so it is easy for people to get here from all around the Bay Area.

To get attendees, you can use a platform like Meetup (www.meetup.com) or post announcements on a community email forum. Eventbrite, which does online ticketing and payments, also sends out announcements about upcoming events. You can use the social media, such as Facebook, if you have already built up a following.

In general, I have found the Meetup platform is ideal for creating interest groups in a particular topic and announcing a program to the group. After you create your group, select a catchy name for it which is clear about what you are doing, such as "A Meeting Place for the Newly Divorced and Widowed" if you have written a book on relationships for the this group. Also, it's best to create your first meeting within three days of setting up the Meetup platform, since that's when Meetup announces your group to all those who have selected corresponding categories of interest (such as relationships, singles, dating). Create appealing copy to describe your group, and in your bio information, include information on your book. Include a program with bullet-points of the main topics you will cover, so potential attendees know what to expect.

Initially, it is best to make your first meeting and any program you present free to introduce the new group and build interest. Then, start charging, starting at about $10 per person. After a couple of successful programs, you can go to $15, $20, or even more.

When you organize your own program, allow about 15-30 minutes before the program for individuals to arrive and network with each other. Then, start with short introductions in which you ask people to take about 15-30 seconds each to say what they do in the real world and what they hope to gain from your program. Briefly introduce yourself and begin your program. Unless you want to make the meeting interactive, ask people to hold questions until the end and present your program. Leave about 15-30 minutes at the end for questions and a more informal discussion based on what participants are most interested in knowing about.

Afterwards, get any written testimonials. Invite people to send in their testimonials later if they wish, though try to get theses testimonials now, since most people don't send them in later. Perhaps give out a sheet for comments, so attendees can easily write their testimonials and other comments now. Ask for evaluations as well, so you can make your next programs even better, and asked people to either write these down or tell you personally.

## Building on These Programs for the Future

Eventually, you can start doing PR for these programs, though initially do the first few programs to polish your presentation. Ehen you record these presentations, you can use the audio tracks or videos to create online programs which you can sell.

If you are still polishing up your program, consider the first presentations to local groups as a trial run.

Once you are ready, you can turn the material in your programs into packages you can sell. This is also when to start doing PR about your programs to obtain even more attention and sales for your book as well as your other materials.

# CHAPTER 10: CONTACTING THE LOCAL PRESS

Once you have a published book and start doing local programs, you can contact the local press to start building your portfolio to use in your promotion, get paying speaking engagements, and gain wider exposure in the media.

There are four ways to develop local press interest:

1) Get an editor, reporter, or local radio/TV producer or host to do a story about you.

2) Send in an article which gets published with your byline and bio information at the end.

3) Build up recognition for your expertise in a certain area, so reporters call on you to ask for your opinion and quote you in a print article or radio/TV news piece.

4) Tie what you are doing to a story in the news and contact the press by phone or email to let them know of the local angle.

## Getting an Editor, Reporter or Local Radio/TV Producer or Host to Do a Story

To get interest in a story about you, think about what makes you, your book, or the programs you are doing especially interesting. You might include your one-sheet in your follow-up information. Also put together a press release (or hire a publicist or writer to do this) in which you highlight the most interesting facts about you.

One approach for you or someone who is good on the phone is to call first to present your story in a 15-30 second elevator pitch. If the contact is interested, you can follow up with your one-sheet, press release, and anything else the press person asks you to send. If you don't have anyone to call for you, it can be more effective if you call as your assistant, because you can better promote yourself and talk about how good you are at what you do, whereas if you call your praise of your own accomplishment may sound too self-congratulatory.

An alternate approach is to send an email with a brief introductory letter , which is adapted from the information in the press release but turned into a personalized letter.  Such a letter can be especially effective if the contact is hard to reach, since after getting a personal letter, he or she might call you.  If you don't hear anything, follow up in a day or two to check if the person got the email and wants to know more.  If he or she didn't get anything, resend the letter – and this time the person should expect it and is more likely to get it and respond.

## Send in an Article for Publication

To send an article for publication, prepare a short article of 500-1000 words on the topic in your book and invite the editor of the newspaper, magazine, or Internet publication to use it, along with your bio information and link to your website.  Ideally, the publication will include your website in your bio, though some publications may not be permitted to do this.  Usually you can include your company name, and as long as your website is under your name or company name, readers will be able to find you.

While some authors get paid for articles and columns, these are usually staff writers or already nationally known columnists with syndicated articles.  So generally, consider any articles you submit as a form of PR to get you increased visibility that could turn into more book sales, interest in your seminars and workshops, and other programs.

One way to offer these articles is to send a letter to selected editors with a copy of your article and bio at the end, along with an offer to send a series of articles in the future. Generally, writing these weekly or every two weeks is a good timeline. Sometimes the editor will want first rights in a particular area until the article is published, although commonly, since you aren't getting paid, the editor will publish on a non-exclusive basis and won't ask about your offers from other publishers. So generally, you can offer an article to multiple publishers in an area, and if the first rights question comes up, you can select the preferred publication.

You can use a similar approach in contacting editors nationally about using your article. In that case, a service that sends out a blast of personalized emails such as the PR and Networking Connection (www.prandnetworkingconnection.com) is a good way to quickly send out an offer of your article to multiple publishers at the same time. For example, I did this after an article about income equality today compared to conditions in the Middle Ages appeared in the Huffington Post. I sent out a blast and the article was picked up by about 40 newspapers and Internet publishers, which contributed to my getting a deal to publish a book on the subject.

You can also offer these articles to bloggers, since sometimes bloggers use these articles as a guest blog.

## Build Up Recognition for Your Expertise

To gain recognition for your expertise, you can do much the same things as in pitching editors on writing an article about you or sending in your article for publication. The key now is to keep on doing this. You want to keep your name top of mind, so editors are likely to call you when they need someone to give them an expert opinion for an article they are writing or want a quote they can use for a story on some recent news developments where your expertise might be a good fit.

You can also send a letter or press release about you as an expert in certain areas, so if a writer needs a source, you can help. In this case, highlight the main subjects you can talk about, using bullet points for each topic. In some cases, sending a short letter and the copy in your one sheet might be all you need to get your name and topic in front of an editor. Then, every month or so, send in another letter or press release to remind the editor of what you are doing, so you stay top of mind.

## Tie In What You Are Doing to Something in the News

A great way to become quickly prominent is if what you are doing can be tied to something in the news and you can emerge as a spokesperson on that topic because of your book. You might potentially go national quickly if the story gains traction, and other national news people call on you to further comment on the story.

So look for news stories where you might contribute your expertise. For example, if a research study shows a new breakthrough in understanding memory and your book is about how to improve your memory, call and/or email a science or news editor to offer the findings from your workshops to add to the story. So check out the news each day in your local paper or on the Internet to see how you can add to the conversation.

## Using Multiple Approaches and Building on Past PR

You can use any one or a combination of approaches. Multiple ways to contact the press is a good idea, because it increases your visibility. It's the squeaky wheel approach to the news – the wheel that squeaks more often and louder is more likely to get more oil.

However you contact the media, document any press coverage. Include it in a page of press coverage in a printed or PDF press kit, or record this material online on your website. As you get additional press notice, add this to your one-page press notice or your press kit. Put the listings in reverse chronological order to feature the most recent press coverage first.

Once you accumulate a dozen or more press features (which can include being quoted in an article or being on a talk show panel), divide the coverage you get into categories, such as:
Newspapers
Magazines
Online (or Internet) Media
Radio and TV

As your coverage expands, you can further divide this by the press features in different areas (such as in different regions of the U.S. or even different countries).

Initially, include all good press coverage, but as your media campaign expands, include only the latest or more important features in the highest circulation or most well known media. Consider selecting which items to include like curating a museum or art gallery show. Pick your best items that give the best impression.

All of these approaches can be applied to get national and even international press, but the goal of starting local is so you build up some local coverage which will help you gain national interest. Otherwise, you might easily get lost in the sea of eager authors and other hopefuls seeking to get noticed and featured in the press.

Consider the process like building a relationship. You may not get immediate coverage, but local press people will start to remember you, so when you contact them again, they may be more receptive. Also, they may recall you when they are working on a story or need a quote from an expert on a subject for an article.

# CHAPTER 11: BUILDING YOUR PORTFOLIO

As you start doing workshops and seminars for local groups and start getting press coverage, collect this material together into a portfolio which could take several forms:

1) a print portfolio, which you can put in a binder to show at one-on-one meetings or turn into a PDF to send to media contacts,

2) a PowerPoint presentation, which you can show at group meetings,

3) a photo video, in which you use still photos to illustrate what you have done at events, on your website, and your social media pages,

4) a video with clips, which you can show at events, on your website, and on your social media pages.

Portfolio building is extremely important, because it demonstrates the growing interest in what you are doing to multiple audiences who might be interested. These include organizers and meeting planners who might invite you to do a program for their organization, speaking bureaus that might want to represent you, news reporters and editors who might write about you or print your articles, and potential customers for your book or programs.

Having a portfolio helps to show you are professional and reinforces your credibility and presence as an expert in your field. Also, a portfolio helps to open the doors to even bigger organizations and media coverage.

Think of your portfolio as a changing and evolving collection of information about yourself, your book, your programs, and your media coverage. So as you do more programs and get more press coverage, feature the most recent items and the ones from the largest and most noteworthy organizations, publications, and press people first. In this way, your portfolio grows and evolves as you gain more and more recognition for what you are doing.

Putting together a print portfolio is a good starting point to get together the various materials, which you can later scan to create a PDF. You can also scan these materials to create JPEGs you can use in a PowerPoint, photo video or video with clips. The basic materials to include in your portfolio are the following:
- a one-sheet about your book
- a one-sheet about your programs
- a photo of your book
- photos of you doing your programs or from your book
- a press release – or two, if about different stories or angles
- a list of programs for different organizations, including the names of the organizations and groups – and if a significant number of attendees (say 50 or more) include the numbers
- a list of frequently asked questions – or the questions you would like the press to ask you.
- copies of articles which have appeared about you in the print media or online
- a list of articles you have written
- a list of publications that have featured your article
- a list of media appearances, including the names of the publications or the talk or news shows, and the host and date for each show.

You can select from this portfolio what you feel is most relevant to include for a particular pitch – or in some cases, use it all.

After compiling this material about your publications and media appearances in a file, you might create an Excel file to keep track of this information. Set up a column for each publication or appearance, along with the name of the editor, producer, or host, the date of the publication or appearance, a phone number and email for further communication, and other information about that appearance.

In creating a PowerPoint presentation, pull out the highlights to create the slides for a 5 to 15 minute presentation – typically about 6-24 slides. If you print out handouts, put 6 on a page. Besides showing this presentation to a group that might be interested in what you are doing, such as a business to business leads or referral group, you can turn any presentation into a PDF or series of JPEGs.

To create a photo video, insert a series of JPEGs into a photo video program, such as Animoto (www.animoto.com). You can add music from the photo video application or obtain royalty free music from the many royalty free music services, such as Pond5 (www.pond5.com). I have used both of these services to create a dozen photo videos of books I have written or helped clients sell to publishers, and then I have posted these videos on YouTube and I have included some on my websites.

You can use photos from your books or workshops to illustrate the main topics you cover in your programs. It's best to keep these photo videos to about 2-3 minutes each, where the video features each photo for 2 or 3 seconds and then goes on to the next. You can add in a voice-over commentary if you want as an advanced feature in these photo video programs. The 2-3 minute format is good for a photo video, since this is the typical attention span of someone who comes to your website or listens to you do a presentation.

Finally, a video is ideal for showing the highlights of your portfolio along with clips of you putting on your program or doing of media appearances. Often you can get the clip of our video from the TV station airing your interview; or you can arrange for a video service to record your interview on the air. The TV station may have a recommendation of one or more services who do these recordings, or you can search on Google for a video service in your area that does this.

To make a video with clips, unless you are skilled at video editing, go to a professional video service to edit together your clips. A photo video is ideal to put on your website – or post it on YouTube or on Vimeo with a link from there to your website. You can use this video with clips of you and your book and programs if you make pitches to organizers and meeting planners to put on programs, to business groups to show what you do, and to prospective clients in one-on-one meetings. These videos are also ideal if you are in a trade show and have a laptop and monitor where you can show your video.

In sum, start gathering together material for your portfolio featuring information about you and your book, programs, publications, and media appearances early on. This portfolio will help you in increasing your visibility, the power and reach of your programs, and the money you can earn from your book and additional programs.

# CHAPTER 12: CONTACTING SPEAKERS BUREAUS AND MEETING PLANNERS

Once you have begun building your portfolio or platform as a speaker and are ready to expand your programs nationally – or even internationally, you are ready to contact speakers bureaus to represent you and meeting planners to hire you for events.

To contact either, you need at least a one-sheet featuring a photo and bio, your main topics, and some references or testimonials.  In addition, you need a video featuring clips of your programs, along with some introductory copy about what you speak about.  Even if you have used some video samples before to show one or more previous programs, if you don't already have a professionally produced video, you should invest in one.  Figure on about $1500-2000 for a good video, which will not only include your best clips from previous programs and any TV programs, but strong graphics and copy introducing you and your topics.

For example, one professional speaker video that impressed me showed the speaker appearing on the stage to loud claps in the background.  The copy then introduced the name of the speaker and the focus of his talks – "unleashing the leader in you" – which was featured in large, swirling type followed by an explosion of fireworks and stars.  The next part of the video was divided into sections, where each section began by announcing his major topic followed by a 15-20 second video clip of him talking about that topic.  Finally, the video concluded with contact information for more details and to arrange a booking.

Your other materials might include more details, such as what you might include in your press kit:
- a page or two of testimonials and endorsements,
- a list of PR appearances,

- a list of published books,
- articles,
- some photos.

Plus you might include other relevant items to help make the case for hiring you.

Additionally, put together a short letter to introduce yourself in an email or write up a very short phone script introduction, such as a sentence or two of up to about 50 words, so you can quickly state your pitch to be a speaker. Include your name and topic and 1 or 2 highpoints to entice the speaker bureau contact or meeting planner to want to know more. Once they request more information, that's when you send your one-sheet, a link to your video, and other material in your information packet.

You can target some speakers bureaus and meeting planners in your field to contact individually. Other sources of speakers bureaus include the International Association of Speakers Bureaus (www.iasbweb.org) and a directory available from the Complete List of USA Speakers Bureaus and Lecture Agents that was compiled by Lilly Walters, the daughter of Dotty Walters, a long-time supporter of the speaking industry. (http://www.paidpublicspeaking.com). You can also do a search for individual speaking bureaus that feature a wide variety of speakers or specialize in a particular topic through Google.

It can take some time to make these individual contacts, and many lists don't include emails, though you can find them by looking on the websites for each bureau. To save the time and expense of obtaining all of this information yourself, you can use an email query service that has already created a database of speaking bureaus and can send out a personalized query for you, such as Publishers, Agents & Films (www.publishersagentsandfilms.com).

Similarly, you can contact meeting planners individually. One way to do this is to join the Meeting Planners International ([www.mpiweb.org](www.mpiweb.org)) as a Supplier Meeting Professional, which is a person or company who provides and/or sells products and services to the meetings industry, including being a speaker. This membership will enable you to obtain access to MPI's online directory, where you will find meeting planners listed by city, country, and chapter, based on different regions of the United States or other countries. In addition, you can participate in activities with you local chapter, which include various workshops, seminars, and networking events. The cost is about $500 a year. Alternatively, if you are looking for meeting planners in the U.S., you can use the email query service noted above, Publishers, Agents & Films, ([www.publishersagentsandfilms.com](www.publishersagentsandfilms.com)), since it has a database of U.S. meeting planners, and can send out a personalized query to planners in selected areas of the country.

Generally, speakers bureaus don't require an exclusive relationship, though some of the larger ones may request this, although they are more competitive in getting representation with them. If a speakers bureau does ask for an exclusive, clarify what they will do for you in return to help you decide. Typical fees for setting up speaking engagement are about 25%.

Even if you do get representation by one or more speakers bureaus, don't expect to get all of your bookings from them. Typically, they account for 10-20% of a speaker's bookings, and they are better able to book speakers who are active in pitching their own bookings and have acquired a strong reputation in their field. So even if you find a speakers bureau to represent you, continue to contact meeting planners and other event organizers to set up speaking engagements, workshops, and seminars.

Finally, to get more information about being a professional speaker and meet with other speakers, you might join the National Speaker's Association ([http://www.nsaspeaker.org](http://www.nsaspeaker.org)). The organization has chapters all over the U.S., which have meetings in major cities, and there is a national convention each February. As a new speaker, you can join their Academy for Professional Speaking for a $175 initiation fee and $49 a month, which will provide you with all sorts of tools and techniques for becoming a professional speaker. The professional membership after the initiation fee is $465 a year, and to qualify, you have to have given at least 20 paid speaking programs or earned at least $25,000 from speaking in a year. Should you have products or services that might be of interest to professional speakers, you can join as a Professional Affiliate.

# CHAPTER 13: PUBLISHING IN MULTIPLE FORMATS

You can increase the money for each book you self-publish by publishing on multiple platforms. If you have a traditional publisher, it will be up to the publisher as to what you can do, unless your publisher is only doing print or ebook publishing, so you can publish on other platforms where you have the rights. If you have a contract with a publisher, check what rights you have, and if you get back the rights, such as after the publisher decides to no longer publish or doesn't publish your book within the time limit indicated to publish in your contract.

When you self-publish any books, include a link for more information about you and your other books and programs. You can include links to your website, squeeze page, or sales page inside your book – ideally up to three times, once in front on your author information page, another in the middle, when you mention other sources of information, and at the end of the book, with your contact information. Just don't overdo it, so your book seems like a sales piece.

Typically, pricing for ebooks on different platforms is around $2.99, though you can charge more for specialized content, such as if you are publishing books with financial tips on investing saving money, or mortgage financing – perhaps charge $3.99 up to $9.99 for those. However, you can also set a lower $.99 or $1.99 price for more exposure, especially if you are selling a novel, although sometimes a low price on a nonfiction book can suggest the book may not be that good. Try experimenting with different prices to see the audience response – and you can always raise or lower the price.

Another strategy is to make your first books free, at least for a time, to generate leads for other books and programs, when readers click on your links inside your book to your website, squeeze page, or sales page.

Any of these books, and especially the books you are using for leads, can be fairly short – say about 5000 to 10,000 words, which works out to about 25-50 pages.

## Getting Started

A good starting point is first publishing on Amazon. I personally like publishing on CreateSpace, which is owned by Amazon, or on Kindle. CreateSpace offers a great print-on-demand package at no charge if you create your own Word or PDF file to upload. You can use one of their templates plus a photo of your choice for the cover, or create your own design. Examples of about 40 books I have created through CreateSpace are at www.changemakerspublishing.com, and I help others publish their books on CreateSpace. Or you can use many other self-publishing services, which usually start with a Word or PDF file, though most have charges. By contrast, the CreateSpace program is free, though they have their own design services.

One of the advantages of CreateSpace program is that it is linked directly to Kindle, so with a few clicks you can publish there, and you can indicate that Kindle should use the cover you have already created in CreateSpace. Kindle will also convert your CreateSpace Interior file, though you can upload your interior file directly.

Alternatively, if you first publish your book in Kindle, you can easily publish it in CreateSpace. As with CreateSpace, you upload a Word document or PDF.

When you publish with Kindle, don't enroll in the Kindle Select program, since that gives Kindle an e-book exclusive for 90 days, and then it automatically reenrolls you for another 90 days. The program is designed to make your book free during this period for Amazon Prime members. As Amazon describes it:

> "KDP Select is an optional program for you to reach even more readers and gives you the opportunity to earn more money. If you choose to make a book exclusive to the Kindle Store, which is a requirement during your book's enrollment in KDP Select, the book will also be included in Kindle Unlimited (KU) and the Kindle Owners' Lending Library (KOLL). You can earn a share of the KDP Select Global Fund based on how many pages KU or KOLL customers read of your book. By enrolling your book in KDP Select, you will also be eligible to earn 70% royalty for sales to customers in Brazil, Japan, India, and Mexico."

However, in my experience, you don't make any additional money this way and you are unlikely to make sales in the four countries listed anyway. The big problem is the exclusivity to selling on other platforms. So don't enroll in the first place, or if you do, sign in and go to each book in your Kindle Account, click on "Manage my book on KDP, open up the drop down Book Actions menu to the right, click on KDP Select Info, and uncheck the box that says: "Automatically renew this book's enrollment in KDP for another 90 days." Your book will need to remain in KDP select for whatever term you have left, and then you are no longer enrolled.

## Preparing Your Interior and Cover Files

Depending on which platform you use, you need a Word, PDF, or epub file to upload, as well as a cover.

When you use a Word document or regular PDF, you will sometimes get an error message about the fonts not being embedded properly, so the program has tried to find as close a match as possible, which is usually fine. However, if you create a PDF from Word, go to Print and then to Properties, and instead of Standard, click the down arrow, and select PDF/X-1a2001. This will give you a printer-ready PDF, which embeds the fonts. It's best to keep your formatting simple, such as using only Heading 1 and 2, and possibly Heading 3, and limiting the number of JPEGs in the document.

If you use the Word or PDF files for a Print-on-Demand book like CreateSpace, be sure to format these for whatever size book you have selected. While 6x9 is the standard, other common sizes are 5.5x8.5, 8x10, and 8 1/2x11. Whatever size you select, set your page size to that format, and set the margins to those you expect to use in the final book, such as .75 for most 6x9 books. Resize any pictures to fit in these margins. You will see the required margin sizes once you know the number of pages, so if your book is 400 pages or more, you need a wider margin. Perhaps use a large book size in that case for a lower page count

One of the reasons I like starting with CreateSpace (or other print-on-demand program) is you can create the cover with a template or graphic designer. Once you publish your book, you will get a JPEG of your cover which you can use for your e-book, and you just download this cover JPEG into Kindle.

If you start with an ebook that accepts Word or a PDF, you can upload the original, since the program will reformat the book to the standard ebook reader size on a phone or tablet. It will be a responsive format, so it can adapt to the size of the phone or tablet.

The other file format to use for publishing on other platforms is an epub file. This can be difficult to format yourself, so it's best to outsource it to someone who does these conversions. One recommended source is Fiverr (http://www.fiverr.com). To find providers, put "convert files to epub" in the Fiverr search engine and you will find over a dozen people who will do a conversion for $5. It's worth trying out a few of these people at $5 each until you find one you like for converting additional files. One man who does these conversions and is recommended by Debbie Drum, an online marketing expert who publishes about a book a week, is tlmason, who has this offer on Fiverr below.

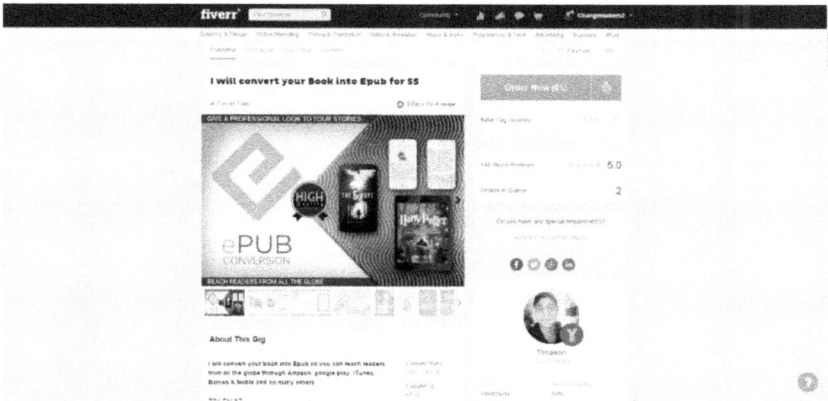

So now you're ready to start signing up for accounts and uploading files onto various platforms, as described in the next section.

# CHAPTER 14: POPULAR PLATFORMS

Once your files are ready, you can publish them to various e-publishing platforms, though you can set up your accounts before then, so you can publish when you are ready.  These major platforms include:
- iTunes (from Apple)
- Nook (from Barnes and Noble)
- Kobo
- Draft2Digital (an aggregator for multiple platforms)
- Smashwords (another aggregator for multiple platforms)
- Scribd

While it can be more profitable to sign up with these sites directly and your book might be listed more quickly, it might be worth connecting through an intermediary like Smashwords or Draft2Digital, because of the big savings in time, rather than creating your own account on each one.  After spending an hour trying to set up an iTunes account, only to learn you can't publish directly there with a PC, I think it's worth the commission – about 15% -- these intermediaries take.  Plus these intermediaries have their own sales platforms.  Perhaps publish some books direct and others through an intermediary to see what works best for you.  You can always select which platforms an intermediary should exclude from their sales if you already have some directly published books on a site.  You don't need an ISBN, since generally these digital publishers assign one to you.

Since you have a nonexclusive with all of these platforms, you can potentially agree to have a new company distribute to a store where you already distribute direct through another company.  If so, set the same price with each distributor.

You can set the price, or if you wish make it free, and you can change the price at any time, which could be a good way to test the market at different prices.

## iTunes

The only way to publish on iTunes in the iBookstore is if you have a Mac, create an account, and sign-up as a producer. If you don't have a Mac, you have to go through a third party aggregator, and Apple helpfully provides a list of its partners. There's no charge to list each book and you don't need an ISBN. The iBooks Store only accepts books created with iBooks Author (.ibooks) or books in the EPUB (.epub) format. The reason you can't upload an .epub book if you don't have a Mac, is that you have to install iTunes Producer from the iBooks Store, after you log into iTunes Connect and see its dashboard, and you can't install that app on a PC. While iBooks can only be sold in the iBooks Store, the books in the .epub format can be sold anywhere.

If you have a Mac, you can get a free iBooks Author app, which can help you create a beautiful book. You can use the iBooks templates, and can drag and drop text, graphics, movies, charts, tables, and more. You can also choose from custom fonts, liven up the text with video or audio, and add in animations, scrolling sidebars, and pop-over widgets. When you drag and drop in images, your text automatically flows around them. Plus you can import Adobe InDesign and ePub files and edit them in the program. When you are ready to publish, the Author program guides you through a step-by-step process, so you can sell the book or make it available for a free download. You can also export your book in an iBook format to give to anyone with an iPad or Mac. While you can use Mac in the Cloud (http://www.macincloud.com) to create an iBook with their $1 an hour or $20 a month plan, you still can't get the iTunes Producer without a Mac, as the iTunes customer advertising service rep the phone.

So if you don't have a Mac, too bad – you have to use an aggregator. Thus, the following description of creating an iTunes account to sell your book there only applies if you have a Mac..

The first step is to create your account on Apple (www.apple.com) to get your Apple ID and password by filling in an application with your name, contact information, ID, password, some security questions, and your tax and credit card information. Indicate that this is for an individual account if you are using a SSN, not for a company, even if it is a DBA, since then you need a Federal Tax ID. Once you provide all of this information, you can sign in with your Apple ID and password and apply to be a seller, after which the acceptance process is fairly quick.

If you don't have a Mac, you can work with any of Apple's Book Partners, who have various requirements. Mostly they are for Word or PDF documents, and some accept other formats, including Indesign and Quark, though some may have special requirements for formatting the document. For example, Smashwords requires the Word document formatted according to a special style sheet, which can take about 5 to 6 hours to format a 150 page manuscript. Other partners based in the US include Bibliovault, Draft2Digital, Aptara, Zoodigital, and Newgen. Others are located around the world. You can check out the different services at the following link. The biggest ones which are recommended by many writers are Smashwords and Draft2Digital. https://itunespartner.apple.com/en/books/partnersearch

## Nook

Nook (https://www.nookpress.com) is a relatively easy platform to sign up on. In fact, if you haven't written your book, you can write it on Nook, and publish it, using their Manuscript Editor. Or if you have your book, you can upload in multiple formats – Word, epub, txt, rtf and even HTML. You can create

Print-On-Demand books from a PDF at no charge and then order the book, though the cost is a little higher than CreateSpace. Once you upload your book, you can edit it in the Manuscript Editor and preview it as it will look on Nook. To sell it, you need to set up a vendor account, where you add in your contact information, tax information, and bank account so you can be paid, once your royalty is $10 or more. You receive a royalty based on the list price – 40% for books priced at $.99 - $2.98, and 60% for books priced at $2.99 to $9.99. For $10 or more, you get 40%. It takes up to 72 hours to get your approval after filling out your vendor information.

## Kobo

Kobo (http://writinglife.kobobooks.com) is also easy to sign up to sell one or more books. You sign up for an account, enter your contact and bank information to get paid, and you don't even have to include your tax or SSN information. Kobo sets the sales price at $2.99 or more, and you get a 70% royalty. You get paid after you have earned $50 or more twice a year. If the book was previously published, you just have to indicate when. To publish, you upload a cover and epub, Word, wobi, or .odt document, indicate the book's category from a list of possibilities, and write a description. While there is an option to preview the book, it is now in an epub format, so you can't see it unless you have that software.

Kobo also provides stats, so you can track how your book is doing. You can see the number of books sold and the amount earned each month, as well as see a graph with your day-to-day sales, the activity by location on a map of the world, and the unit sales for your top 10 titles. All in all its a fairly quick process, and it took me only 20 minutes to set up my account and upload my first book. After this, I would estimate about 10 minutes per book.

# Draft2Digital

Draft2Digital is another extremely easy to sign up and use platform that has 8 partner stores, which include iBooks (iTunes), Barnes & Noble (Nook), Kobo, Inktera (formerly Page Foundary), Scribd, Osyter, Tolino, and CreateSpace. You can easily specify which stores you want Draft2Digital to contact for you, so if you already have made a direct contact with a store, you can exclude them. Some pending arrangements include 24Symbols, Overdrive, Ingram, Are and Omnilit, Google Play, and Amazon. If you have already published with another distributor, you can still use Draft2Digital to expand your reach and make it simpler to manage your project with other digital stores.

The setup is very easy, since all you need is a Word document, rtf file, or text file. Or if you already have an epub file, Draft2Digital can accept that, too. There is no charge to sign up, and you can assign any publisher name you want.

The fee for distribution is approximately 10% of the retail price, which is 15% of the net royalties. After you create your account, you can opt to get paid by check with a mailing address, PayPal with an email address, or a direct deposit with the account routing information. You get paid by check once your royalties amount to $25; or for digital payments, you get paid once you earn $10 in royalties. If you are in the US, Draft2Digital will not withhold any taxes, but it will report earnings to the IRS.

Once your account is set up, just follow the prompts to upload your file, cover JPEG, author photo, book description, and other author information. Within about 20 minutes your book is published, and the next books should be even faster.

The only style guide for the interior is to mark the chapter breaks with something distinctive and be consistent. Make the heading for the book centered, bold, or in a larger font, or use a

Heading style in Word. Once you do something to clearly indicate your chapter titles, the company will do the rest.

If you haven't already published a paper-back at CreateSpace, Draft2Digital can convert your manuscript into a professional quality paperback with the check of a box, and your only charge is the cost of a book.

Once your book is accepted in any of Draft2Digital partners, they send you an email to let you know your book is now available in that store.

## Smashwords

Smashwords is the granddaddy of the ebook publishers and distributors arena. It has published over 350,000 ebooks, with about 280,000 in its premium catalog, which is distributed to major ebook retailers. The books that get into this catalog meet certain formatting standards, which are outlined in its detailed style catalog. Among other things, your book has to meet certain standards, such as having a quality book cover image, a professional-looking book description, a copyright page that says it's the "Smashwords Edition" or "Distributed by Smashwords," and no hyperlinks pointing to other retailers. It also has to have proper formatting, such as no more than five consecutive paragraph returns anywhere in the manuscript and no page numbers in the table of contents. Some stores, like Apple and Kobo require an ISBN, but you can obtain or assign on through Smashwords' ISBN Manager. The company also has its standard catalog and its Atom/OPDS catalog, amd reaches major mobile app platforms and contains all of the books by Smashword authors.

Unlike Draft2Digital which formats your book from almost any Word, rtf, or text document, Smashwords has extensive formatting requirements, such as no fonts over 14pts, and a table of contents without any page numbers. So you can't upload any Word file; rather it takes about 5-6 hours per book to properly format it, though you can hire someone to do this, as I have done. The steps to formatting your book in Word is in Smashwords' style guide (http://www.smashwords.com/books/view/52) or you can hire a low-cost formatter recommended by Smashwords. While Smashwords now accepts an .epub document, using this file format has some limitations, such as no online sampling, which is required by most retailers – generally at least 10% of your book.

Once Smashwords gets an acceptable file from you, it turns it into a series of formats. Most important is the epub file, since the company distributes this to the Apple iBookstore, Kobo, B&N, and others. Smashwords also turns your original Word document into a .mobi file for Kindle, as well as a PDF, rtf, Plaintext, and HTML document.

If you get into Smashwords' premium catalog, which about 50% of its authors do, the company distributes to major online retailers, including Apple, Barnes & Noble, Scribd, Oyster, Kobo, Overdrive, Baker & Taylor, Inktera (formerly Page Foundry), and Library Direct. The royalty rate for books priced at $.99 and up varies depending on the retailer, though it is typically 60% of the list price. The rate is 70% through Library Direct, or 45% through library aggregators such as Baker & Taylor's Axis 360 and OverDrive. For books sold through the Smashwords store, you get 85% of the net. However, Smashwords distribution through Amazon is limited. If your books are in multiple channels through other distributors, make sure the prices are the same in each one.

If you distribute directly to other retailers, Smashwords recommends consolidating your distribution through them, since their commission is only 10%, and they have some exclusive tools. For instance, Smashwords distributes preorders to Barnes and Nobles, but if you upload directly to Barnes & Noble, the store don't offer preorders.

Normally your book is automatically opted in to all of Smashwords' channels and to any new ones added, though you can opt-out to any of them as you wish through Smashwords' Distribution Channel Manager. You can set your price in their Pricing Manager, which is set by default to $4.95, though you can set any price from $.99 up to $39.99 at the Apple Store, or you can make your ebook free. However, $2.99 is a common price point on Smashwords as on other ebook sales platforms.

## Scribd

Scribd (www.scribed.com) will accept direct submissions if you are a publishing company with a substantial title count (perhaps 50 or more). If you qualify, you make arrangements with their acquisition team. You fill out a form about yourself with the name of publishing company, website, name, number of book titles, genres, and format (epub or PDF). If you are an independent author or publisher with only a few titles, they ask you to sign up with one of their recommended publishing service providers or distributors, which include Smashwords, Draft2Digital, Inscribe Digital, and Book Baby. However, if you want to publish and make your own content available for free, you can upload it at https://www.scribd.com/upload-document. While it's free to publish through Smashwords and Draft2Digital, Inscribe Digital and Book Baby charge for their services and take a percentage of earnings.

If you have enough books to make arrangements directly with Scribd, you get 80% of the revenue and you can set your own price, as well as change it. You get paid by a check or via PayPal. If you want to list your book initially for a free preview to entice readers, you can do that. Once you have published, Scribd will let you know whenever someone makes a purchase, or you can track your earnings directly on your profile. The company has built-in viral marketing, so you can share previews of your items for sale by using Scribd's social features, which are available on most mobile devices. The site also strives to combat piracy through "BookID," a technology that helps to prevent the upload of unauthorized works onto the site, which was a problem in the past due to Scribd's upload anything for free feature.

## Setting Up Accounts and Working with Distributors

While you can set up your own accounts at these different services, the two major aggregators – Draft2Digital and Smashwords – can make it easier for you. Though they take a small commission – 10-15% for their services, it can be well-worth it, given the time savings in doing it yourself for each of your books. So I would recommend doing it yourself or using an assistant to post your books for you.

Whatever services you work with, figure that getting your books distributed in multiple platforms is half the battle. You still have to actively promote and market the books yourself to see significant sales.

# CHAPTER 15: CREATING A SUPPORT TEAM

The many things you need to implement a marketing and PR campaign for your book may seem overwhelming, especially when you already have to think about creating additional books and programs or publishing one book on multiple platforms. How can you do everything, as well as, in many cases, earning money from your regular work? Can you really earn the kind of figures that some of the top online marketers claim to be making from their own books and programs? Are those really realistic goals for you, and how can you do it?

First, to answer your question about emulating the online marketing successes to achieve success. To be realistic, these huge online publishing successes have not only followed certain powerful marketing strategies, but they have found a niche in which others will pay not just for books but for programs, personal consulting, and more to succeed themselves. While their marketing strategies may lead to phenomenal successes for them, with earnings of $30,000, $40,000, $50,000 and more a month, those kind of earnings may not be realistic for others writing for a different audience, where you may not find people willing to pay $50 to $500 for a course. However, while your sales may not reach those stratospheric numbers, you can use their techniques, many of which are described in this book, to make more money from your own books and programs in whatever niches fit for you.

So that raises the initial question – how can you do it all? How can you do everything required to achieve a great success in marketing and promoting your book and programs? The key if you can't do it all yourself – and  you really can't – is to bring in a support team to help you, and as necessary take a hour or two or a few days to provide the training they need to become effective in helping you.

Thus, the next question is what type of support team do you need? And how do you recruit and train them?

## What Type of Support Team Do You Need?

The type of support team you need depends on the number of books and programs you have and how actively you are promoting them. Another consideration is whether you are working with a full or part-time assistant at your location, or whether you can farm out some or all of these tasks to one or more individuals or companies. With that caveat, here are some suggestions for what to look for in creating your team. I've listed the tasks you can hire someone else to do, and these can be split up between different individuals or combined.

There are some companies that have inhouse or outsourced individuals to carry out these different tasks, though it will be more expensive, often much more expensive, than if you can recruit the team yourself. The big advantage an established company with a good track record has is that they have tested out the people working with them. By contrast, you may have to do more to test out how well people do the job for you, though past reviews and references can help you choose the best people to work with.

- <u>Posting Comments and Links to Your Material on the Social Media.</u> Postings on the social media can be a hugely time consuming task but it can be turned into a relatively routine process requiring little specialized skill, so this is an easy task to farm out. You get someone to post your comments and include links to your material online or hashtags (#) to your Twitter site to see additional information. You have to supply the initial and follow-up content which the person is supposed to post. On a limited basis, the person can respond to questions or can turn these over to you for a more detailed follow-up. The same content can be used on multiple social media sites. Figure on paying about $8-

10 an hour for this locally, since you can use students and first-time job seekers, or even $4-5 an hour if you outsource this work to individuals in other countries.

     - <u>Collecting and Organizing Your Email Responses and Other Data</u>. You can automate some of this email traffic by having an autoresponder or customer response management (CRM) software attached to your website, squeeze page, or other site collecting emails. Additionally, you may get emails from other sources, such as the business cards you collect at networking events or the contact information you obtain from industry directories, subscription services, and websites. After collecting these emails from various sources, bring them together into a mailing or database program, such as Access. When you gather these emails together, indicate where you got them (such as which sales page or offer the prospect responded to, which networking events you attended and collected emails, or which directory you purchased). For example, I use Access to create databases from different types of sources, and I have an assistant who imports Excel or .cvs files into Access and copies, pastes, or types these emails from different sources in one column and indicates in another column where these emails came from. After testing, the assistant eliminates any returns, requests to be removed, or individuals who have retired or left the field. While some of this database clean up can be automated, someone still needs to do much of the work in cleaning up the database.

     - <u>Making Phone Calls to Obtain Information and Responding to Requests for Information from You</u>. For making phone calls, you need someone who can act as an executive assistant and is good on the phone. This assistant can ask for email contact information or talk to customers who have questions about your book or programs. He or she can also carry on email exchanges to answer customer questions, send out attachments with more information, and the like.

- Scheduling Your Activities and Keeping a Schedule. If you start doing different programs, such as workshops and seminars face-to-face or online, you may need someone to keep your schedule – by setting up appointments for you and letting you know what you need to do when. It's one of the jobs executive assistants do, and you can hire someone part-time to do this for an hour or so, along with other activities, such as making phone calls and responding to requests for information.

- Handling Other Tasks. As your success in marketing your book and other materials grows, you may need additional team members to help you. Make a list of what you need, and as possible, give these tasks to people already on your team to handle for you. Or determine what other jobs you need someone to do and what type of person has the necessary skills to do these tasks. Also, figure out what tasks might be grouped together and estimate how long it will take to do them, so you have an accurate picture of what you need when you recruit support staff for these roles.

## Recruiting the Support You Need

Depending on what type of support you need, there are various ways to obtain this. These include the following:

- Contact the Placement Offices at Your Local Colleges or High Schools. For many of these tasks, you don't need sometime who is trained, such as for posting contacts, entering information in databases, and making phone calls. You just need someone who can type quickly and accurately for some tasks or is good on the phone for others. Many high school seniors and college students can be hired to do this for about $8-9 an hour, and I have used students I originally recruited through a Mayor's Summer Jobs Program for high school seniors.

- Announce Your Job through Your Local Business or Community Connections. This can be a good source of getting someone who people already know and can recommend, rather than posting a listing in a newspaper, online forum, or Craigslist, where you don't have any connections. Often people will know someone with the needed skills who is looking for a job, and having a personal referral can provide extra insurance that you will be hiring someone who can be trusted. For example, I got several referrals that led one woman down the street to contact me about posting some books on Smashwords, and other contacts referred me to illustrators for kids books.

- Outsource Your Job Needs to Websites that Connect Freelancers with Employers. Outsourcing can work for jobs where you don't need someone locally to do the work, such as social media postings. However, I would not recommend this for email management or data collection, where you need to keep close control over the information, since an outsider working for you could easily take this information and use it for other purposes – even to start their own company or resell it to a company that might compete against you. If you do any outsourcing, some of the companies which have a network of freelancers are Fiverr (www.fiverr.com), Upwork (www.upwork.com), and Guru (www.guru.com) .

- Hire a Company Specializing in the Services You Need. Another possibility, if you have the budget for it, is to hire a company that can provide your needed services. For example, social media companies have a team of people who can put together a social media campaign for you. Local recruiters can provide you with part-time office workers create databases or make phone calls for you. Often you will find such companies at local business networking meetings, or you can look them up through Google search by putting in the types of services you need. If you want to hire a local company, add in the name of your city or metro area, though many of these companies can work with you long-distance or have a nearby branch.   Many of these companies can provide excellent services, others not so much, so check them out through their website profiles and packages, and ideally talk to a salesperson on the phone about how they might work with you. Then, compare their offers and decide who you feel would be the best fit for working with you.  In some cases, the owner or an employee of these companies may offer to work with you as a guide or coach, which could be a way to gain their guidance but cut down the cost of hiring them to supervise your whole campaign.  Be prepared to pay more because you are working with a professional company and their referrals than if you hire people directly to work for you.  For example, a typical cost for a professional campaign lasting a few weeks or a month or two might be $2000-5000.

## Hiring Support Team Members

When hiring support team members, ask for resumes from potential employees and look at the sales literature and recommendations from companies you are considering.  In both cases, review the individual's or company's past track record.  In the case of prospective employees, you might give them a short test to see if they can do what you want on the job.

For instance, to test the ability of a job candidate to type accurately and quickly, as well as show their ability to respond well to a question from a prospective customer, I ask candidates to take about 5 minutes to type a letter for me.  I ask them to set it up like a regular letter with a salutation and close, and write it like they are pitching any product or service of their choice to an individual customer or company.  The letter is designed to see how much they can type in 5 minutes and how accurate they are. Secondly, it is designed to look at their creativity in figuring out what to say in the letter.  If they are at least fast and accurate I may hire them, but I will be more directive in telling them what to do.

But if they can write a good compelling letter, I might hire them and give them more freedom to take their own initiative, which I think is ideal, since I'm looking for someone who can work well with as little direction as possible from me.

As for hiring a company to take over some of these functions, I recommend calling some of their referrals, or in some cases, these companies will offer a one-hour free consultation or a free trial of their services for a few days, which can be a way to try them out and see if what they do will work for you.

## Training and Supervising Team Members

After you hire an employee, you need to provide some training. One approach, which I have found very helpful, is to prepare some basic guidelines for what to do, whether you write them or you obtain them from a platform you are working with. For example, for employees who are collecting emails or entering information in databases for me, I have written up a manual on exactly what to do, which includes some screenshots of the online and offline forms they will work on. It includes a step-by-step procedural guide for exactly how and where to enter data, as well as how to indicate when an email has been returned or a contact has requested a change in who to contact.

When employees get started, beyond giving them guidelines to follow, it's a good idea to demonstrate the process while they watch. Then, ask them to do it, while you watch what they are doing. This way you can make sure they are following these guidelines, and provide them with input when they make a mistake, such as skipping a step.

If the company has its own guidelines, such as Smashwords does for formatting and publishing a book on its platform, I give employees those guidelines and leave it up to them to work it out, since in this case, I have not learned those detailed guidelines myself. Should the employees make an error when they try to publish something, Smashwords tells them what's wrong, so they can make the necessary corrections.

Once employees start following the guidelines on their own, let them know you are available if they have any questions, and it's a good idea to check in from time to time to see how they are doing, perhaps once every hour or so initially. As they seem to know what to do, you can check in less frequently, perhaps every two or three hours.

You also need to work out payment arrangements. If you exercise a great deal of control over their work and require them to work certain hours, you need to treat them as employees and make the necessary arrangements to pay them accordingly. You also need to prepare the necessary forms and take out the taxes as required by law, which works out to about 33%. Alternatively, if you allow the people you hire to choose their own hours, work as long and as little as they want, and determine the best way to do the job, you can hire them as independent contractors. If so, there is no need for all this paperwork and deductions. I'd recommend going the independent contractor route if you can, though get a business license, since you are no longer just a writer pitching your own books and programs, but you have people working for you.

# PART II: CONDUCTING AN ONLINE SALES CAMPAIGN

# CHAPTER 16: PUTTING YOUR TEAM TOGETHER FOR YOUR CAMPAIGN

Once you have published your book and developed your programs, the next step is marketing and selling them. Many writers, speakers, seminar/workshop leaders, and consultants don't like to do this. But once you have a general idea of what to do, you can farm many of the tasks to an individual or team who can handle your marketing and sales for you. So before describing what to do to create an online marketing and sales campaign, consider the team members you might get to help you if you don't want to do it all yourself.

## Hiring an Experienced Marketing Coordinator

One approach to creating a team is hiring an experienced marketing coordinator who can handle all aspects of your marketing and sales campaign, including bringing in a team to do the routine work, such as posting your comments and links to your blogs and reports on the social media. Often freelance marketing and sales professionals are looking for part-time work and will regard you as a client, rather than an employer. This might be a good fit when you are first getting started – so having someone organize your campaign by working about 3 or 4 hours a day or a week might work well. Or you might look for someone you can hire as a part-time employee, where you provide more direction and supervision.

Often you will find such marketing and sales people at business networking and referral groups, sometimes calling themselves consultants. You might also find marketing and sales employees through the placement service at a local college or university. In this case, look for business administration or marketing/sales majors. Another source is the resumes posted on job sites, such as Monster Jobs (www.monsterjobs.com), ZipRecruiter (www.ziprecruitor.com), Simply Hired (www.simplyhired.com), Indeed (www.indeed.com), LinkedIn (www.linkedin.com), or even the Craigslist (www.craigslist.org) for your area. Or you can create your own help wanted list to post on those sites. ZipRecruiter will post your listing on over 100 other sites, including Monster, Simply Hired, and LinkedIn.

As with hiring any employee or independent contractor, especially one who will assume a lot of responsibility, check out the person's credentials and track record. Ask the prospective recruits to give you their ideas on how they might market your book and programs, and how they can organize and operate that plan for you.

In some cases, marketing and sales pros will be more like consultants and advisers, who can suggest what you need to do and what type of people you need to hire, which could be useful if you want a second opinion from a professional. Otherwise, look for someone who can put together and supervise a team to do the day to day work for you.

## Hiring Assistants to Do the More Routine Work

An alternative approach, which I have used, is to hire assistants to do the more routine work of doing postings on the social media, compiling email databases, and making phone calls to get leads. Alternatively, you can farm out some routine tasks to organizations that outsource tasks to individuals around the world, such as creating squeeze pages, sales pages, and marketing copy for flyers. Some of the companies that might be good to find such employees include: Upwork (www.upwork.com), Guru (www.guru.com), and Fiverr (www.fiverr.com ).

Other sources for employees and interns include college and university placement services, and business and marketing departments. Or try calling your local high schools about posting your announcement, since some of the older students, most notably seniors, may be interested in a starting-level job. I found several assistants this way through the Mayor's Summer Jobs Program when I lived in Oakland. Still another source of help might be the business referral and networking groups, where someone might know someone who is looking for such work.

When you hire low-level employees to work for you directly, figure on spending some initial time training them so they know what to do. Ideally, write up some guidelines so they can use after your initial training, so they can follow-along as they do the work when they get started. These written guidelines can also help them after they are trained, so they can train others to do what they do. Ideally, turn your guidelines into a detailed training manual, which includes a step-by-step description of what to do for each task. For added explanation, you can include scans or screenshots that show what a person might see as he or she engages in various tasks from creating databases to developing materials to sell or promote your products or services.

If employees are local, you can readily meet with them, and even have them work in your office at another computer and phone. Additionally, you can hire individuals who work effectively across the country – or even in another country, where people know English.

# CHAPTER 17: USING THE SQUEEZE PAGE AND FREE GIFT APPROACH TO ONLINE MARKETING

One common approach to successfully marketing your book webinars, and other programs, is using a squeeze page and free gift approach to online sales. You can get people to your website in other ways, and offer your book and other products there. But this squeeze page-free gift method is an effective way to get people to purchase a program you are offering for $40-to $50 or more.

This approach may not make sense if you are only selling copies of your book for $20 to $25. But once you use your book to create other programs, such as a $97 webinar or online workshop, this two-step process is ideal for gaining interest and making a sale.

## The Key Elements of Your Campaign

The key elements in this online marketing approach include the following:
- Your end goal, which is the program, product, or service you want to sell,
- A list of individuals who have expressed interest in these offerings,
- A free gift, such as a report or book chapter, which you offer people in return for their email,
- A squeeze page (also known as a landing page) which is your sales page for whatever you are selling, along with your form for collecting emails and free gift offer,
- A thank you page where you thank people for their interest and leads to your sales page ticket offer,

- A form that connects your squeeze page with your other elements,
- Follow-up e-mails to those who have not yet purchased your program, in which you offer additional products and services,
- A test to see that everything in your system works.

Presumably you have already selected at least one end goal to start, though you can use the same system for multiple emails. Consider each goal as the end of a sales funnel which is designed to attract a prospect to see your offer on your squeeze page, become interested in what you are offering, and finally buy that – or more, if you have additional products or programs

## Using a Spreadsheet or Table

Use a spreadsheet to track your progress for each squeeze page campaign. Start with your end goal and write down all the elements and steps you need to complete to launch this campaign in the first column. In the next column indicate what you will do; in the third column indicate when you plan to do this; in the forth column include the date you completed that step and use the last column for any comments.

Your spread sheet or table should look something like this:

| Online Sales Campaign Plan | | | | |
|---|---|---|---|---|
| Activity | Description/Link | When to Do | Date Completed | Comments |
| Create Squeeze Page | | | | |
| Create Free Gift | | | | |
| Create Sales Letter | | | | |
| Create Thank You Page | | | | |
| Test of Links | | | | |
| Send Emails to Contacts | | | | |
| | | | | |
| | | | | |

## Setting Up Your Domain and Hosting

To start the campaign, you need a page, website, or free-standing domain for your squeeze page. Any of these locations is fine, but preferably select a domain name for your squeeze page, so you can send prospects directly there. If the squeeze page is on your website but you have bought the domain name from another provider, you can use an URL referral or forwarding from any domain name provider, such as Go Daddy (www.godaddy.com), Dotster (www.dotster.com), BlueHost (www.bluehost.com), or eHost (www.ehost.com). Or you can buy an available name through your hosting services.

Any of these approaches work:

- Create a free standing domain, with the same hosting company hosting other sites for you, or set up your domain and hosting with another webhosting company to test it out,

- Set up a squeeze page and other pages on your current website,

- Obtain your domain name from your website hosting company, or purchase your domain from one provider and your website hosting from another.

For example, I used Hostcentric to create about 20 websites (www.hostcentric.com) using a master account and reseller package, where each additional name up to 25 is about $3 a name. But for my squeeze page, my web designer recommended another service, BlueHost, which he uses. Also set this up as a stand-alone website – www.monetizingyourbook.com, since not only will I be selling this book I am writing, but I will be creating a series of workshops and seminars based on it and using the process of creating a marketing campaign for that to help in teaching you what to do.

In the next sections, I'll describe in more detail how to develop all of these elements into your own online marketing and sales campaign.

# CHAPTER 18: DEVELOPING YOUR SALES CAMPAIGN PAGES

The purpose of your squeeze page, apart from any sales you do from your website, is to collect people's emails, which they have to provide to get your free gift and more information about your offer. You can use this email to send further information and offers.

Typically you offer a free gift for people to learn more, or you can offer something which is available now, usually at a lower price if they order now or within a short time. In some cases, it works well to immediately sell your book or program from a squeeze or sales page. But often this two-step process is more effective, since it gives people a chance to learn more about you and your book or programs to convince them to make a purchase.

In the pre-video days of squeeze and landing pages, a typical approach was to have a long page of copy which featured some highlights and benefits of the book or programs, followed by a buy button, more highlights and benefits, another buy button, and so on, to convince the prospect to make a purchase along the way. If the person wasn't initially convinced, the additional information and buy buttons were used to provide more persuasion to convince the person to buy. Often the offers were laced with incentives to buy now, such as a deep discount for an immediate purchase.

Now squeeze pages commonly have much less text. Instead, they typically include a photo or short promotional video of the product or service. Additionally, the text features the benefits in a paragraph or two, possibly with bullet points, followed by a form to enter your email to click through or get an email to get your free gift.

Commonly, the free gift is related to the book or programs

you are selling. They are like an introduction that entices people to want more, much like doing a free introductory talk, seminar, so attendees sign up to learn more. When people don't know much about you, having this free introductory offering is a way to give them confidence in you, so they feel comfortable paying for more information. A series of blogs or articles by you serves a similar function; they raise your profile and make others more receptive to buying from you.

To set up your squeeze page, you should do the following:

## Determine Where You Will to Put Your Squeeze Page and Thank You Page

If your squeeze page will be a page on your current website, create another page for it and for the pages you will link to that, such as a page for your sales page, another for your thank you page, and a third for your free gift. If your squeeze page will be on a new site, pick out your domain name from a service that sells names such as GoDaddy (www.godaddy.com), Dotster (www.dotster.com), or your hosting service. Then, arrange with a website host to post your site. This could be a hosting site connected to the service selling your name or it could be another hosting service, such as Hostcentric (www.hostcentric.com), which I sed, or BlueHost (www.bluehost.com), which my webdesigner has used and recommends.

Other top websites listed on rating sites include:
- eHost (www.eHost.com),
- iPage (www.page.com),
- HostClear (www.hostclear.com),
- IdeaHost (www.ideahost.com),
- SiteBuilder (www.sitebuilder.com),
- WebsiteBuilder (www.websitebuilder.com).
If you are setting up WordPress, Blue Host and SiteGround

([www.siteground.com](www.siteground.com)) are especially recommended for hosting your site. Generally, hosting costs are about $2-4 a month.

Besides setting up the URL for your squeeze page, set up an URL for your "Thank You" page. These different pages can be anywhere, but ideally keep them together on the same site. Don't call your squeeze page a "squeeze page." Find some other creative name for it, such as calling it what it is – ie: reportonsavingmoney" or simply or "thankyou." To keep the search engines from finding your page, since it is supposed to be a private page for those giving you their email, string the words together as in the example, rather than separating them so they are search engine friendly, such as "report-on-saving-money."

For example, I am setting up my website for Monetizing Your Book programs at [www.monetizingyourbook.com](www.monetizingyourbook.com) and the squeeze page at other URLs to be determined, such as www.monetingyourbook.com/monetizepowerpoint, and the thank you page at http://www.monetizingourbook/thankyouandfreegift.

## Select Your Free Gift

Decide what you want to offer based on what your book or programs are about. Some good possibilities are:
- an introductory lesson for an email course, webinar, or video training program,
- a chapter from an ebook,
- a PowerPoint presentation with highlights of your book,
- a sample white paper,
- a certificate or coupon for a free product or service related to your book (for example, if your book is about how to relax using yoga, massage, and other techniques, offer a coupon to a branch of a fitness chain in the prospect's area.
It's best to select a free gift with a low cost to you.

## Create Your Form

You use a form to collect the emails of those opting-in to receive your gift or requesting more information from you. Some programs, such as Instabuilder (www.instabuilder.com), enable you to easily create a squeeze page through WordPress. You can create this page before or after your thank you page, but determine the thank you page URL in advance, so you can indicate this link in your email collection form, which is already present on the page or pops up and asks for the person's email once he or she clicks to obtain your free gift.

Besides copying the form code to create the form, fill in the requested information. Commonly, this will be the name of the website with the form, which will be something like: www.domainname.com/dmsignup. Then, link to the URL of your "thank you" page.

## A Thank You Page

Set up your thank you page so you immediately thank the person for signing up to get more information and for your free offer. Usually, people will put in a valid email to get directed to this thank you page, though sometimes people will put in a fake email to get your gift. To reduce the chances of getting a fake email, indicate that you will email them a link to their free gift, though many email marketers only ask for an email to access the free gift.

There are two ways to set up this page.
- You provide the opportunity to purchase, commonly called the "upsell," on the thank you page. For example, lead off with a short video, PowerPoint presentation, or PDF where you provide valuable information, and immediately send them a link where they can buy your complete book or programs, after getting

a taste of theses through the video, PowerPoint, or PDF.

    - You provide them with both the free gift (ie: video, Power Point, or PDF) and the opportunity to purchase them (the upsell) on the thank you page.

    For example, in one of her squeeze pages, Debbie Drum, a specialist on affiliate sales and online marketing since 2010, begins with an invitation to watch a video for *The Secret to Higher Conversions and More Sales*. In it, she combines a 4 minute PowerPoint video of text with an audio track on how to make yourself memorable to your target audience by using a few short videos to show that you understand your audience and are comfortable connecting with them. At any time while you watch the video or after watching it, you can order *The Secret to Higher Conversion* for only $10 by clicking an "Add to Cart" button. Should you try to leave the page to go to another website, you will see a "Leave this page" button come up. If you press "stay," you will see an detailed description of the program in the form of a traditional sales page, with highlights of the program, extra tips, and a half-dozen testimonials. Plus, you can take advantage of a limited time deal for only $10 on how to become a marketer who gets remembered. I found it an effective sales pitch, since I got a copy after seeing the video.

    In another example, Drum begins with a free gift on how to recycle your content. You just click to download it. Then, below the listing of that item, there are links to four other programs, including a blog on using the social media to get more traffic, a site with various programs for selling products online, a consulting program to work with Debbie directly, and an interview with a marketing expert on Kindle. Thus, Drum uses the same techniques she teaches others featuring a squeeze page, free gift, and sales pages with different offers for available programs provided by her or her affiliates.

## Connecting It All Together

Once you have these pieces prepared, connect your email form with your squeeze page, so prospective customers go directly from your squeeze page to your thank you page. What do you put on your squeeze page? The next section discusses what to do.

# CHAPTER 19: DEVELOPING YOUR SQUEEZE PAGE

In the modern squeeze page, less is more, and it's designed to easily show up on a mobile phone. As previously noted, the goal of a squeeze page is to convince or "squeeze" a visitor into providing a personal email address, so they opt in to get more information about your offer and hear from you in the future.

Besides using a squeeze page to collect the emails of people in targeted industries and fields, you can collect theses emails in other ways, such as by creating a database of reviewers, bloggers, speakers, or anyone else, by going to their website, getting a directory, or using a query service that has already created these databases like Publishers Agents and Films (www.publishersagentsandfilms.com).

But in collecting the email in these other ways, you are emailing people cold. The advantage of creating the squeeze page is that you draw people to want to come to you because of the books, programs, and other materials you provide. So you have to design this page to have this appeal – and then you need to build traffic to it, just as you might seek to draw people to your website. The reason to draw them here instead is because this is a dedicated page which provides a gateway to your sales channel. It starts with you offering a free gift or other incentive to get people to give you their email. Once you have that, you can persuade them to want more from you.

## Creating Your Content

Once you plan the other pieces to link to your squeeze page – your thank you page, sales page or website URL, and email capture form – the next step is creating the content for your squeeze page. In the free gift approach, you use this page to gain interest to get their email and connect them with your thank you page to get their gift and see your offer for your book and other programs.

In the past, the squeeze page had extensive content on it to get you to buy with the repeated highlights, benefits, and buy buttons, but now extended copy on this page seems less common. One of the few times I encountered such a long sales page was when I first tried to leave the initial squeeze page for Debbie Drum's *Authority 3X* book on how to be more memorable. While I could have immediately clicked "Add to Cart" and added this for $10, when I left the page, I got a "Do You Want to Leave" notice, and when I clicked "Stay on Page," I saw a detailed sales pitch which went on for about 20 pages, much like the old marketing pitches that were commonly this long.

## An Example of a Sales Page

The basic message of the pitch with a large header with white lettering on black – "3 Easy Step Process To Become The Marketer Who Gets Remembered" -- was that emails from someone unknown were likely to be ignored or considered spam, because they were coming from a stranger. But by using her method, I could turn strangers into friends. To explain, Drum compared the benefits of an in-person meeting for closing a deal to creating a sense of trust through an introductory video so people get to know you. Then, in bold type she announced: "Here's My Special Offer," followed by a large picture of her *Authority 3X* book. Next the pitch indicated in bold type "Here's What You Get," featuring the highlights of the "turn strangers into friends" approach through video. After this, the ad featured in white and bold type the headline: "Who Is This Perfect For," followed by a list of the target market, which included authors, publishers, blog owners, and product creators, with another powerful message: "Copy This Strategy and Dominate Your Market." After this she explained how the purchase process worked by leading the customer to a download page to obtain a PDF and the assurance that "Folks Love My Trainings and My Marketing Style"

Drum concluded the pitch with a half-dozen testimonials from people who used her method successfully, followed by a 100% risk free 30-day money back guarantee for the introductory price of only $10. After the sales pages noted this was a "very limited time deal," there was another "Add to Cart" button, followed by three PSs, indicating that this was the last time I would see the author, that I should get the book now before missing the deal forever, and that this evergreen information would be good today and in the future. Plus the pitch concluded by telling me I could make 1000 times the low price being offered of only $10, so "Add to Cart." Finally Drum repeated the benefit of the book that opened the pitch: "3 Easy Step Process To Become The Marketer Who Gets Remembered."

In short, it was a very effective pitch that repeated the highlights, benefits, and appeal of the product in a number of ways. Further, Drum bolstered the credibility of the pitch with some testimonials, and she used several buy buttons in the form of "Add to Cart" invitations. She also repeated the headlines that conveyed the basic message that this was a 3 step process to become a marketer who gets remembered, and now was a special offer to get the book for a very low price. Plus she indicated the target market.

Drum set up the squeeze page to provide a one-two punch. This way if I didn't order right away from the squeeze page with the video, she had another shot to sell the book through a long-form sales letter which explained the message in more detail.

Another selling point was that as soon as I ordered I could immediately download the book, which is an important part of online marketing your book and programs. People want to access their purchase almost immediately – either with a link in the immediate confirmation of their purchase, or with a link in a email to the email they used in purchasing the product.

After I bought the book, the confirmation notice included still other offers for more advanced and expensive programs, with a few more incentives to introduce me to what Drum was offering and entice me to want more. For example, one bonus was a series on Book Publishing Riches, in which Drum used links to three introductory free videos to illustrate how one could make more money by publishing to a variety of platforms other than Kindle, such as PubIt, CreateSpace, and Smashwords. Another bonus was for book on how to make money by ghostwriting for others and how to get one or two others to pay for an ad in your book. In addition, a link to the main site for Book Publishing Riches opened up still other articles that provided more tips followed by an offer to get more information, such as a $100 series on how to publish on multiple platforms.

In short, this multiple offers a method offered a fairly low cost book as an entry to learning more advanced information at a higher price. And this approach was certainly an effective way to sell a program on how to make more money by publishing and marketing your books. Likewise, you can use a similar approach to guide people to want your product or service, using a squeeze page along with a long-form sales pitch for those who don't watch the video.

# CHAPTER 20: CREATING YOUR SQUEEZE PAGE

In creating your squeeze page, use a strong title and subtitle, a few short paragraphs or a half-dozen or so bullet-points to highlight the benefits to the buyer. Include a photo or short video that quickly conveys what the buyer will get or the expertise of the author or presenter. End with a form to capture the email and a link to click to immediately see a demo, get a free gift, or learn more.

For example, in her article on"How to Create Squeeze Pages: What Makes an Awesome Squeeze Page Design," (http://www.wordstream.com/blog/ws/2013/09/16/squeeze-page.) Megan Marrs conveys the basic essentials. Her key points include:
- Keep your content to a minimum, at least above the fold, which is what you first see when you open a browser to a page. It's much like on the top half of a newspaper – hence the term "above the fold."
- Create a convincing offer to make it worthwhile for a person putting in an email address, such as by offering a valuable free gift, which provides a brief taste or introduction to what you are offering, although not everyone provides a free gift. As an alternative, some marketers offer a big discount for orders places now, while others offer a money-back guarantee if you're not satisfied, with 7, 14, or 30 days being typical times for you to decide if you like something or not.
- The main type of squeeze page offers include an email course, ebook, white paper collection, templates, or design aids. Sometimes you can offer video trainings, though prospective customers are used to getting videos for free or finding them on YouTube, so if you offer a video series, make them private, password protected or viewable only to selected emails. Email courses, such as one based on your book, are ideal. In these, you

provide information in smaller segments, which are easy to put into practice and thereby give the user good value. If users finds your course useful from the initial video, they will look forward to future emails, so you build a positive relationship, making users more open to follow-up offers. You can add value to the course by including video sections, which can be as simple as you speaking for a few minutes on a webcam or smart phone. Providing, an email course makes sense, since you have asked for the person's email on your squeeze page.

You can create your squeeze page manually as you would with any other website page. Alternatively, you can use a Squeeze Page Generator, such as WordStream's Landing Page and Leads tool, which enables you to use different squeeze page templates, colors, and themes to create forms, copy, thank you pages, and tracking codes (www.wordstream.com). Another plugin for easily creating a squeeze page is Instabuilder (www.instabuilder.com), or you can use several WordPress squeeze page plugins with templates for creating a WordPress squeeze page. These plugins include a WordPress Landing Page Plugin to create and track landing pages, an Easy Sign Up Plugin to create a sign up form for newsletters and offers, and a Squeeze Page Creator, with squeeze page templates.

The common forms of squeeze pages are pop-ups, a splash page on your home page, or a stand-along squeeze page.

- Pop-Ups. These pop-ups appear over content you are reading and ask for your email before showing you more information, such as a "free gift" that provides a taste of your program. If you use a pop-up, use one that's quick to read, such as having an enticing header like: "How to Turn Your Facebook Page into a Sales Machine," a few bullet points about how to do it, a place to put in one's name and email, and a button to click for Free Instant Access. Provide someone who isn't interested an out, so they can quickly click an "X" button on top to close the pop-up.

- Splash Page on Your Website. This is a custom page that opens up on your website with an offer, though a risk is that people might click away if not interested, so they don't go to your real homepage. One way to prevent this is to include a big "no thanks" button, so people can go directly to your home page. The idea of this page is to quickly give people an offer, such as for your book or program based it. If you create a splash page, design it to look like your regular home page, and include a cookie, so when people visit your site again, they go immediately to your home page and don't see the splash page.

- Stand-Alone Squeeze Page. This is the traditional approach of using the landing or home page of a website to directly offer your book or program without any links to other pages.

# CHAPTER 21: DESIGNING YOUR SQUEEZE PAGE

The squeeze page should be designed to fit into a small area that can both appear above the fold – what you see immediately in a browser – on the first page of your smart phone. So it should have limited text and include these key elements:

- a compelling title that conveys the offer,
- a subtitle that expands on the benefits of the offer,
- a photo of the book cover, a video thumbnail linking to a short video, or a photo of the target market enjoying the program, product, or service,
- a statement of the value of the offer and the savings,
- a few bullet-points or lines indicating what the book or program offers,
- a button to click to "Gain Instant Access" to the free gift.

## An Example of an Effective Squeeze Page

An example of a successful squeeze page is Debbie Drum's ad which features a photo of the book cover, followed by this copy which is attractively laid out to the right of and below the photo:

FREE VIDEO REVEALS 5 WAYS TO
INSTANTLY GET MORE EXPOSURE FOR
YOUR BOOKS
($47 VALUE)
Top Sites Revealed–See Where Book Buyers Are
Really Hanging Out
GET INSTANT ACCESS BUTTON
Whether you are a beginner or a seasoned publisher,
use these 5 sites immediately to gain the exposure
you need for your books!

START TODAY TO GET THE GREATEST
RESULTS FOR YOUR PUBLISHING EFFORTS
Site 1 reveals how Apple helps you get more book
sales
Site 2 reveals how Google helps you get more book
sales
Site 3 reveals a little known source of hungry book
buyers
Site 4 reveals a site that most publishers have never
heard of…but the buyers are there!
Site 5 reveals a way you can capitalize on a new
group of book buyers
GET INSTANT ACCESS BUTTON

In short, the ad has a compelling photo to draw attention and copy that lists the key benefits that its target market – writers and publishers – will want to know about. Then, it offers an opportunity to immediately learn more. For those who click the button and enter their email, they can see a short 4-minute video about these different sites with hints of how much more they can learn, followed by an "Add to Cart" button inviting the viewer to buy, which I did.

## The Elements of a Successful Squeeze Page

More specifically, the basic elements of a successful squeeze page are these, as described by a blogger for Backlinko (http://backlinko.com), a company that specializes in providing SEO strategies to drive traffic to a site, and WordStream (www.wordstream.com), a company that helps website owners get more results from paid search and online advertising.

According to Brian Dean, founder of Backlinko in an article: "How to Create a Squeeze Page that Converts at 21%,

116

(http://backlinko.com/social-squeeze-page) , the key is to have a beautifully designed squeeze page which is optimized for social sharing with sharing buttons for Facebook, LinkedIn, Twitter, and other popular sites. The squeeze page should also have a "Magnetic Headline." The article includes a link to a very effective ad and video which Backlinko has used.

The squeeze page is on the Backlinko website, so the top of the page includes links to the Home page, About page, Contact page, and a Proven SEO Tips newsletter.

Then, splashed under the navigation bar, there is the headline: "How to Rank for Any Keyword (This Is the Exact 1-2 Punch I used to Rank #4 for Backlinks)," followed by an invitation to "Click the play button to see the EXACT step-by-step process, so you can see the video next on the screen.

The video features Brian at a white board explaining this 1-2 punch which involves providing an "expanded link post" which gives a lot of detailed information about what to do in the first three steps. But then the video offers to send the viewer additional information to his or her email, so the viewer has to enter an email to see the rest of the video, as Brian did in his video. After he explained the expanded link post tip for about 4 ½ minutes, the first half of the video, a pop-up announcement suddenly appeared indicating that the viewer should "Put in your email to view the rest of the video, and I will email you Part 2 of the Case Study."

Presumably, someone could put in any email to open up the rest of the video, but then one wouldn't also get the emailed information. Thus, just like most viewers interested in learning more about this 1-2 Punch, I put in my email, and the video continued. Brian then explained the "content roadshow," comparing it to the way movies did out of town screenings, and then gathered word-of-mouth and good reviews to spread the word about the movie. But now, this content is useful for publishers, too. For example, Brian recommends sending a "Thank you email" to anyone you mention in your material, which might lead them to mention and link to you. Another strategy is to go to industry specific forums, which have thousands of users in ones target audience. Also, he recommends using a heads up email where you let people know about your content. If you just post your announcement on the social media you can get lost. But he recommends searching for the top 200 results for your keyword and emailing those contacts about your content, but don't be pushy by asking them to share it with their own contacts. Instead, leave any response up to them. They may then share it or provide a link to it, because you have shared something of value. He also emphasizes how you need to get backlinks – people linking back to you, not just you to them – to go up in the rankings. Then, if you do send your email, you will get future actionable content on free link building strategies, SEO tips, and marketing case studies.

Then, whether or not I finished the video, the squeeze page ended with an invitation to get more valuable content if I provided my email. As the squeeze page announced:

> "Want more awesome SEO and content marketing videos like this?
> "Sign up to the Backlinko newsletter right now and **get exclusive access** to link building and content marketing case studies just like this one.

### Hop On the Backlinko Newsletter (Free)

This was then followed by a box where one could enter their email, and if they still hadn't put in their email, there was an additional announcement:

> "If You Enjoyed This Post, Sign Up for Free Updates
> (And get SEO case studies, videos and insider tips not found on the blog)

Lastly the Backlinko site featured a picture of some newsletter pages, which included a more detailed article on **How to Rank for Any Keyword** and the top of a graph showing tracking for responses. Then, the website featured another "Enter your email" box, followed by a space to add a comment, along with my name and email, though my email address would not be published.

Again this was an effective approach, and after entering an email, one could see another video showing a 3-step process to publish a high-converting Social Squeeze Page on one's site. How? While Dean was sharing information that anyone could use to pitch his own service, the video showed tips to create an effective squeeze page to convince people to give you their email to learn more about your book and programs.

To summarize, the key tips for a Social Squeeze Page are these:

1) Have a topic that your target audience really wants to learn about which has actionable things to do with good results, so people want to give you their email to learn more.

2) create a video of you talking or use a screen capture where you add your audio to slides or images on the screen  (some of these screen capture programs are TechSmith.com (www.techsmith.com), Movavi.com (www.movavi.com), Screencast-O-Matic (www.screencast-o-matic.com), CamStudio (http://camstudio.org), TinyTake (www.tinytake.com), Hongkiat (www.honkiat.com), and SourceForge (www.sourceforge.net).

3) Create a strong short headline and subheadline.  The headline should give the specific benefits of watching the video, while the subheadline creates an information gap, which leads you to want to know more, such if you state that you will provide the exact 3 steps to achieve something.

4) Add in an opt-in form just below the video, so users can respond immediately.

5) Add in another opt-in form at the bottom of the page, so readers can remove themselves from future mailings.

6) Ideally, use a program that can embed a form to capture emails within your video, such as provided by Wistia (www.wistia.com) or Lead Pages (www.leadpages.com).

7) Add in social sharing and comment buttons, so people can share your email easily on the social media, such as Facebook, LinkedIn, and Twitter, and add in their comments. The more comments you get, the more these increase your credentials, since the positive comments show that others have recognized the value of what you are sharing.

# CHAPTER 22: CREATING COMPELLING CONTENT FOR YOUR PAGE

Since the squeeze page is designed to capture the person's emails, you have to provide a good reason for them to give you that. Just offering a free e-book, article, or video isn't enough. You have to entice the prospect with a reason to want it in about 3-4 seconds, or he or she is gone. That's because, as noted in an article on "How to Create a Squeeze Page that Converts at 21.7% (http://backlinko.com/social-squeeze-page), market researchers have found that on average 8 out of 10 people will read headline copy, but only 2 out of 10 will read the rest. These are the key steps to follow to get readers to read more:

## Creating Your Topic and Headline

The secret to creating a compelling squeeze page lies in what Brian Dean of Backlinko calls the "Magnetic Headline". The first step to creating this great headline is to find a topic that your target audience very much wants to know about. Generally, they want actionable information that they can put to use right away. In Backlinko's case, their target audience is entrepreneurs, professional SEOs, and bloggers, who wanted to create their own powerful websites and squeeze pages to attract customers.

You can apply these same principle for creating a great squeeze page to any topic. For instance, if your target market is health conscious people, yoga enthusiasts, and those seeking spiritual fulfillment, you want to figure out what they want that they aren't already getting from others in the field. An example might be a unique new product based on brain and nutrition research that will feed the brain, so you not only live longer but think smarter. Then you highlight that in your headline. Or if you are in the financial field, and you have read about the potential for a worldwide economic collapse, your headline might relate to how you can help people save their assets in the event of the coming financial debacle.

In short, your goal for the page, according to Dean, is to "choose an in-demand topic that your audience has trouble finding reliable information on." Then, your headline should quickly indicate in a short catchy way that you can provide this information. You might even test out possible headlines on business associates in your target market. If you are in a business networking or referral group, that can be an ideal place to do such a test. Then, use the feedback you get to know if you've got a great headline and subhead, just a merely good one, or if you should go back to the drawing board and start over.

## Creating an Interactive "Social Squeeze Page"

One way to create a powerful page in todays world of social media is to invite people to interact with the page, from viewing a video to adding comments – and, of course, adding their email to your growing collection. This page will include 8 key elements, which look something like this, as you scroll down the page.

| POWERFUL, COMPELLING HEADLINE | |
|---|---|
| SOCIAL SHARING BUTTONS (such as the logos of Facebook, Twitter, LinkedIn, or Pinterest) | SUBHEADLINE Plus some copy creating an information gap, such as your secret for some information your target audience wants to know, which they can only obtain by watching your video with that information. |

| A CALL TO ACTION (Such as an invitation to see your video to learn more) |
|---|

| YOUR 3-10 MINUTE VIDEO (In it you provide key information, such as a few key tips, a case study, or a brief tutorial, so people will want to learn more by buying your book or program materials, or signing up for a webinar or personal consulting. You can embed your video directly from YouTube with the appropriate coding, or you might host your video with Wistia or Lead Pages, so you can collect emails from within your video. An example of doing this is to let viewers see half of the video. Then, it stops and they have to enter their email in a form to see the rest of the video. If you have provided viewers with valuable tips, they will want to give you their email to see more. |
|---|

| OPT-IN FORM #1 This form should appear right below your video, where the viewer can most readily see it on looking away from the video. If he doesn't provide an email there, you'll have another chance at the end of the squeeze page. |
|---|

## A COMMENTS OR KEY TIPS SECTION

The Backlinko approach is to provide a comments section, on the theory that the more comments your page attracts, the more social proof you have to build your credibility. The positive comments will also lead people to want to see your video, share it, and opt-in with their email. But the downside of allowing and encouraging comments is that you can get a lot of junk comments and people may write a comment to pitch their own products and services. An alternative is not to include any comments or carefully moderate the comments, so you allow in only appropriate comments. Instead, you can use this section to feature a few key tips drawn from your book, workshops, video training, or other programs. Then, if people appreciate your information, they will want to know more.

## ANOTHER OPT-IN FORM

This form is to give viewers still another chance to opt-in, if they haven't done so before. But now that they have seen even more on your website, they may be even more receptive to learning more. So this final opt-in form encourages them sign up or buy now. As the Backlinko team suggests: "More opt-in forms, more e-mail subscribers."

# CHAPTER 23: USING THE 8 KEY ELEMENTS IN CREATING YOUR SQUEEZE PAGE

Here are more details on each of the 8 elements, recommended by Backlinko (http://www.backlinko.com).

1) **A Good Headline**. Keep this short and appealing. Emphasize the benefits the person will be getting, such as: "How to Improve Your Memory Without Drugs in 3 Simple Steps."

2) **Include Social Sharing Buttons.** Add the social sharing buttons from Facebook, Twitter, LinkedIn, Reddit, Pinterest, and other social media site near your headline, such as to one side of your subheadline.

3) **Create an Information Gap in Your Headline or Subheadline**. This gap represents the difference between what you know and want to know, since researchers have found that people don't like information gaps and want to close them. So having that will make people more likely to want more information from you, such as by watching your video and joining your email list to learn more. For example, after the Backlinko's headline "How to Rank for Any Keyword," the subhead includes the wording: "This is the Exact 1-2 Punch I Used to Rank #5 for "Backlinks." What is the Exact 1-2 Punch? That's the information gap. Similarly, you can create your own information gap, such as by referring to your "3-Step Solution," "10-Point Program," or "Secret Ingredients" you use in teaching others through your book or programs.

4) **Provide a Specific Call to Action.** Tell the person what to do next. If you have a video, ask the person to "click the play button to see the video about whatever you are offering (such as by

saying: "Click the play button to see the exact step-by-step process."

If you don't have a video, list the key benefits of your program, so people want to learn more.

Make your call to action very specific about what want to person to do. For example, it's better to say "click the play button" than "watch the video," because it is more specific in stating what you want the person to do, which is to play the video. If the video isn't embedded on the squeeze page but is on another page, specify what the viewer should type to get there, such as "type in _____ URL." Avoid a more general call to action, such as "Sign up for a free trial" or "Get started."

**5) Ideally, Add in a Video – Preferably from 3-10 Minutes.** Now that the world has gone video, it's ideal to include a short video, such as one with you enthusiastically explaining what you are offering, and you might hold up a book or write on a white board as you share this information. Another video approach is to feature a voice-over as the speaker's words appear on the screen or a hand with a pen writes down the words. An alternative to using a video is using a strong photo with the key highlights and benefits of what you are offering next to the photo.

At one time, the videos were typically 1 to 2 minutes, but the trend has been to use a longer video of about 3 to 10 minutes with some valuable tips, highlights, and benefits of your program. A key reason is that a 1 to 2 minute video may seem too much like a hard-sell video on a squeeze page, whereas a longer video with valuable content will help people to want to know more. But don't make the video any longer than 10 minutes, since people will start to tune out.

As Brian Dean of Blinko puts it:

"My #1 goal is to provide **so much value** that people can't help but move their mouse cursor to my signup form and type in their email…A longer video gives me the opportunity to drop more value…which brings in more conversions from people that actually are about my message."

One good approach to this more informational video is to feature a case study where you show people the results which you or a customer achieved, and how you did it. If you don't have a case study, you can provide a step-by-step tutorial about how to do anything, such as how to apply some of the ideas found in your book or program.

Additionally, it can help you get more customers if you embed an opt-in email form in your video, which you can do through the video hosting site Wistia (www.wistia.com), using their Turnstile feature. The company incorporates a live AWeber form in the video, and as viewers watch, the video stops at that point, such as halfway through the video. You indicate in the Turnstile menu how many seconds into the video you want to stop it, and viewers have to enter their email to continue watching.

Also, in your text you can offer to send the viewer additional material via email – still another reason to give up your email. Providing this additional email mailing is important, because otherwise people can easily put in a fake email, since they don't care about getting any more information emailed to them. For example, the Blinko message in the video is: "Enter your email to watch the rest of this video training. I'll also email you part 2 of the case study." According to Dean, 29% of the people watching the video entered their email at this point.

**6) Add an Opt-In Box Below Your Video (or Add It Below Your Photo and List of Benefits If You Don't Use a Video).** If you have a video, include an opt-in box to collect emails below this video. If you use a photo with bullet points that feature the highlights and benefits of your offer, include the opt-in box next to that. Also include some text to encourage people to give you their email to get your offer, such as a chance to see more great content with tips such as in the video they just saw or the opportunity to gain access to a newsletter, report, or other useful content. For example, the Backlinko opt-in form includes this text: "Want more awesome SEO and content marketing videos like this?...Sign up to the Backlinko newsletter right now and **get exclusive access** to link building and content marketing case studies just like this one.

7) **Consider Whether to Add a Comments Section or An Additional Content Section.** While Backlinko recommends including a space for comments on the grounds that the more comments you have, the more credibility your site gains as a popular, interactive site, my web designer recommends against including comments, because this opens the door to getting spam postings. Although you can reduce the possibility of that happening by moderating the comments and indicating that you have to approve any that get printed, hackers might still get through. Also, if you get comments, it takes time to reply to them. So use comments or not, as you choose – though if you do include comments, be careful to keep the spammers out.

As an alternative to the comments section, you might add an additional tips section or feature an interesting case study or your own story.

8) **Add Another Opt-In Box if You Have Comments or Additional Content Section.** Consider this a last opportunity for people to leave their email if they haven't already.

So there you have it – the basic elements to create your squeeze page. Some other tips on what to include and how to design your page are these:

1) If you have testimonials and success stories from happy customers, include these to show your offer is of value. It's like providing social proof of the worth of your offer.

2) Make a good use of color, so you have good contrast and plenty of white space.

3) Make your content easy to read, using headlines and bullets to feature the most important information. Since a majority

of people will see the page on a smart phone, keep your text short and compact in the middle of the page, so it will be quick to ready and easily scroll on a smart phone.

4) Keep your most important content "above the fold," – what's seen in the browser window when you first open a site in it. This way, viewers see this information immediately without any scrolling. This helps draw readers into looking more closely at your page, and then they can quickly see the basics, such as the video, main bullet-points, and opt-in forms. You can add additional content with keywords below the fold, so you get an added SEO boost.

5) Encourage people to jump on your offer now, rather than waiting, by providing an extra discount for a limited time, such as offering a video program for $24.95 now versus $74.95 later.

6) Add in images of your book, programs, and any products.

7) Use a statistic if it shows a high number of likes or downloads, such as "over 10,000 likes in 10 days on Facebook." But if you have only gotten a small number of likes or downloads, leave this out.

So now, go to it. Create your squeeze page. You can even plan it out and write your copy before you set it up on your website. Once it's up, the next step is to promote it to build traffic to your site.

# CHAPTER 24: GETTING PAID WITH A PAYMENT PLATFORM

Once you are ready to start selling your book and other programs, you want to get paid. If you are selling digital products, it helps to use one of the payment platforms, though there are other payment methods.

## Common Payment Methods

You can arrange to receive a payment directly through a payment processor, such as PayPal, WePay, and Amazon Payments, where you set up an account and include payment buttons on your website. Then, payments either go automatically to your bank, as with WePay, or you request a withdrawal to your bank, as with PayPal. Alternatively, you can give someone your account email, as with PayPal, and the person can send you money by making a direct deposit in your account or use their credit card.

Another payment alternative when your books or other programs are listed on some services, such as CreateSpace (www.createspace.com), Amazon, or Smashwords (www.smashwords.com), is that platform will keep track of your sales and send you payments via PayPal or make a deposit directly in your bank. These services also provide for any fulfillment, such as shipping physical books from CreateSpace or Amazon, or providing downloads to the customer from Smashwords, which also provides your book files to a dozen other digital book stores and collects any payments from them.

The disadvantage of these payment processors and services when you don't want to limit your book sales to certain digital distribution channels or have other programs to sell (such as video and DVD training programs) is that you have to handle the fulfillment yourself. For example, if you get a payment for $30 from PayPal for a digital book, you have to send an email with an attachment or a link to Dropbox, Hightail, or other service which has the file, so the customer can access it.

But if you get these special payment platforms, the service will handle the fulfillment, along with sending out receipts, reminders, thank you, and follow-up emails to customers, so you don't have to do that individually. Then, too, some of these platforms provide you with links to other vendors who might become affiliates who will sell your book or programs; or they may have products and services that might appeal to your contacts, and you will get a referral fee for those sales. Plus, some of these platforms will do PR for their more popular products, which might help your sales, too, if your book or programs are selected.

Thus, if you integrate one of these dedicated payment platforms into your website, it can help to streamline the process, as well as handle any refunds from customers who subsequently decide they don't want your book or other programs. (Probably there won't be many refund requests; but you may get a few, and once you give the okay, these services can readily process a refund for you.

## The Major Payment Platforms

Dedicated payment platforms have a number of advantages. They are integrated with your autoresponder, and addition to taking payments, they can collect emails. They also permit you to make arrangements with affiliates, so when you sell something for an affiliate, you get paid a commission, just as they get a commission when they sell one of your books or programs. Some of these platforms have their own online storefronts, where they can sell your products, too.

The disadvantage of these platforms is they take a percentage of the sale on top of what a payment processor like PayPal charges. It also can take some time to learn how to set up and use the platform, which has its own login, so that's one more user name and password to remember. But you can create a chart to keep track of your passwords, and you can always use a password recovery feature by putting in your own email and getting a link to set your password again.

Five of the most common platforms include:
- ClickBank
- Zaxaa
- Nanacast
- JVZoo
- E-Junkie

I'll describe each in turn to help you choose for yourself.

## ClickBank (www.clickbank.com)

ClickBank is probably the most popular and widely used, and it's easy to open up an account. I did so within minutes by creating a username and verifying my email. Besides books, ClickBank sells all kinds of products. As the company describes on its website, it started over 17 years ago and has delivered lifestyle products to customers around the globe. Amazingly, ClickBank has a library of over 6 million unique products, 200 million customers around the world, and a network of 500,000 digital marketing experts who could become your affiliates in over 190 countries, so your book or other products can reach customers worldwide.

The company can support ongoing subscriptions and monthly membership, and if someone has already bought your book or other products, ClickBank will re-market additional offerings from you to create return customers and more sales. Plus the company is set up to help you create joint venture partnership and split profits.

However, while ClickBank states it offers simple flat rate pricing, with "no hidden fees or surprises," it has an initial start-up fee of $49.95 to provide a legal compliance review for product approval for your product materials, sales funnel, marketing/promotional copy, and price points. So this initial approval fee could become expensive if you have multiple products and programs, unless you can arrange for this approval to cover the different books and programs you are selling, now and in the future.

Assuming your book and other products are accepted, the ClickBank fee is $1 for a transaction fee, plus 7.5% a sale. The average affiliate commission is 50% and sometimes as high as 75%. While this platform is good if you want to do affiliate selling of other people's products, it could be overly expensive when you are just starting up and have few products to sell because of the $49.95 start-up fee. Still, it's easy to use and get started.

## Zaxaa (www.zaxaa.com)

Zaxaa is an ideal platform for getting started, since there's no charge when you sign up under it's Instant Automation Plan. Then, it charges a 3% fee per sale, besides what your payment processor charges (it's about 4% for Pay Pal. While the company is fairly new, it's easy to set up with an auto responder integration, and it's easy to set up affiliates, though it doesn't have the vast number of connections as does ClickBank, and it's not as big as JD200, to be described next.

As the company describes itself, it is a "shopping cart platform to instantly set up profitable sales funnels and sell digital products online, instantly deliver them to your customers, and instantly recruit affiliates to help sell your products." You don't even need a website or installation on a webpage. You can simply post unlimited products directly on the Zaxaa site, though the benefit of having a squeeze page is to entice people to buy your book or programs, whether they are featured on your site or on Zaxaa. Additionally, Zaxxa has a WordPress membership plug-in, so you can create a membership site for products offered to members. And you can set up monthly, yearly, bi-yearly, bi-monthly, weekly, and daily subscriptions. If you want to test out your copy and pricing for two different advertising pitches to potential customers, you can create trials, too, to see which ad pitch works best. Another plus is an incentive for others to sell your products, since you can set up an instant payout of commissions to affiliates, so you don't have to manually calculate and send the payments to them. Thus, it's easier for you, and affiliates like this instant payment arrangement, since they want to get paid fast.

Another benefit of this platform is that you can instantly create your hosted front-store to showcase all of your products. You just direct everyone to your sales funnel, which is your user name (ie: mine is changemakers) and Zaxaa's website (ie: changemakers.zaxaa.com). While most sellers promote a single product one at a time, having the front-store means that someone can come back to purchase later, and people can choose which products they want to buy at their convenience. You can also instantly build your customer list by integrating the platform with various form and mailing programs, such as Aweber, GetResposne, MailChimp, iContact, SendReach, and more. When customers purchase anything, they get added to your list, so you can easily contact them about new products. Then, too, the company offers an opportunity to create discount coupons, so you can limit them to a certain time period or to selected customers. If you have limited quantities of a product or program, such as if you want to limit a webinar to 25 or 50 people, you can do that, too, which can increase sales, because people can feel they are getting something of greater value because the quantity is limited. Should you run into scammers and fraudsters who try to cheat you, you can ban affiliates from promoting your products or can stop customers from purchasing from them. Later, as your sales increase and you sign up for Zaxaa's Premium Automation Plan, you can get all kinds of metric reports to see how your retention rate is going for recurring products, how many unique visitors you have, your conversion rates, and more.

The company also offers video tutorials to help you set up your store, such as how to create a front-end product or add a OTO (one-time-offer) product to your sales funnels. Other videos talk about how to create a coupon to give discounts, pay out commissions, integrate your payment processors/gateways with Zaxaa, and see how well your products are selling.

Once you start seeing large sales, you have two other options -- $77 a month with no transaction fee, discounted from its usual $99.95, or $499.95 yearly, discounted from $924 per year. For now, sign up for Zaxaa's free option, which allows you to have unlimited products, upsells and downsells, sales funnels, affiliate programs, customers, and affiliates. Plus you can take recurring or one-time payments, and you can use PayPal Adaptive, where commissions can be paid out at the point of sale, and you can have up to 3 partners. Some other arrangements are only for those with the Premium Automation monthly or yearly plan, such as taking payments using Authorize.net, Strike, 2 Checkout or PayPal Standard, and taking offline payments. With this premium plan, you additionally get certain metrics, such as a prediction of your income, retention metrics for recurring products, and embedding payment forms on your own site.

Choosing among the different plans can sound quite complicated, so keep it simple and don't worry about these other possibilities until your 3% fee to Zaxaa is over $40 a month.

# CHAPTER 25: SOME ADDITIONAL PAYMENT PLATFORM

So you have a full range of payment possibilities, here are a few more platforms to consider, especially as your sales pick up.

## JVZoo (www.jvzoo.com)

JVZoo has a number of advantage, including no out of pocket costs to sign up as a seller. You can create as many buy buttons as you like and add as many products as you want in return for paying a 5% fee for each sale. You can create a sales funnel for all of your products, and create urgency to buy with countdown buttons to the end of a sale. You can even create a website on one of the company's sales generators, and the company will host the page for you. You can then instantly add customers to your list when they purchase one of your products.

For simplicity sake, the company arranges for all payments to be handled by PayPal, the biggest payment processor, and after the purchase, the company's customer portal will instantly deliver your books or other products for you. The service makes it easy to recruit affiliates, since you list your product and interested affiliates contact you. Once you agree to work together, you can give your affiliates either an instant or a delayed payment to make sure customers are satisfied with their purchase, so you stay in control of any refunds. Should you have partners, the company can pay up to three joint venture partners for each transaction. The company additionally provides you with tracking information on your dashboard, which shows the number of clicks and sales. Should you sell online courses, the company has software  for building a membership site through its Membership Software Platform, so you can deliver your courses to targeted customers.

In short, it's an easy to use site with good features, including autoresponder integration, with an emphasis on Internet marketing generally. It has a smaller number of affiliates than some other companies and a slightly higher commission rate than Zaxxa.

## Nanacast (www.nanacast.com)

Nanacast has many great features, and it offers a free trial to get started. But after that it has fairly high monthly costs, from $97 a month for its Viral Package to $147 a month for its Viral and Elite Premium Package, though the Elite Package may go up to $247 a month. Also, it can take more time to learn this system than the other platforms. An upside is that there is no percentage taken from your sales.

This platform has all kinds of great features if you have enough sales for this to make sense. For instance the platform integrates with all of your autoresponder tools, and merchant accounts, including PayPal and Stripe. You can easily turn any existing website or blog into a membership site using a built-in Nanacast membership wizard. It also has its own WordPress plug-in, and you can quickly and easily integrate with any third party tools, such as Joomla, Drupal, Vbulletin, and the popular marketing automation platforms. In addition, the Nanacast platform is designed to automate everything. This includes automating any sales funnel, including upsells, downsells, and bundling offers. You can automate payment collections, such as recurring, trial, and continuity payments. You can additionally automate any client communication, including "thank you" emails and billing information, and set up split test order pages, so you can see which approach works best when you vary the advertising message, price, or other features. Then, too, you can automate your revenue, profit, tax, expense, and commission reports.

The platform additionally permits you to customize the checkout page with your own branding and logo, unlike other platforms such as JVZoo and Clickbank. Plus you can customize all the pages in your sales funnel so they match your brand, whatever designs you use. You can also add 1-click upsells and downsells to your page, along with sales funnels where one page leads readily from one page to another. Nanacast enables you to monetize everything, even your free content, by creating a blog teaser that entices people to want to know more, so they have to pay for full access. You can also create a paid subscription podcast, as well as custom affiliate links for your partners that link to any URL on your website or blog posts. Then, too, Nanacast can help you build a large team of affiliates to promote your material with a strong affiliate program. Another advantage is that the platform is integrated with the leading third party services many online marketers use, including Aweber, Getresponse, Mail Chimp, iContact, Constant Contact, and others.

In sum, it's a great program, although when you are just starting, the basic cost of $97 a month is high. Though you may get an initial free trial period, after that, until you have significant sales, this program makes no sense.

## E-Junkie (www.e-junkie.com)

Finally, E-Junkie is good for selling tangible goods, like DVDs, as well as digital goods. It includes inventory management for physical goods, which means it can offer shipping. Like the other platforms it provides autoresponder and affiliate support, and it is integrated with different payment processors, including PayPal, 2CheckOut, Authorize.Net, and ClickBank. Also, it has a number of pre-integrated services, including Google Analytics, Aweber, MailChimp, GerResponse, and PublishMyMedia. If you want to ship something, it is integrated with the U.S. Postal Service and UPS.

You can start with a 1 week free trial to try it out, and thereafter it is only $5 a month with 10 or fewer products, and up to 200 MB of storage space for your download files. As you have more products and need more storage space, the monthly cost goes up, though there's no charge when you participate in other sellers' affiliate programs. Making it more affordable, there is no set up fee, no transaction fee or limit, and no bandwidth fee or limit. In the event you have files to download from another location, you need to sign up for a monthly plan at $20 or more, and you can have even more products – 60 or more. So this could be a good platform, especially if you have physical products and want to download files from another site, such as your website, though otherwise, you can readily store files on the e-Junkie platform. The platform also appears to have a number of ebook sellers, along with artists and craftspeople selling their wares – and you can check out the 500 or so affiliate products on the site. But the other sites have more established affiliates with higher end products, if you want to do affiliate sales.

## Different Payment Processors

Besides PayPal, which all of the sales platforms appear to take, many take other payment processors, such as Amazon Payments, and some can integrate with your own credit card payment platforms or processor. Some also take Stripe, which has no monthly fee and is easy to use and set up.

## Where to Put Your Sales Page

While some platforms provide a sales page where you can post your product, it is best to have your own website or sales page, so you can post your product on multiple platforms. You just have to duplicate your sales page and set up different buy buttons for each platform. Putting your sales page on multiple platforms is also a good way to test out which platform works best for you, though look for platforms with just a transaction fee or a low monthly fee to get started, and initially, when you just have one or a few products, pick one platform to start.

For more information, go to the websites of these different platforms.

# CHAPTER 26: BUILDING TRAFFIC TO YOUR SQUEEZE PAGE WITH VIDEO ADS

Once you set up your squeeze page, you need to get people to find it among about one billion websites out there – and about 3 trillion Internet users. Do you doubt the numbers? There is even a website with a counter for the number of websites (http://www.internetlivestats.com/total-number-of-websites) , and the day I checked, the counter indicated about 929 million websites online, with another few websites added every second  Whew!

## Different Type of Ad Approaches

In any ad campaign, direct your message to targeted traffic – individuals who might be interested in your books and programs – and get them to go to your squeeze page or website.

Many types of Internet ads do this. These include:
- text ads that appear on a search engine, usually with a headline, a few lines of copy, and a link to your webpage;
- display ads, which generally appear in a box on the top right;
- pop-up ads, which jump up when you move your mouse over a certain area or click on a news article;
- sponsored ads which appear on a news feed, such as on Facebook. They include a photo, headline, and copy, which look like other headlines which link to articles or webpages, but they include a notice that this is a "Sponsored" ad to indicate this isn't news or a posting from a Facebook friend. These are all ads where you pay based on the number of clicks and the price per click.

Another advertising approach is to advertise on a website of an individual or organization that appeals to your target market.

For example, if you have a weight loss product, you might look for websites that promote healthy diets and nutrition. Then you work out with the website owner what they charge for different types of ads.

Still another source of advertising is Meetup groups in your specialty and geographic region, since some group organizers have sponsors. In return for a flat fee or monthly charge of about $50-$100, they list their logo, a few lines of copy, and may include information about them in emails to their members. As an example, I found sponsors for some of my film Meetup groups who paid $50 a month or $75 for 2 months to promote their film festivals and other events. Besides giving them a logo listing, I sent out a newsletter with a featured announcement about their programs.

## Using Video Ads

Aside from these text, display or other types of ads on Facebook and other platforms, video ads have been growing in popularity. These are ads that you place on YouTube or Facebook. You use the Google AdWords/Video platform to place the video ads in front of people who are searching for your type of content on YouTube, and you use the Facebook advertising program to place similar videos on Facebook.

On Facebook, your ads are much like an ad with a picture that appears in a news feed for a particular audience. It features the name and logo of the company advertised, followed by 2-3 lines of copy and then the picture or video to click, whether the news feed is streamed on a computer or mobile device. You can set your daily budget for one ad or your total campaign, and you can run an ad for as little as $5, which affects how often the ad shows up to a selected target audience.

On Facebook there is an ad auction where you choose the budget for your ad based on the total amount you want to spend. Also, you choose a bid – the amount you are willing to pay to have customers see your ad and click it or take some other action. You can opt to pay a specific amount a day, such as $5 per day, and enter your budget amount. Or you can create a lifetime budget for your ad, and you ad will run continuously until that budget amount is reached or your ad end date arrives. Facebook also has an option called "Optimized Bidding," where Facebook automatically bids for you while staying within your chosen budget and offers your ad to the people more likely to take action, and will bid at the lowest possible price. Or you can choose your own bid price, and Facebook will suggest a bid range based on the audience you want to reach.

On YouTube, your ad looks like just another video, and it appears before, during, or beside the video you want to see. However you arrange for these ads through the GoogleAdWords videos, it's called a TrueView video campaign.

There are two types of video ads:

Display ads, where the video appears next to YouTube videos, on YouTube search results, on video plays on YouTube channels and on publisher sites across the Display network. You use this format to promote a video when people are searching for or browsing videos on YouTube and across the web. You are charged when a viewer clicks on your ad and begins watching your video.

In-Stream ads are commercials that appear before, during, and after Internet videos. The most common are linear ads which look like television commercials. They delay or interrupt the video and typically last 15 to 30 seconds, sometimes as much as 40 seconds. Those that run before videos are called pre-roll ads. Mid-roll ads occur during the video, and post-rolls display at the end.

Nonlinear overlay ads are superimposed over the video, so the user continues watching while the ad is displayed.

Not all videos have ads and start to play right away. But commonly, the most popular videos have ads, though typically users can skip the ad after 5 seconds if they don't want to watch it. That means you have up to 5 seconds to quickly attract the viewers' attention with content that makes them want to see your whole ad.

Should viewers watch the ad all the way through, the last page will include a link to your squeeze page, as well as an option to replay the ad. If they click on that link, they will go there, and you will be charged for that click. You will also be charged if viewers watch for longer than 30 seconds, but if they watch less than 30 seconds, you don't pay. Once they go to your squeeze page, it should have a form to capture their email, along with an offer for a free gift, and more information on your book and programs.

## Targeting Your Ads

As in any kind of ad campaign, target your ads to your target market. To do so, think about who is most likely to be interested in your book or programs and what keywords they may search for to find information or view videos. Think of what questions they might ask to find information on what you are offering.

For example, if you have a book about diet and nutrition, you might come up with some topics and questions, such as "How to lose weight," "How to have a healthy lifestyle," or "Where can I find diet supplements?" Then, turn those topics and questions into keywords or phrases, such as "lose weight," "healthy lifestyle," and "diet supplements."

Also, be aware of the differences in the way Facebook and YouTube do their targeting, when you use keywords. Facebook target people based on what they indicate they "like," and you can additionally target your ad based on audience characteristics, which might include location, demographics such as age and gender, interests, activities, hobbies, and what people buy online and offline. You fill out a profile of who you want to see the ad, and Facebook targets the ad accordingly. On YouTube you use keywords, and AdWords targets people with those interests.

## Deciding What to Say

Create your ad to match what people are searching for. You have to be really specific. So your ad message should directly target what people need or want with a short question or statement. To take the weight loss example again, don't say something vague like: "Now you can be healthier than ever" or "Here's a new way to feel great." Instead, use a header like: "A new method to lose 20 pounds in 30 days," or "A new healthy way to lose weight in record time." Support your headline with a message that explains the headline and points up the benefits of the product or service.

More specifically, organize your video into a series of short 3-5 second segments, where your copy is very short (say up to 40 words) and combined with a video image that attracts attention and interest. It should look professional, so your message comes across with an air of credibility and authority.

## The Different Advertising Platforms

As described, the two main ad platforms for video ads are Facebook and YouTube, and Facebook has regular display ads too. Though they work slightly differently, you can create the same ad for both, with some tweaks.

Some video ad companies can create ads for both, such as VeeRoll (www.veeroll.com) , which can make a video for you in a few minutes using templates. That saves you the cost of hiring a professional video service, and they can help you put up your ad in either or both platforms.

# CHAPTER 27: CREATING AN ADWORDS TEXT OR VIDEO CAMPAIGN

There are two types of ad formats for AdWords campaigns. One is the traditional text and display ad campaign, where ads appear based on a search on Google and its website publisher partners. The other is a video TruView campaign, where the video ad comes up in a search. But while a cost per click (CPC) model is used for determining the cost of a text or display ad, in a video ad campaign, the payment is based on a cost-per-view (CPV).

Either approach can work well, based on how well you target your ad and write your copy to appeal to your target market. In both cases, you can limit your budget per day or for of the whole campaign. However, the maximum amount you set for each click contributes to how often your ad will appear and in what position on the page, so you can expect more response with a higher budget.

## Using a Text or Display Ad

In the online text or image ads, customers on the web can see your ad, read its text, and click your URL to go directly to your squeeze page or website. Such an ad may sometimes appear on the top right of the page or it may go above the other search results. In either case, it is clearly labeled a sponsored ad or includes the "Ad" logo in a small yellow box to the left, above, or below the ad copy.

In such a campaign (http://www.google.com/adwords, you have three basic elements, a headline to attract interest, such as "Freshly Brewed Coffee," "Hunter's Specialties Blind Materials" or "Waterfowl Migration Map," with the phrase "Sponsored" or an

Ad logo near the website link in the ad. Then, you have another two lines to further entice the user, such as "Already perfectly brewed coffee/The perfect way to start your day." In some cases, you can include a small picture, about 1" x 1" next to your ad copy, as in the example below. When someone does a search, using key words in your ad, such as "fresh coffee" or "duck hunting" your ad may turn up.

## Freshly Brewed Coffee

Ad cafe.example-business.com
Always perfectly brewed coffee.
The perfect way to start your day.

## Shop for duck hunting on Google

Sponsored

Hunters Specialties Blind Material 12 ft. - Wheatfield

**$24.99** from Cabela's

World's Foremost Outfitter - Since 1961

In placing your ad, you use a form in which you put your Headline, link to your website or squeeze page, and two lines of text. Next you choose the search terms or keywords that will result in your ad showing up in the Google search results, based on the words you select. You can further fine tune your ad wording, keywords, locations, and other settings – such as if you only want your ad to appear for individuals living in certain regions or cities near where you are conducting a workshop on your book. Then, you set your daily budget and your maximum bid.

Most people choose a cost-per-click, or CPC bid, which is the preferred bid for driving traffic to your website, though there are two other ways to set bids. One is the cost-per-impressions or CPM bid which is only available for Display Network campaigns and is based on the number of impressions or times your ad shows. This approach is mainly used for increasing brand awareness. The third strategy is the cost-per-acquisition or CPA bid, in which you only pay when someone takes a specific action on your website after clicking on one of your ads. This method is mainly used by experienced AdWords advertisers who are interested in conversions, such as purchases or sign-ups.

Once you set your bid, Google uses a formula to decide where to place your ad and how high in the search results, based on your budget and others bidding on a particular keyword. Should there be more than one person bidding on that placement, the one with the highest bid gets to display their ad. However, that person may not pay the full amount of that high bid, since he or she will pay just above the next highest bidder, which would be just enough to be the highest bid. For example, if you use the CPC bidding strategy and bid $1 per click and another person bids .50, you would only be charged $.51 per click.

Later, you can get stats on how well your ad is doing, where you see the number of clicks and cost of each ad, so you can learn the average cost of each click and how well these clicks have converted into sales. Then, you can determine how much value and ultimately profit you are getting from the clicks and therefore the effectiveness of the whole campaign.

## Using a Video Ad

For a video ad, you need to create video of about 15-40 seconds that is hosted on YouTube. Then, you arrange to have it play through AdWords on YouTube or on one of Google's partner's websites. Or you use a similar approach in arranging for the video ad to appear on Facebook. Since YouTube is still the most popular platform for video ads, I'll focus on that.

AdWords uses a similar cost-per-view (CPV) arrangement that is much like the CPC view for the text and display ads. You similarly set the price you'll pay for your TrueView video ads when created through AdWords, which is only one way to arrange for ads on YouTube. But these other ads are much more expensive, and typically they are bought via ad agencies working with larger companies and larger budgets. So initially, just think of creating your video ad through the Google AdWords platform.

You need to provide a completed video, rather than inserting the contents in a text or display ad, so AdWords can generate the ad. Google will determine where the ad appears on the screen based on the type of ad selected – In-stream or Display, and the frequency and placement will depend on your keywords and budget, based on how much you are willing to pay for a view.

In creating your video ad, the ad should be appealing to the target audience, so they view it and ideally click to go to your squeeze page or website, though if they watch less than 30 seconds or don't watch the whole shorter ad, you don't pay.

The two types of ads appearing in a different context are:

- In-Stream ads, where your video ad appears before, during or after other videos on YouTube or on the DisplayNnetwork, which includes other video publisher sites, games, and apps. You pay when a viewer watches 30 seconds of a longer video or for the whole video if it's shorter than 30 seconds, or engages in other video interactions, such as clicking on a call to action overlay (CTA), cards, or companion banners. On these ads, you will see an "x" button, which enables the person to stop seeing your video and go to the original video he or she wants to see.

- In-Display ads, where your video appears when people search or browse videos on YouTube and across the web, through YouTube search results. They also might appear on publisher sites on the Display Network. You are charged when a viewer clicks on your ad and begins watching your video.

## Setting a CPV (Click-Per-View) Bid

For either type of ad, you set up CPV bid, which is the highest price you want to pay per view. This is called your maximum CPV bid or your "Max. CPV. For example, if you think it worth 30 cents for someone to watch your video, you can set 30 cents as your maximum CPV. You can set a different bid maximum for your in-stream and in-display ads.

This max CPV is used in an auction, much like the CPC auction, to determine your chances of winning the auction and appearing to viewers. This bid maximum can also affect your ad's position among other ads on the search results page. The higher your bid, the better your chances of your ad appearing and being in a better position compared to other advertisers' ads, so it will gain more views.

Because of the way this auction works, you may not have to pay the full amount, since wherever possible, Google will charge you only what's necessary for your ad to appear on the page. So this final amount you actually pay for a view is called the "actual CPV."

Google also includes your quality score and your ad rank in its formula for figuring out your payment. As Google describes it, your "Quality Score is a measure of how relevant your ad is to a customer, and includes multiple performance factors like view rates. Once Google determines your Quality Score, this is multiplied by your max CPV bid to rank your ads among other advertisers to determine your rank. In the auction, the highest ranked ad wins, and the cost for a video view of this ad is just above the CPV of the next ranking ad. In any event, if you didn't follow all that, just know that Google has a complicated process for determining how and when your ad will appear, and the higher your max CPV, the more likely it is that your ad will appear more often in a higher position.

To further determine your ad placement and frequency, your ad is grouped with other ads in that same format (all in-stream ads or all display ads). Then, based on your bid and the bids of the other advertisers for a particular keyword along with other characteristics you have selected, such as location and age and gender demographics, Google figures out where and when to place your video.

How should you decide how to bid? One way is to base your bid based on the traffic forecasting data Google provides as you select your settings for your target audience and your max CPV, so you can see the likely forecast based on your maximum bid. Alternatively, you can base your bid on the value of a view to you, depending on the nature of what you are selling. For example, if you are pitching high valued workshops and seminars, price it higher, than if you have a lower cost book for sale.

Besides setting this maximum CPV, you can control how much you spend each day or for the whole campaign. That way you don't suddenly find you are getting charged for a huge number of clicks without them converting into a sign-up or sale.

## Learning the Results

To learn how your campaign is doing, you can see the results, including the number of clicks or views and costs, on a day by day basis for each ad. Then, you can assess the value of the ad you based on the amount you have invested, the number of views, the cost per view, the number of impressions, and the number of click-throughs to determine the cost per click (CPC). After that, look at the conversion factor based on how many people clicked to obtain their free gift and how many of those people ultimately bought your book or other programs. Finally, look at your proceeds compared to your investment to decide if the ad campaign was worth it.

As Matthew Peneycad reported in *Social Media Today:* "YouTube TrueView Ads: Anticipated Results and Tips" (http://www.socialmediatoday.com/content/youtube-trueview-ads-anticipated-results-and-tips), he got the following results for a test buy.  He invested $250, got 5500 views, had a CPV of 45 cents, had 32,500 impressions, and a CPC of 57 cents.  Given the high rate of response, he spent the $250 in 2 hours, and he reported being "fairly happy with the results."  He was happy to obtain a CPC which was competitive to Facebook's suggested bid for his targeting selections, and he was very happy with the targeting options.  Though he ended his article with some cautions, most notably to set a daily spend limit for a campaign with a longer duration, since otherwise,  you could quickly spend a lot of money.  Additionally, Peneycad recommended combining a video campaign with other traffic and view drivers, including paid media, supporting advertising campaigns, PR, gaining support from influencers, and seeding programs to give your content further exposure.

In a quota.com forum (https://www.quora.com/What-is-a-good-average-cost-per-view-CPV-on-YouTube-or-CPM), a half-dozen people chimed in on the average CPV and the results.  The general view was 10-30 cents was a typical amount for locally-targeted campaigns, while one man felt 7-8 cents was a good CPV for the US with some targeting, and they reported an average of 15-24 cents, and as little as 5 cent.  The view rate was about 20-25%, though one man reported an average view rate of 23% and a 54% view rate on more than 50% of his video ads, reflecting the importance of having an appealing video to increase viewership.

So generally, people reported good results after spending a relatively small amount for each view.  However, to fully assess the value of your campaign, determine how many of those views and clicks turn into conversions, where people want more information or make a purchase from you.

# CHAPTER 28: INSTALLING WORD PRESS ON YOUR SQUEEZE PAGE OR WEBSITE

Once you select your domain name, you can to set up your squeeze page or website with WordPress. After that, you can use Instabuilder or any sitebuilding program to make it easier to add in different features, like graphics, videos, and text boxes. While you can do this setup before you have your copy, I found it helpful to prepare the copy for the initial pages of the site in advance to be ready to add them once the installation was complete. Later, you can add additional pages and copy.

## Creating Your Initial Pages

These initial pages for a sales pitch as described earlier are:
1) the squeeze page with a photo or video where you direct traffic
2) a form for collecting emails, which will be on the squeeze page
3) a thank you page, which includes a link to the free gift
4) the free gift (report, article, book chapter or PowerPoint presentation)
5) the sales page, which people can go to after getting their free gift; it will include a link to place an order, plus links to one or more additional pages for other programs
6) additional pages for further programs or products

While you can send your traffic directly to your sales page, the advantage of the free gift, along with the form for collecting emails and the thank you page with the free gift link, is to increase interest, gain trust with your gift, and collect an email for continued promotions. I recommend preparing the copy for these pages in advance so you have something to put on the pages.

Once you have the domain name, you can set up the site by installing WordPress and any sitebuilding program you are using, such as Instabuilder. Then, you can wait until you have your copy to continue finalizing the site, such as picking a theme and adding your copy.

While you can create your website using any kind of platform, WordPress is now used on about 70% of all websites, is very easy to set up, and has many simple to use buttons for creating pages. Also, it is easy to install various sitebuilders, such as Instabuilder or WordPress. Thus, I will focus on using WordPress here, and in the next section, I will discuss using Instabuilder.

## Installing WordPress

One of the easiest ways to install WordPress is using the Mojo marketplace, which some hosts like BlueHost, my website provider, use. If you aren't able to use the Mojo marketplace, you can follow some more complicated steps where you have to create a new database, new user, assign the user to the database, and disable automatic database creation. In this case, check with your website hosting support team on what to do. Ideally, though, you can readily install WordPress, especially with the website hosts that have a one-click installation process.

The basic steps to install WordPress through the Mojo marketplace are these. BlueHost also has a 3-minute video on how to do this, which can apply to the basic steps with any host that permits this easy set-up. You can see it at https://my.bluehost.com/cgi/help/wordpress. The steps are:
- Log into your Control Panel.
- Go to the Website Builder section.
- Choose "Install WordPress."
- This brings you to the Mojo Marketplace. Click "Install."

- Select the domain you want to install WordPress on. You can choose any domain in your account or which is pointed to your hosting account from your domain name provider. You can specify a subdirectory within your domain if you wish in the box to the right and create a name for it, such as "book sale." Or leave it blank it if you want WordPress to be installed on the site's main page.

- Next click "Check Domain."

- Then click "Show Advanced Options." This will allow you to change your site name or title, which you can also change later. The important thing is to change your user name to one which you can remember and isn't simple like "admin." You can use your email or a user name which you create.

- Now create a password. You can use one that is automatically generated or create your own. If you do create one, it should be very secure and strong, such as if you use a capital letter, a mix of letters and numbers, and some symbols such as a "," or the "@" sign.

- Next check "Automatically create a new database."

- Check that you have read the terms and conditions.

- Click "Install now," and you can see WordPress installing on the menu bar on top of our screen.

- Once the install is complete, click "View Credentials." This will show you the new URL for your site, as well as the admin URL you need to log into the site, along with your user name and password.

- Now you can go to the URL and make sure you can log in after you put in your user name and password.

Then, you are on WordPress. Once you are logged in, you will see a display that looks like this, and will let you know the latest version of WordPress that you are running (ie: 4.3.1 as of this writing).

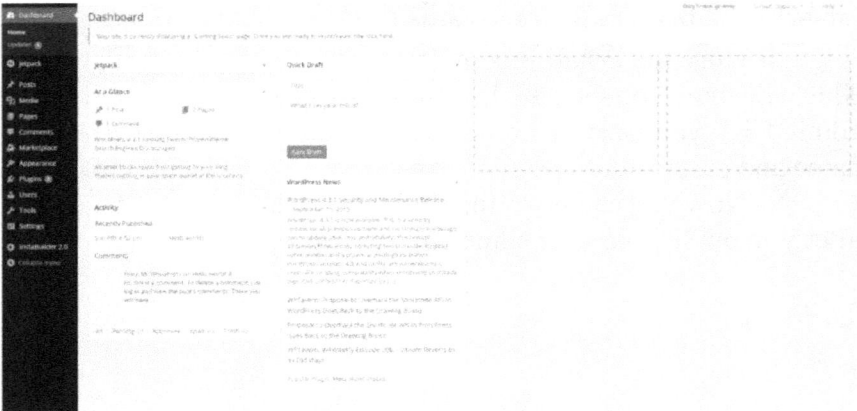

The next steps according to my web designer are these:

Add in "Home" for your first page, "Blog," if you plan to include a blog, and a separate page for your squeeze page (though don't call it that), thank you page, sales page, and any other pages you plan to link to, such as a workshops and seminars page. Click "publish" or "save" as you make these changes. You'll notice that the button for "Enable Instabuilder 2.0" is off. That's because I installed it, but didn't turn it on yet, because I wanted to explain how WordPress works first. Then, I'll describe how to install and use Instabuilder, which can help you in creating your squeeze and sales pages, rather than just using WordPress.

Here's what the page looks like when you start adding new pages on WordPress. You click "Add New Page," than add a title and the copy for that page. Or create the pages you want and add in the copy later.

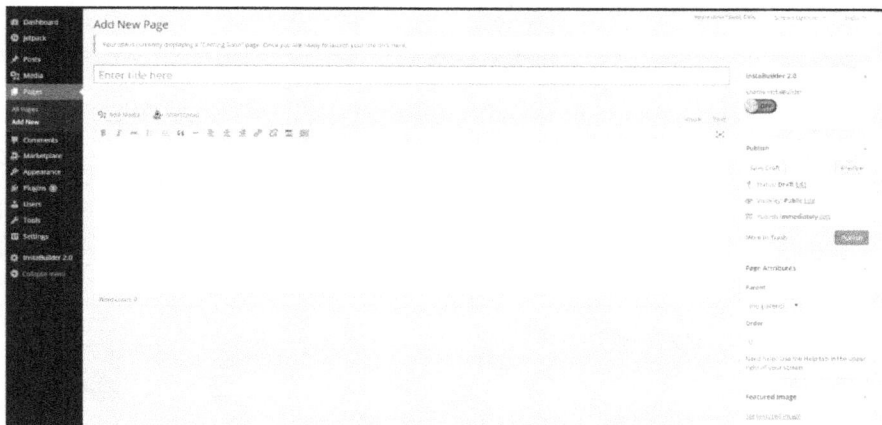

After you add each new page click "Publish" to add that to your site. For example, here's how I set up my squeeze page, though I called it "Exciting New Book" so the URL doesn't say "squeeze page." Similarly, give your thank you, free gift, sales page, and other pages other titles.

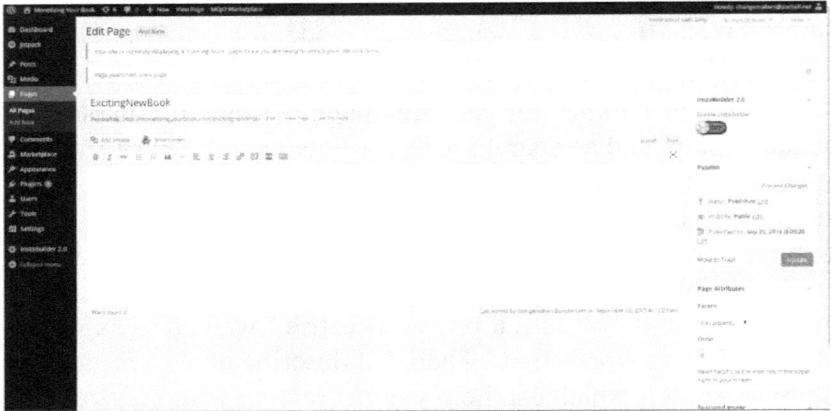

After you add in your new pages, if you click the All Pages button, you will see a listing of all the pages you have created. Since you have changed the names to something more exciting, it is helpful to print out the pages and write down the new name you have created and change the original copy file (ie: from "squeezepage" to "excitingnewbook").

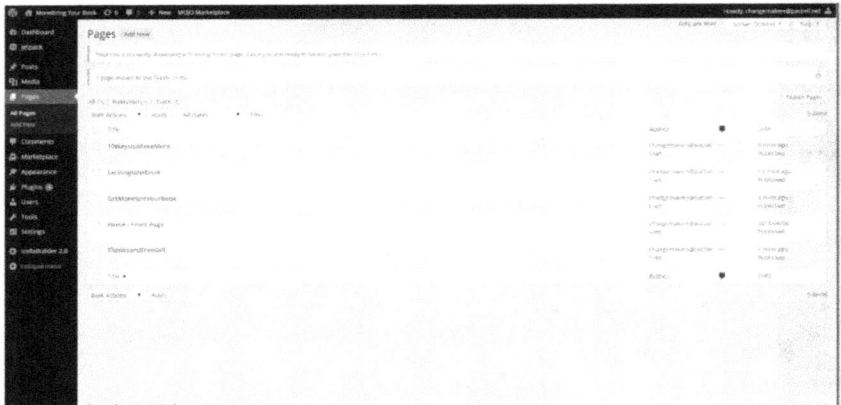

Next, go to "Settings" make the following changes, and click the "Save" button after every change. You'll see six submenus under this for General, Writing, Reading, Discussion, Media, and Permalinks. Here's what to do for each one.

162

General Settings

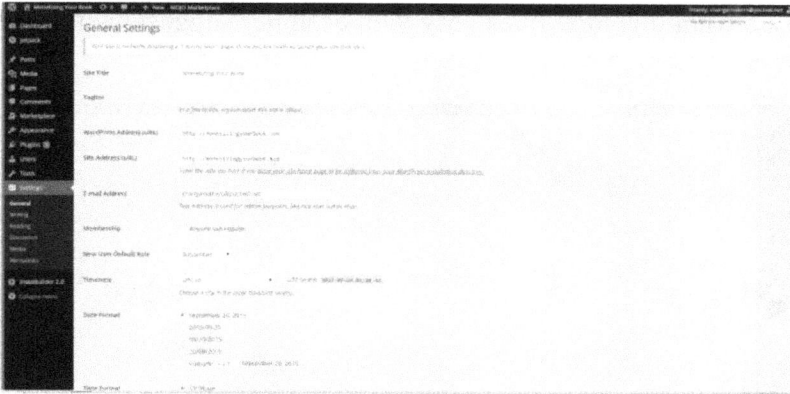

You can type in your site title and tagline and admin email address. Also, un-check "anyone can register" and select your time zone. Your time zone is based on the UTC standard for Coordinated Local Time, which starts at "O." It is the same as Greenwich Meantime, which starts in the UK and you add -1 as you go West, +1 as you go East. For example, if you are in California, the correction would normally be -8, but due to Daylight Standard Time, it is -9. Adjust your time accordingly, and you will see an indication of UTC time and local time, so you know if you have done this correctly. You will see a number of other buttons, which you can leave in the default position for the time format, date format, day the week starts. Keep it at Monday unless you prefer Sunday, site language (should be English), and some buttons for the MOJO Automatic Update Manager.

Most critically, NEVER change the WordPress Address (URL) or Site Address (URL) or you will break your site!!!

## Writing Settings

This is what this look likes.  My web designer suggests you leave it as it is.

## Reading Settings

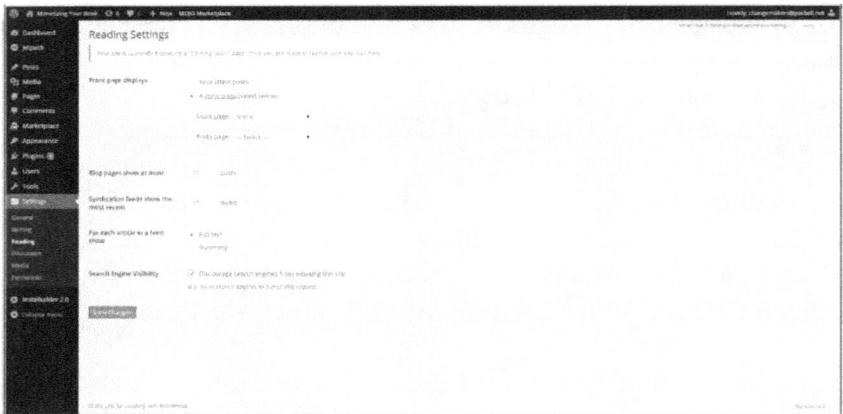

On this page, change the setting for "Front page displays" to "static page" if you are creating a regular website, which you are, except that your home page is your squeeze page, which you can use for this free gift and sales page arrangement, or it could be a single selling page with enough detail to get viewers to order now. If you select "Static Page," you must also select the "Home" page and the name of your squeeze page from the drop down menu to be the first page. For example, I called my squeeze page "ExcitingNewBook," so that becomes the home page.

Until you are ready to launch the site, check the "Discourage search engines from indexing this site," since you don't want the search engines finding a site with no content. But once you are ready to go live, uncheck this, so the search engines will now find you.

Discussion

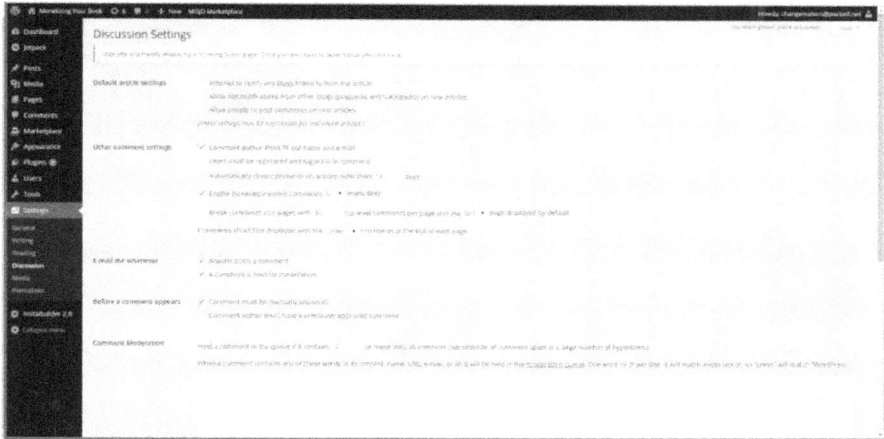

This section is designed to permit others to make comments on the site and for you to get email notifications when others post comments. Importantly, uncheck the first three check boxes or you will be quickly spammed, and you don't want anyone to add a comment unless you manually approve it. Also set up this page so anyone who comments has to fill out their name and email and you have to moderate and manually approve any comment. You also have the option of indicating that certain words in the commentator's content, name, URL, e-mail, or IP are spam. But there is no need to use this filter if you are manually approving all comments, so you can leave this blank. Finally, my web designer recommends disabling any avatars for faster loading.

In sum, the only comments settings you should have checked are these:
- Comment author must fill out name and e-mail
- Enable threated (nested) comments 5 levels deep
- Email me whenever anyone posts a comment (this is in case a comment slips by your screening in moderating all comments)
- Email me when a comment is held or moderation
- Before a comment appears comment must be manually approved.

The page should indicate that you will hold a comment in the queue if it contains 2 or more links, since a common characteristic of comment spam is a large number of hyperlinks.

Media

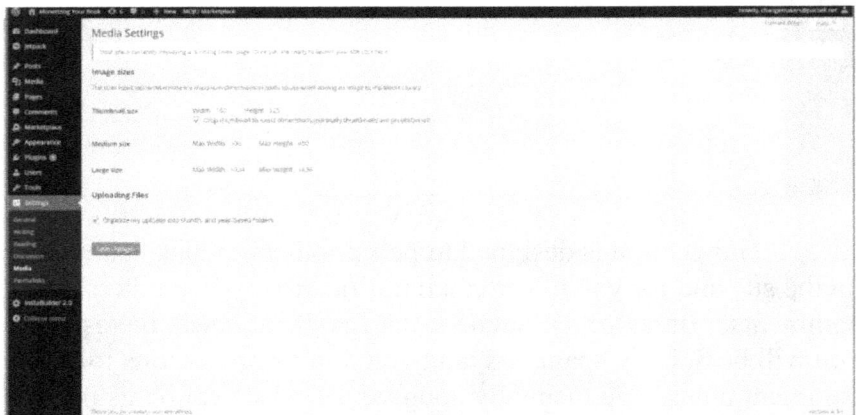

This is where you set the sizes for your images. Generally, the default sizes are fine, except if you are using images of books, change the sizes to accommodate books, which are commonly in a

2x3 ratio since most trade books are 6x9. So instead of a square format for image sizes, change them to be in the 2:3 ratio. For instance, instead of a 150x150 thumbnail, change it to 150 width and 225 height. Instead of a 300x300 pixel width for a medium sized image, make that 300x450.

To more easily find things, check on "Organize my uploads into month- and year-based folders."

Permalinks

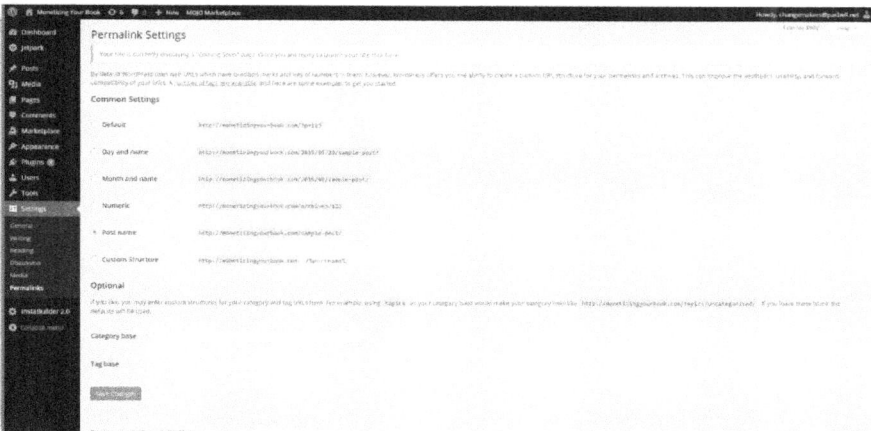

This page gives you the option for how to name your pages. Don't use the default, which gives you a page number. Instead, click "Post name", which is the most "SEO-friendly" option, whereby each post is indicated by the name of your post.

Once your WordPress site is set up, you are ready to select your theme, enter your copy onto the page, and work with a sitebuilder, if you want to design your own page, as described in the next section.

# CHAPTER 29: USING INSTABUILDER OR OTHER SITE BUILDER

Once you have WordPress installed, you can select a theme for your website. You can still sell your book and other programs directly from your website, and use the same traffic building techniques to direct viewers there. This is simply an alternate way to use a squeeze page, thank you page, and sales page to build sales, using methods that have been tested again and again by online marketers who have been found these methods effective in generating sales.

If you are creating a squeeze page, sales page, thank you page, free report, and other material to sell your book or program, you can use your theme for other pages, but when you use a sitebuilder, such as Instabuilder, you will select a template with it's own design. The big difference is that a website theme will have places to put links to other pages on the home page, whereas a squeeze page and sales page are designed to create a single sales funnel, leading the viewer from one page to another, leading to a sale. Along the way, you might have links to other websites, to provide credibility for selling your book and programs, such as by including a link to your main site with extensive information about you and your books. But usually you don't want all that detail using this squeeze page/sales page approach, since you want to direct the viewer down the funnel, rather than wandering to your site to seek more information.

A good way to work with a sitebuilder like Instabuilder is to select certain pages where you turn Instabuilder on. Then, you select from Instabuilder's templates for different types of pages, such as a squeeze page, sales page, and thank you page. But for other pages where you don't want to use a template, such as for your free article or report, use WordPress. You can include your article or report on that page, or you can add a Word or PDF file with that information which someone can download, or do both. Ideally, create this additional page in a separate window, so the viewer doesn't leave the original page. However you set this up, add a link back to the sales page or order page, where the viewer can purchase your material and perhaps get a discount or free gift for purchasing it now. I set up my own squeeze page and sales funnel using Instabuilder, which provided a very professional look, and I used a page on WordPress for the free article featuring highlights from the book, and a link on this page to an order form.

Importantly, you can't do both – you either create the page in WordPress or Instabuilder, when you turn it on for that page. But you can't use a WordPress theme on an Instabuilder page. For each page on which you want to use Instabuilder, you turn it on and select one of its page designs for the kind of page you want to create, such as a squeeze page, sales page, coming soon page, or several others. Then, you use the Instabuilder menu, which is shaped like a TV or video player remote control to add in different elements, including uploading photos and writing, editing, copying, and pasting in text.

To illustrate, here's an example of a squeeze page:

**MONETIZING YOUR BOOK**

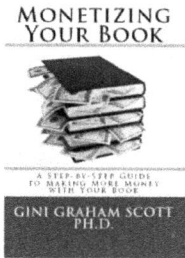

Book Series on 20 Ways to Turn Your Book Into Cash

**Sell more Books and Create Other Income Opportunities from Your Book**

Simply enter your first name and primary address to download the FREE report TODAY!

First Name

Email Address

**YES, I Want The Free Guide**

We'll never spam, rent, sell your information.

A STEP-BY-STEP GUIDE TO MAKING MORE MONEY WITH YOUR BOOK

**GINI GRAHAM SCOTT PH.D.**

Learn how to:

- Create a series of programs from your book content that help you make more money.
- Develop all kinds of spinoff products and services, from articles to workshops, seminars, and audio and video programs.
- Promote and increase the attention paid to you and your book.
- Become an expert in your field and command more money for everything you do.
- Get the tools you need to quickly earn more money than you get from just royalty or book sales.
- To learn more and get a free article with "The 10 steps to Follow to Start Making More Money from Your Book," just fill in the form and you'll immediately get your free article.

http://www.monetizingyourbook.com

Here's an example of the "thank you" page I created.

**Thanks! Here The FREE Article ...**

It's called "10 Steps to Making More Money from Your Book" and it features highlights from *Monetizing Your Book*.

**MONETIZING YOUR BOOK**

**GINI GRAHAM SCOTT PH.D.**

**⬇ CLICK HERE TO DOWNLOAD THE REPORT**

* remember to bookmark this page in case you need to download it again...*

http://monetizingyourbook.com/thanksandfreegift

Here's the beginnings of the sales page, which continues as you scroll down to highlight what's in the book, why I have the credibility to write it, the benefits for the buyer, and an offer to get a discounted priced. Sprinkled through the copy, which goes on for several pages, are a half-dozen forms for how to buy now.

http://monetizingyourbook.com/getmonetizeyourbook

If you want to put on webinars, you can create a page for that, such as the following:

Live Webinar

## Discover the Secrets of Making More Money from Your Book

To Be Announced

I'm Going To Show You

✓ How to get more reviews for your book from book reviewers and book bloggers

✓ How to use blogging and articles effectively to increase your sales.

✓ How to develop programs based on your book, such as workshops, webinars, DVD and video training materials, and more.

✓ How to use the social and traditional media to draw attention to your program and build your platform.

✓ And Much, Much More . . .

**Gini Graham Scott, Ph.D.**

She has published over 50 books with major publishers and published over 40 books through her own company. She helps clients write books and proposals, find publishers, agents, and film producers, and find ways to market and promote their books

If you aren't ready for something, you can create a "coming soon" page:

*Monetizing Your Book*

### Stay Tuned!

**We'll Be Publishing Additional Books in the Series Very Soon...**

Book 1 has just been published. Books 2, 3, and 4 will be published over the next two weeks. We can let you know as soon as they are published if you want to Get on the Waiting List, and you can also to put in your advance order for all four books at a 56% discount.

First Name

Email Address

**Get On The Waiting List**

Your Privacy is SAFE

**ADD TO CART**

**Click Here To Order**

Privacy | Disclaimer

Notice that each of these pages has its own URL, as does the report page. In naming these pages, it's best to use a few words that describe the page and are separated by hyphens, such as monetizingyourbook.com/coming-soon. By separating the words, they can be recognized by the search engines, although if these are private pages, you can indicate that, so the search engines don't index these pages. Another way to keep the search engine from recognizing the pages is to combine the words together or use letter combinations creating non-words, such as if you want to set up a private seminar page that only those who pay can access, such as monetizingyourbook.com/seminarmakingmoneylg.

If I was creating these pages, I probably would be more low- key. But online sales and marketing professionals have found out what works to sell anything, so I have deferred to their approach. So I have used their templates and kept much of their salesy wording in creating my own pages.

After you create all these pages, you have to link them together, so the squeeze page goes to the thank you page, which includes a link to the free gift, such as an article with highlights from the book. Then, the thank you page, free gift page, or both link to the sales page, which provides a way to order your book and any programs based on it.

Besides creating these pages, you still have to set up the forms for getting orders and payment, which is where the autoresponders and payment programs come in.

# CHAPTER 30: HOW INSTABUILDER WORKS AND SETTING IT UP

If you are considering using a sitebuilder to create a squeeze page, thank you page with a free gift, and sales page, here are more details on how the program works, so you can easily adapt it to your own purposes. While there are other sitebuilder programs, I have used Instabuilder, which is a good and inexpensive drag and drop software program for building the sales campaign pages.

A decade ago, the sales process was much simpler. You could set up a sales page and sell the product directly from that, or combine a sales page and a thank you page to sell a single product. They were fairly simple long pages with multiple offers to buy as you went along, and I set up several of them through outsourcing to someone from Australia who was skilled at quickly creating these pages.

However, now with the development of YouTube, Facebook, and sales videos, these sales approaches have evolved. One driver of these changes is that online selling has become very competitive, so you need more than a single book or other product for this to work effectively. You need your book, plus a variety of programs you have developed from it. Ideally, you have developed some advanced specialized programs which provide more value, so you can charge more for them. So think of your book as a door opener for other programs and services.

Another feature today is that many online sales offers have count-down times, so prospects have to act before a certain time to get the extra bonus, discount, or other special offering. These pitches also offer multiple materials for sales and deep sales funnels, so as you go along, you get multiple offers to buy. You can readily adapt these methods for selling your own books and programs.

You only need a few basic pages to start selling, and you can easily add more pages with more items to sell as you go along, including books and programs from others, so you benefit from affiliate sales commissions. These affiliate sales are essentially the online version of creating partnerships for face-to-face selling, such as when a friend with a booth at a festival opts to sell your book.

## The Advantages of Using a Sitebuilder Software

A big advantage of using sitebuilder software like Instabuilder is that you can create professional looking sales campaign pages without hiring a website designer or spending money on special software, such as a graphic program like Photo Shop to edit your images. Additionally, you don't need tech skills for using this software, since you just need to point and click your mouse to drag over and select different design elements, such as text boxes and media boxes for importing images and videos.

Another advantage is that you will find many templates – over 90 in Instanbuilder – so you can create the different pages in a sales funnel – from squeeze and sales pages, webinar and coming soon pages. Each type of page offers a variety of styles, and you can choose pages that are text and photo only or those which include videos. The trend is to feature videos, which variously feature you talking, images of your product, or a sales message written over attractive graphics as music or a voice-over presents the sales message. If you don't yet have a video, you can use a photo – and after you get a video, you can always add it to the page. Should you want to build your page from scratch you can do that, too. Or you can start with a template and delete sections you don't want or move these elements around.

What I especially liked about Instabuilder is its drag and drop interface, where you can add an element you want anywhere on your page. Thus, so you are not stuck using the original layout if you want something different. But I found it helpful to use a template as a starting point rather than creating a page from scratch.

Still another advantage of the program is that the pages are designed to be 100% responsive, which means that they can look good on a smart phone as well on as a desktop. You can see how this works when you visit a page in your browser in the "restore down" screen position, which makes your browser display smaller than the full screen. If you move your mouse all the way to the right, you can see the small arrows pointing in opposite directions, so you can resize the windows. Then, move the right side of the page as far as you can to the left. A responsive page will stack up the elements that are spread out on the page so they all flow down on the smaller mobile screen.

Then, too, the pages you create in Instabuilder are SEO-optimized, based on what online marketers know helps to increase online rankings. You can additionally customize the pages to be more search engine friendly. Or you can turn off the SEO for more private pages, such as for a thank you page, a page with a free gift, or a "member's only" area.

Instabuilder also enables you to do a split test of pages with different headlines, copy, and offers, so you can determine which one has the best results. You can readily duplicate any page and change a section of a page for a split test campaign, until you find the page copy and design with the most appeal.

If you aren't ready with to sell your book, follow-up books, or programs, you can create a "coming soon" page, and invite people to sign-up for your mailing list to be notified as soon as the site is ready. This way you contact sales leads to keep them involved for the future. Alternatively, you can invite people to place advance orders with a buy now button. If you know when the book or program will be ready or want to limit the time for a special offer, you can add a countdown timer which you set for the time when the offer ends. Then, the prospective customer will see the counter counting down the hours, minute, and seconds until the end.

Should someone leave without buying anything, you can set up what's called an "exit site redirect," in which they will see a pop-up inviting them to reconsider leaving by giving them an extra-special offer, such as a trial offer or free gift, which marketers have found increases sales by about 10-20%.

Then, too, you can insert already created opt-in forms, whereby someone has to enter their name and email in order to click a link to another page to get a free gift, such as a report or article, or see a helpful video.

Should you later want to use this page anywhere else, you can save your WordPress page into a HTML format.

Once you create the page, you can set it to work with any autoresponder, such as AWeber, GetResponse, iContact, or MailChimp. You just need the autoresponder's HTML code.

A further advantage of Instabuilder if you are not sure this will work for you is that you can try it out for 2 months with a 60-day money back guarantee. The basic cost for up to 3 domains is $77, or $97 for unlimited domains, and if you work with clients, you can assign licenses to them for the $197 package. These are one-time fees, so once you have the software, you can continue to use it, with a low yearly renewal fee if you want continued technical support.

## How Instabuilder Works

To get started, turn Instabuilder on for each page where you want to use that rather than using the basic WordPress theme on your site. You can use any theme you want for the other pages on your WordPress site. When you want to use Instabuilder, turn it on for that page and it takes over.

Once you turn on the program, to your left, you will see a long black bar that looks like a TV remote with icons on it. If you can't tell what they represent by looking at them, hover over each one with your mouse, and you will see the name for that icon, such as "navigation," "text element," "image element," and "opt in form."

You can upload own photos and graphics or choose from the program's library of graphics and icons. The program also has a variety of sales buttons, such "Add to Cart" and "Click Here to Buy Now." You can add a link to indicate where the person needs to go to make a payment.

It can take a few hours until you feel at home with the different elements of the program, though the basic drag and drop function makes it easy to operate. What takes some time is finding out what different buttons do and how to add in or delete sections of copy, as well as replace placeholder copy with your own.

This is the way the dashboard looks.

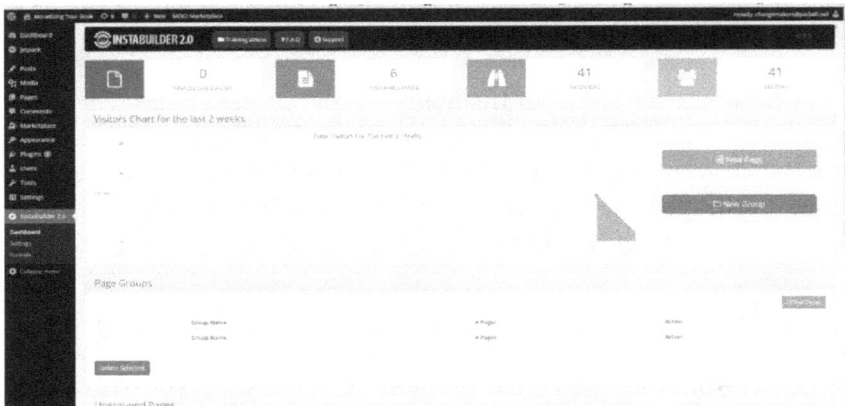

If you turn the program on for a WordPress page you have already created or click "New Page," you will go to the opening screen to create your page. Any pages you create in Instabuilder will also show up in your list of pages in WordPress. Once you have created them in Instabuilder, you have to turn on Instabuilder on that page to see them.

The next step is to choose a template for the different pages you want for your sales campagin.

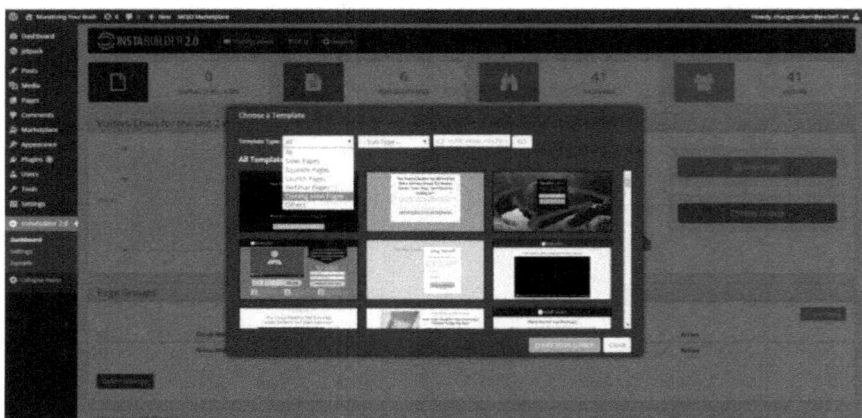

Once you choose your template or choose to create your video from scratch, you go to the screen where you can adjust the template for your own purposes. For example, I selected the "launch" template and selected one template from 6 possibilities. Thereafter, I was able to edit the copy, insert my own video, and add other widgets.

Next use the panel on the left that looks like a TV remote and has the icons which you can drag and drop onto the template. You can use the settings button on the top right that looks like a gear to select from all kinds of graphics.

This settings bar also provides a variety of designs and settings. For example, you can choose the background color of the page, add an attention bar, change the font style, and so on. You can experiment with different possibilities.

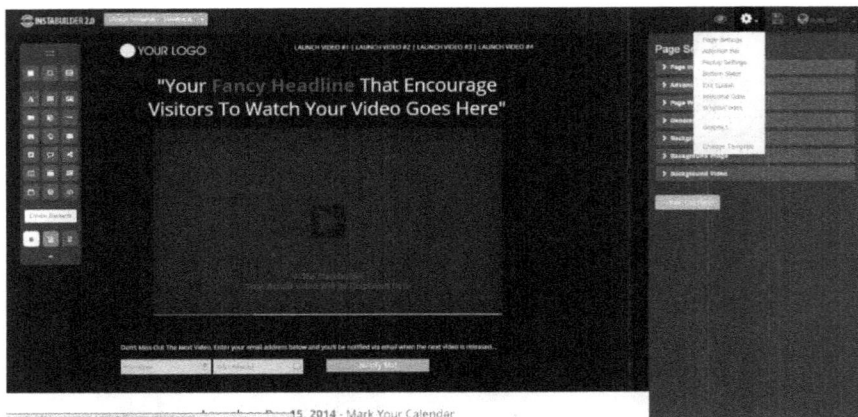

As described on the Instabuilder site, the plug-in includes these various features that help you make very professional-looking sales pages fairly quickly – and even more quickly as you become more familiar with the programs features.

- Your pages are instantly mobile friendly, since they are 100% responsive.

- You have over 90 templates to choose from which include: Squeeze Pages, Mini-Squeeze Pages, Video Squeeze Pages, Sales Pages, Video Sales Pages, Launch Pages, Webinar Pages, Thank You Pages, Download Pages, Upselling Pages, and Coming Soon Pages.

- You can customize all of these templates, and can control the font, design, and placement of everything, just by clicking on the elements you want to use and dropping them where you want.

- Alternatively, you can create your own template from scratch and save any changes you make, so you can use that for other pages in the future.

- You can build landing pages which are designed to help you build opt-in lists, when someone enters their name, email, and other information into an opt-in form.

- You can create lead-generating surveys where you ask people what they are interested in.

- You can use a built-in image editor to make your images look even better.

- You can select from dozens of graphics that help to build sales, such as header images, call for action buttons, and icons.

- You can quickly create multiple page variations, so you can split test different pages where you vary such things as the headline, photo, video, and offer in order to see which pages have higher conversion results.

- You can add an Exit Popup feature to provide visitors who leave without buying anything with another incentive to buy now, which increases your leads.

- You can create scarcity buttons, where you urge visitors to act quickly before the offer runs out and combine that with a countdown counter. You can further test the placement of these buttons by placing them on different places on the page.

- You can promote the social sharing of your page, with Social Share Buttons for the four major social media sites – Facebook, Twitter, LinkedIn, and Google Plus.

- You can add animations to selected elements on your landing pages to increase visitor engagement with your site.

- If you want to include these pages on a non-WordPress site, you can save the page as an HTML file with graphics.

- You can publish selected pages to Facebook.

- You can customize your pages with high-level SEO editing, using keyword targeting features, and you can make your pages more search friendly for maximum exposure and sales.

- You can integrate with virtually every major autoresponder, by just using the simple HTML code for that autoresponder.

- You can easily create webinars, since the system integrates with the largest webinar provider in the world – www.gotowebinar.com.

- You can organize the pages you have created so you can easily find them again, such as by grouping the pages by project type or by split test variations.

- You can automatically generate legal pages to comply with sites like Google and Facebook, so you can quickly add disclaimers, privacy policies, terms of service pages, and more.

- If you work with clients, you can build pages for them and export them to your client's sites.

In short, I have found Instabuilder a great program to work with, and you can try it out for 60 days to see how well it will work for you.

# CHAPTER 31: USING THE SECRETS OF THE ONLINE MARKETING PROS

Besides using squeeze pages and sales pages, online marketing pros use a number of other techniques to sell books, courses, video packages, and other materials, that you might apply in your own sales efforts. Whatever their particular products and services, they use the same basic principles of online marketers in selling their own programs or that of their affiliates.

Some of these marketers appear to have become fabulously successful in pitching to writers and publishers, by using the techniques which they are teaching to others on how to make more money by selling their own materials and showing others how to do the same thing. In turn, you can use many of these same techniques to more actively create an online marketing campaign.

As previously discussed, a first step is to put more time into creating an arsenal of related products and services you can sell in addition to your book, and then though an online marketing and sales campaign, you can substantially increase your income,. For even more detail, you can sign up for courses offered by these marketers (which average around $97, $197, or $297 for each class. These include a mix of video trainings, PDFs of slides used in the videos, notes that highlight the content of many videos, and short ebooks – and somehow, costs ending with "7" seem to be the magic number).

For this approach to succeed, you need the right material to appeal to a niche that is willing to pay substantial fees for the special information you have to offer, such as if you are writing about real estate, investing, health, success, and making more money in different ways. Then, customers can feel it's worth it to spend substantial sums for these programs to increase their income, health, or success. But if you are writing novels, kids book, memoirs, or nonfiction about social issues, or topics that don't lend themselves to creating extensive additional books and programs, these methods may not work for you.

## Some Major Success Strategies

Here is a summary of the major success strategies, including many previously discussed in more detail.

- Collect the emails from the people who sign up on your squeeze page, blog, or website, and mail them every few days or at least every week or two with a new offer from you or one of your affiliates for a new book, video, or other program that will help them be even more successful.

- Have a compelling call to action title in your subject line and in the course you are offering, such as "How to Double Your Sales in 24 Hours (or 48 Hours, 72 Hours, 3 days, 1 week, etc.) or Less!" Other compelling titles are words and phrases such as "Here's a Proven Template for (add in your program)", "A Three-Step Strategy for Increasing Your Sales When You Launch (Your Blog,)" "Discover the 10 Publishing Essentials," or "How Working (30 Minutes/1 Hour/2 Hours) a Day Can Transform You into a High-Earning Online Book Marketer." Still other titles might suggest this is a "Special," "Secret," or "Unique" program, therefore worthy of the high cost for participating.

- Emphasize the benefit and value you are providing, such as how much more the person will gain in money, power, prestige, losing weight, etc., rather than promoting the features of how the program actually works.

- Pitch your offer on multiple channels, so if someone doesn't respond on one, maybe they will on another. For example,

I got offers for the same $197 program from a few emails with different pitches, which included a link to a video I could view with some tips from the program. Then, in case I missed seeing the video, I got an offer to watch a replay, and below the video, if I didn't want to watch it or wanted a recap, I could download a PDF with some tips. After that, to learn more, I had to sign up for the course.

- Show how much value there is in the program by listing what the person is going to learn from this step-by-step program. Use bullet points to highlight what the person will learn, using phrases like "a complete step-by-step program," "a strategy to guarantee success," "how to quickly develop the content," "how to increase your rank," and "how to scale your program."

- List the benefits the person will get in the form of special bonuses that have high value. Point out how he or she can get these bonuses by acting quickly before the time is up. You might even put a limit on the number of bonuses that are available, such as only offering bonus 1 for the first 10 people to sign up, bonus 2 to the next 20 people, bonus 3 to the next 30, and so on. So the quicker a person signs up, the more bonuses he or she gets.

- Place a high value on each bonus, but reduce the total amount for those who register before the time is up. To further demonstrate the great value of the offer, keep adding up the bonuses to show the small amount to pay for all these great benefits. For instance, the value might be about $2000 for a step-by-step home study course, about $900 for creating the perfect package, about $500 to learn about outsourcing, another $900 for setting up everything in advance, about $1000 more to learn the secrets of upselling, so the total value is about $5300. But then, the offer for the whole package is only $500, and to sweeten the pot, there is a 30 day money back guarantee, and even better, another personalized group training program valued at $500, so you are really getting a program valued at $5800 for this low price.

Then the offer concludes with a statement about what you might lose out on, if you don't sign up now, such as "Can you afford not to sign up if you might make an additional $1000 a month for only one product?"

- In addition to describing the benefits, value, and low cost of the program, compared to the benefits and value offered, describe briefly how the individual will get the content, such as through a series of recorded trainings in the member's areas, private questions that will be answered by the trainer, immediate access to the training, and an ability to access this training for a lifetime.

- Describe the costs of the different programs which are part of the training with the magic number of "7" at the end of each price point. For instance, the cost isn't $199.95, $195, or $200 – it's $197. It isn't $499, $495, or $500 – it's $497. And so on. For some reason, these offers today end with a "7," perhaps because marketers have found in testing that customers respond to that number more than other price points below or above it.

- Point out how transformational and life-changing a program might be, such as by announcing that "Just listening to an introductory video for the next 60-90 minutes will change your life."

- Describe your background in a short introduction that shows how successful you have been in using the technique you will teach. For example, you have been making $50,000 a month, have sold over 100,000 ebooks without any affiliates, and are now working with some of the most experienced online marketers. It also helps if you can show how you struggled early on, such as growing up poor and then starting a business with no money, experience, or knowledge, but now you have all the elements of a successful life, such as living in a huge house with a large pool and view of the valley below.

- Create the desire to make money with limited time and effort and gain a passive source of income without having to spend a lot of money. Point out how this program will help participants make real money without wasting time and money on approaches that don't work. Invite the prospect to think about what their life will be like when they are able to earn several thousand dollars a month in 30 days or less, without doing much work, because once they set the new system in motion, they can relax.

- Use visual images of charts and graphs to illustrate how sales can go up from day to day, once you start applying the techniques you will learn in this course.

- Provide some initial tips, which give prospects some immediate benefit of participating in the whole webinar, such as:
-- sell in several smaller niche markets that many sellers don't know about rather than sell in a high volume sales arena where there is a lot of competition;
-- sell information on Amazon, since this is a relatively untapped market;
-- sell your content in physical books, which is still a much bigger and more profitable market than ebooks; plus you will have less competition with physical books;
-- choose the best keywords to appeal to your audience and use Google's Keyword Planner to find the best keywords for marketing your book and other programs in your niche.

- Create a sense of scarcity by suggesting that the offer will go away as of a certain date and time, and put a counter on your sales page or webinar page that shows the time ticking away.

- Use a simple video format for a webinar, which you can create quickly and inexpensively.
-- One approach is using PowerPoint slide images, where you have a few words or a sentence or two on a slide, which are accompanied by a voice over saying what's on the slide. After the

presentation, besides offering a replay, turn these slides into a PDF which a prospect can easily print out.

    -- Another approach is to be in the video yourself, where you talk directly to the prospect, and from time to time, turn from the camera to a blackboard or flip board, which is featured on the screen, as you talk.

    -You don't need a high production value for these webinars and courses, and you can make them very quickly – sometimes by recording a webinar you conduct or just talk directly into the mike.

    - Make your course materials quickly and inexpensively by using PowerPoints or talking directly to the camera, with a blackboard or flip board to highlight your major points.

    - Offer a money-back guarantee for 30 or 60 days, which will help to build trust in what you are offering; this will help convince people to sign up and see for themselves if the webinar or course you are offering is as valuable as you claim.  Generally, you can expect only a small percentage of people – perhaps 2-5% -- to ask for their money back.  Return any money quickly to those who request it, so you don't have problems with your merchant account or bank thinking you are running a fraudulent business.

    - If people don't respond right away, continue to email them with additional free gifts in the form of more tips and reports about the success of your method, which might result in your finally convincing someone to sign up.  As an alternative, offer a downsell which they can obtain for about $10 or $20, which can be a low-risk proposition to try out your program and help convince them to pay $200-500 for the full program.

    - Provide testimonials in your webinar, download, or follow-up offers to show how much people have gained from the program.

- Provide a short report with your course highlights, such as the main things to do to have a successful paperback or ebook on kindle, such as:

-- create a great cover with strong graphics, preferably created by a graphics designer;

-- select a good title, such as drawing on the titles of other bestselling books to help people better find you when they use those keywords;

-- choose a less competitive category and start with a low $.99 price to get some sales and reviews;

-- select a niche which has a high demand and isn't extremely competitive;

-- create a book dealing with a need or problem that already exists, where you offer a solution, so you build on what is already working;

-- use a strong description with sales copy and headlines to attract readers to your book; or if it's fiction, provide a preview with highlights of the story that are especially appealing;

-- do regular marketing every day, including guest posts, permafree books, and Kindle Countdown deals for one of your books to attract interest to your other books;

-- seek at least a half-dozen reviews, since people look to reviews in deciding whether to get a book; social proof is an important sales driver in making sales;

-- create an audiobook which you can make quickly, even in 10 or 15 minutes; then you can quickly make more money, as well as increase the perceived value for your other books;

-- don't just publish an ebook; create a paperback both for extra revenue and to increase the perceived value on the Amazon page listing your book. Once you have a paperback, Amazon will cross its price on your page for Kindle and show that your ebook is discounted, resulting in more sales. Plus the hard cover helps to show this is a legitimate book.

- If you have multiple courses, list them with a short 2 or 3 line description, along with a link for more information on each course. Then, direct them to your sales page for that course or book.

- If you create your offer as a course, you can charge more for it, such as $100-500, because you are incorporating videos and other materials that add value – especially when you add up all of the total value and slash the price way down, as described above. By contrast, if you are selling a book, you have to charge much less, such as around $15-25.

- Divide up what you are selling into a series of trainings, webinars, or books, so you can price them individually and charge more for them, than if you put everything into a single book. Moreover, people's attention spans are shorter now, so they tend to prefer shorter books of about 50-150 pages, whereas the preferred length used to be 150-350 pages.

Armed with this information, think about how you might package your own books and programs for sale. Should you be interested in more courses on how to do this, the main sources I have used in writing up this summary of secrets are the following – and I have no affiliate arrangements with any of them now.

The Double Your Kindle Sales System with Mike Balmaceda (www.mikeylightning.com)
60 Minute Marketer with Dennis Becker (http://www.e1kad.com)
Publishing Beyond KDP with Debbie Drum (http://debbiedrum.com)
Guestblogging Strategies with Jon Morrow (http://www.guestblogging.com)

.

# PART III: BLOGGING, PODCASTS, AUDIO BOOKS, AND VIDEOS

# CHAPTER 32: CREATING AND SETTING UP YOUR BLOG

Just about everyone blogs – or posts, as some writers prefer to call it – these days.  You can use these blogs to both promote your book and other programs, as well as make money from them, as you acquire a following.  To acquire this following, you need to create a blog that offers value – and you need to promote your blog to get traffic to it, since just about everyone is a blogger these days.  According to a U.S. News article: "Can You Make Real Money Blogging" by Geoff Williams, there were 181 million blogs at the end of 2011.  Now four years later, there are many, many more.

Generally, figure on posting a blog on a regular basis, ideally once a week, or even two or three times a week, if you have a lot to say and the time to write these.   Initially, it can take time to build up a following.   But keep at it, and over time your following and income will build.

## Creating Your Blog

As a first step, decide what your blog will be about.  Here are some possibilities:
- It could be an extension of your book, which works well if you have a how-to, self-help, relationships, or business book.  In your blog, provide more advice beyond what's in your book, or create a community of people to share stories, ask questions, or provide information to others.
- Another approach if you have a novel or memoir is to write about a related topic based on the setting or social conditions where the story takes place.  For example, if your memoir is about recovering from domestic violence or illness, you might write about the latest developments on that topic.

- Another possibility is to stake out a topic you are particularly interested in, even if it is not directly related to your book, since this will help to draw a following about that, and people may become interested in your book and other programs or refer you to others.

- Share your opinion about developments in your field, and cite others with opinions and point out how you agree or disagree.

- Be an aggregator, where you feature the latest comments or news about your topics.

Whatever you write about, create a blog that is memorable, so you provide new, interesting, and valuable information. If you are in a niche with a lot of readers, such as in finance, health, and relationships, do something to be different and stand out. Otherwise, it will be difficult to compete with already established blogs, much in the same way that you need to write a book and develop programs that offer something new and valuable. So think about how you are unique and different in considering what to write about, whether your blog will expand on your book or is on a related topic. Also be ready to adapt to find new approaches, because the Internet and the interest of users is constantly changing. As Amy Lynn Andrews points out in "How to Make Money Blogging," (www.amylynnandrews.com/how-to-make-money-blogging):

> "The trick in making money as a blogger is selling things you can stand behind and things your readers are willing to invest in…You'll significantly increase your chances of success if you meet a need for others instead of blogging as an outlet for yourself…Always be on the lookout for new income streams, and keep them diverse. The Internet changes constantly. That way, if one stream dries up…you've still got others…Tap into your uniqueness."

While blogs were originally just text, now bloggers are incorporating photos and videos, so consider using these to make your blogs even more appealing.

## Setting Up Your Blog

A good location for your blog is on your website, where your domain name is followed by a page for your blogs called "blog," such as www.yourdomain.com/blog. A good reason for positioning your blog there is that as you attract traffic to it using traffic building techniques, this will increase the SEO on your site, because it has new content, which will help you go up in the rankings. Additionally, when people like what you are saying on your blog, they can readily learn more about you by going to your main site. You can also easily include links in your blogs to pages on your website, such as your home page, as well as to your sales page or squeeze page.

An easy way to set up your blog is to install WordPress on your site. Then, you can use the design that is already on your website or select another design from one of WordPress's many templates. If your website is already set up in WordPress, as about 70% of websites are today, you can go to your website's wp-admin page, log in, and add another page you call "blog."

To keep track of your visitors, include a sign-up form on your blog where people can put their name and email. Perhaps offer them a free gift in return for doing this, such as an article or chapter from your book, much as you might do on a squeeze page.

If you are using your blog to increase your SEO ranking, follow the current Google guidelines for the length of your blog and incorporate common key words that might be used to follow a blog on your subject. Sprinkle these words throughout your blog – perhaps every paragraph or every 100 or so words. The current guidelines are for blogs of 700-1000 words, though at one time the guidelines specified shorter blogs of 200-300 words. If you aren't concerned about SEO rankings, use any length that is comfortable for you or combine shorter and longer blogs, depending on what you have to say. For consistency, strive to write blogs of approximately the same length each time, much like a newspaper columnist, whose typical length is about 700-800 words.

While the average blog is about 700-1000 words, in some fields a longer blog of 1500 words may be more effective, because you can provide more in-depth information on a topic.

Decide if you want to set up your blog for people to make comments, ask questions, and otherwise interact, like on a forum. This interaction can work well for certain types of blogs, such as if you are writing about self-help, relationships, or recovery topics in your book, so your blog can become a support group for people personally affected by your topic. You can also build a following as you interact with the community that develops around your blog. Offering helpful advice based on your expertise will help in building this following and can lead some participants to purchase your books and programs. For example, Amy Lynn Andrews notes that "after proving their trustworthiness, bloggers use their blogs as springboards to launch *other* products that bring in income, such as ebooks, books, speaking, products, etc."

However, a caution in permitting comments, according to my web designer, is that you open yourself up to spammers. At the very least, moderate any comments so they are subject to your approval before they get posted. This way you generally can keep out the promoters of products and spammers, though from time to time they may get through, and you have to delete their post.

# CHAPTER 33: USING YOUR BLOG FOR PROMOTION AND MAKING MONEY

Once you have your blog set up, you can use it to in a number of ways to promote your book and programs and make money, based on my experience and that of several blogging experts. Choose the approaches that work best for you. Here are some of suggestions.

## Using Blog as a Freebie

Use your blog as a "freebie" to attract customers or clients by being an expert, teacher, or entrepreneur. Consider your blog a launchpad for that. According to Jon Morrow, author of "Make Money Blogging: 20 Lessons Going from 0 to $100,000 a month" (http://boostblogtraffic.com/make-money-blogging), "Nearly all 'bloggers' who make a decent income have books, courses, a side career as a keynote speaker, or even software. That's how they make their money." Their blog is one of many entry points to the different things they do.

One of the reasons this strategy may work for some bloggers is you first build up a level of first by giving readers helpful content at no charge. After you do this for a while, you can start talking about your products and services, such as at the end of one of your blogs or in creating an advertising section for one of your programs. You may make less money in the short term, but your long-term profits will be much higher.

## Using Your Blog to Learn What People Want to Know About

Learn what people want so they can solve a problem they already have, such as something you have already researched and started blogging about. With this insight, you can now guide them to your book or program that can help them. Generally, this approach of focusing on what people want now works best rather than trying to determine what you think they need but aren't aware of yet, since it can be hard to first educate people about what they need. When you ask your customers for insights about what they want, a good question to ask, according to Morrow is: "What's your biggest frustration with (your subject) right now?" For instance, if they have a book about diet and nutrition, ask them about that.

## Building Your Email List

According to some marketers, the most important predictor for sales is the size of your email list. Morrow recommends striving for one dollar per subscriber per month in sales. But keep in mind that for any emails to turn into sales, you need good programs and services though if you have them, your blog can act as a sales funnel, much like you might use a squeeze page to pitch same products. So once you start getting subscribers, find things you can sell them, such as more in-depth programs or follow-up books. Preferably feature your own book and programs, though you can add materials by affiliates if you like their work and there is a good complementary fit with what you are doing.

# Creating Newsletters

Creating and promoting a newsletter can sometimes supplement your blog and draw attention to it, along with your book and programs. Often a newsletter is sent out on a monthly basis, and you can use these mailings to supplement whatever you write about on your blog. For instance, a newsletter might include highlights of your latest blogs, announcements of upcoming workshops and seminars, reports of publicity you have gotten, guest blogs you have done, rave reviews for your book on Amazon, and the like. While some of this information might be on your blog, keep your blog focused on providing tips and information of value, while a newsletter is more newsy and timely.

# Getting Sponsors or Underwriters

Writing sponsored or underwritten posts or series can be a source of income, too, according to Amy Lynn Andrews (http://amylynnandrews.com/how-to-make-money-blogging), though if you write these, ideally keep the subject related to your book, programs, or blog. Be upfront in disclosing your sponsor or underwriter, though you can explain why you have chosen to include their information, such as because you admire their work and think your readers will find it useful.

The difference between a sponsored and an underwritten post is that in a sponsored post, you write about a company's products or services, while in an underwritten post, you write about whatever you want, but you put in a plug for the advertiser with an introduction in the beginning or line at the end that says: "Brought to you by…"

If you think something you are writing about will get a lot of response, this can be a good time to pitch a company to underwrite your blog – and this might be a way to get the company to offer your books to clients as a premium if there is a good fit. For example, if you write about financial topics, a good underwriter might be a bank who you credit for its innovative investment programs. However, a caution about sponsored posts. Use a limited number of these, so you don't turn off readers because your blog now seems too commercial.

## Creating Webinars

Webinars are a great way to attract subscribers for your blogs, as well as attract interest for your books and other programs. Alternatively, use your blog to promote your webinar.

A good way to start using webinars to build traffic is to feature webinars hosted by other people, and along with your webinar invitation, invite people to subscribe to your blog. You can also host webinars with others, or host your own webinar and invite guests that relate to your topic and don't directly compete with you.

Often introductory webinars are free – but the webinar offers doorways to other programs, such as coaching, consulting, and more advanced programs. According to Jon Morrow, when he does webinars for other people, he averages 500 new email subscribers per hour invested, and sometimes he gains as many as 1000-2000 email subscribers from a single webinar. A single product might net at least $10,000. Those numbers show the Internet's potential. However, when you are starting out, first organize a few local events to test out your presentation and then start charging a small fee. You can use your blog to promote these events or provide links to an online webinar, where those interested can sign-up online to take the course.

## Selling Products

Selling manufactured products is another potential income stream which you can promote through your blog, website, squeeze page, or newsletter, if there's a good fit with your book and programs. For example, a client with a book on improving a marriage by attending a relationships boot camp talked about his idea for a game in which couples would travel through the board in pairs or in groups of couples participating in various exercises. He thought this could become a limited-run board game that he could sell as an aid to improving a marriage or significant partnership.

When you use your blog to sell a product, such as an ebook or seminar program, some marketers suggest starting with an inexpensive product. Then, if prospects like that, they may want to buy a more expensive product or program from you – which is where the real money is, at the end of the sales funnel, not by selling only a single book.

This strategy works well if you have a number of more expensive products to offer afterwards. However, some marketers, suggest it's more profitable to create and sell the expensive product first, and gradually create less expensive products. An example might be if you have created a webinar, workshop, or weekend retreat, based on write you write about. Then, using Morrow's strategy, you would release the most expensive products first and gradually offer increasingly less expensive ones.

Another tip when you use your blog as a lead in to other products and services is that you should feel comfortable charging premium prices in return for providing premium services, such as helping your customers get results. This approach can work for anything, such as if your book is about having better relationships and you coach men or women in how to have a great relationship. In this way, you go beyond your book, such as by consulting with a client, reviewing their homework assignments, answering their questions, and even sitting nearby as they meet someone in a bar to give them feedback on what works and doesn't.

## Providing an Entry to Your Site with Premium Content and Membership

Your blog can also serve as an entry to an online site with premium content and membership communities. Another way to get to this content and community might be through a link from your squeeze page or website. But your blog can be a good entry point, because it is ever changing as you add new blogs, whereas a squeeze page and website are generally more permanent, apart from occasional updating.

The basic idea of sites with premium content is that you have high-value content that others will pay to access. Since there is so much free information on the Internet, this content has to be truly unique or provide insider information, or perhaps you might provide access to you or other experts in the field, so users can contact you personally, such as through a webinar, phone call, coaching, consulting, or a face-to-face meeting.

## Increasing Your SEO Ranking

While SEO can be important, when people search on Google or Yahoo and find you, initially focus on creating good content, building relationships with influencers, including guest bloggers, and offering your books and programs for sale. Then, your site will gradually rise naturally in the rankings, which is what I found with the Publishers, Agents and Films site. I posted blogs about once a week dealing with different ways for writers to find publishers and agents, self-publish, and find film producers, and after about a month, the site appeared on page 4 of a search with the words "publishers" and "agents." A few weeks after that, the site was on the 3$^{rd}$ page, then on page 2, and it worked its way up from the bottom, so now it is on the top of that page. If I put in other combinations, such as "publishers" and "films," it is number 1 on the first page.

## Sharing Your Blogs on the Social Media

You can put links to your blog, much like posting links to your squeeze page or website, on the social media, such as Facebook, LinkedIn, and Twitter. But along with these links, include some copy describing how visitors will find going there helpful or interesting, so they will click the links. This posting can be on your news feed, updates, status, or fan pages. Then, too, if your followers and fans like your posting, they might pass it on, and maybe these recipients might, too, which is how posts can go viral. If you belong to groups interested in your subject area, try posting information there, too. Today, using the social media is so important that you want to let others know about your blogs in this way.

# CHAPTER 34: ADVERTISING ON YOUR BLOG

## To Advertise or Not to Advertise

While some bloggers use ads, such as through Google AdSense, to bring in money when people click on the ad, you can make more – sometimes much more – using the same ad space to sell your own products or services. Or if you are promoting an affiliate product or program, you can make more selling that. The general consensus of marketing experts on blogging is that it is better not to use ads on your blog, such as display ads, which are like sidebar, header, or footer ads on your site.

Often such ads are provided by ad networks, which are companies like Google AdSense, which pairs advertisers with bloggers and takes a percentage from the profit. If you want to use an ad network, besides Google AdSense, which is the most popular one, other networks are Blogads, BlogHer, Beacon Ads, Federated Media, Sovrn, Media.Net, Rivit, Sway, and many others. But the problem with accepting these ads on your blog site is that you have to be in a unique niche in which advertisers will pay a lot of money for clicks on their ads – say blogging about end of life services and the funeral industry. So generally, you won't make much money for clicks, and your content could get lost in your ads. Another problem is that Google penalizes sites with too many links above the fold in their search rankings.

The one exception to putting ads on your blog site might be using private ads. Typically these are buttons, graphics, or small display ads that appear on the sidebars of blogs, and you arrange to post them directly with an individual, small, business or company. But instead of a pay-for-clicks arrangement, you generally work out a flat fee. While companies might come to you, especially as you get more viewers, generally you need to reach out to them. A good way to do so is to look at other bloggers in your niche and see who is advertising on their sites; then contact those individuals or companies and invite them to advertise on your site. To find out what to charge, look for the advertising pages or media kits of the other bloggers. However, if you do pursue any advertising on your blog, be sure that the type of company and their message is compatible with what you are blogging about. For example, if you are blogging about fishing, since you have a book on becoming a great fisherman, look for advertisers with products about fishing.

## How to Use Ads on Your Blog

While many bloggers don't recommend using ads on your blog, many other do, according to Bill Belew, who writes in "Blogging for Money" (http://billbelew.com/category/blog), that more than 2 million publishers now get paid from Google's AdSense program. I's so popular, because publishers get a higher CPC (cost per click) from Google that on other ad networks. And according to "Make Money Blogging" on Building Your Own Blog (http://www.buildingyourownblog.net), "running ads is the most common way people earn income from blogs." Perhaps you might accept such ads if you don't have products of your own or from affiliates to sell yet. So this is a good way to get started. In any case, here's a brief introduction to using AdSense to get money from your blog, and you can use such ads on your website.

An easy way to get started is to use a service for placing ads on blogs and websites, such as Google AdSense( http://www.google.com/adsense), which can place ads from their corporate connections on your blog. So in a short time, you start receiving a portion of the commissions the advertisers make when people click on the ads. And the more you build readership, the more your income from ads can be expected to increases. On average, figure on about 1-10% of your blog visitors clicking on an ads. The rate Google AdSense pays on ads ranges from $.05 per click and up to many dollars, though on average expect about $.20 to $.50 per click.

To set up a new account on AdSense, click the "Get Started Now" button, put in an email, activate the account, and indicate the page your website where you want to place the ad. After that you wait to hear if your account is approved might take up to a week. After you are approved, you select the style of ad you want, which could be a long horizontal, large rectangle, skyscraper, or medium sized display ad. Also indicate whether you want a text or display ad, and you will get some code from Amazon to place on your website in your ad box. Then, you will start seeing ads appear. Don't click on them to test them, which is not permitted by AdSense, because if an ad gets clicks, that means the advertiser has to pay you, and some online criminals have gamed the system by creating a lot of clicks for an ad resulting in a big payout – to the crooks!

## Key Considerations in Creating and Placing Your Ad

Some key considerations for advertising, according to Belew, are these.

1) To determine the best ad format and size for the ad, you can experiment with the AdSense code for different types of ad.

2) Ads surrounded by content or at the end of each blog post tend to get the most clicks.

3) Don't have too many ads, because users can get turned off, just as if they have to wade through too many commercials to see a TV program.

4) While a natural tendency may be choosing an ad design that blends in with the content on your blog template, you want the ad to stand out so it will get clicks. So experiment with different colors, fonts, and font sizes to learn which ones get the most clicks, but don't spoil the look and feel of your blog.

5) Test out the ad size, too, though wider ads tend to gain more clicks, since readers can more readily read the whole ad without having to read from left to right and move down to the next line many times to understand the copy.

6) Consider the different formats for text or image display ads. Sometimes, the thin and streamlined links work better, since they can be squeezed into small empty spaces and be surrounded by content.

# CHAPTER 35: USING SLIDE SHARE TO GET OUT YOUR MESSAGE

SlideShare (www.slideshare.com) is another great program to feature your message, and you can link to it from your website or blog. It's like putting a PowerPoint presentation on the SlideShare site, which is a global platform reaching over 70 million viewers a month, and you may be able to convert your viewership there into high quality prospects.

Another advantage of using SlideShare is you can integrate your presentation into lead generation sites. Among these are Marketo (www.marekto.com), which provides marketing automation software for organizations of any size, and Hubspot (www.hubspot.com), which features a marketing platform to increase your traffic, grow your database, and analyze and manage your marketing as you grow your business. Initially though, SlideShare is a good way to post your professional content to share with other contacts you already have.

SlideShare is part of the LinkedIn family and is free to use. You just upload any kind of visual formats, including infographics, PowerPoint presentations, documents, and videos. Then these become a source of content for over 70 million LinkedIn users, who can access SlideShare from all over the world (about 50% are outside the U.S.), using either a computer or mobile device. Thus, besides providing a link from your blog to SlideShare, viewers seeking expert content on certain topics might find you, making SlideShare a great source of high quality leads, more website traffic, and other business opportunities.

## Setting Up a SlideShare Account

The process of setting up a SlideShare account is very easy – you just create a SlideShare account, for your business, upload, and share your content. For business users, LinkedIn also has a Lead Generation program to get quality leads, although this starts at $4 a lead, so you probably don't want to use this program unless you are marketing a high value product or service. Instead, just use SlideShare to share your expertise, and if you wish, you can join the SlideShare community, where you follow other users, "like" and comment on SlideShares that interest you, and subscribe to selected topics. You can also gain insights from what others have posted to see how they have used SlideShare to engage their audience. Moreover, if you share others' work, they may be likely to share yours? And the more your content is shared, the more views you get, not only for your content on SlideShare, but on your other online platforms.

To help you use the platform, you'll find guideline for creating great SlideShares, such as by using  vivid imagery to draw in an audience, which is more appealing than just using bullet points and clip art. There are all kinds of apps and tools which allow you to create great presentation, including Keynote, Apple's version of PowerPoint, which you upload as a PDF to SlideShare; Canva, which you use to create blog graphics and presentations with attractive design layouts; and Haiku Deck, which allows you to quickly create visual presentations with minimal text with a few clicks. Still other apps include:
- Google Slides, which is like PowerPoint, but with an interface that allows for collaborative editing;
- Piktochart, which enables you to make an infographic in under 10 minutes, drawing from over 400 templates;
- Infogr.am which lets you put your data into an Excel-style spreadsheet;
- Slide Temple, where you can choose from over 100 customizable icons;

- BeFunky, which helps you create professional-looking photos using various photo effects;
- Skitch, which is part of Evernote, that allows you to add annotations, sketches, and more to make your point.

In short, there are all kinds of design elements you can explore to make great SlideShares.

## Promoting Your Slide Shares

Once you create your presentation, SlideShare will automatically optimize your content to improve your searchability. Even so, you need to promote your SlideShare presentation yourself, such as through your blog, to make it more viral. Then, the more your SlideShares are shared on the social media or embedded on other websites, the more views and reach you will get, leading to even higher search results.

# CHAPTER 36: GUEST BLOGGING

Guest blogging can be another way to draw attention to your books and programs, and you can include a link in your bio to your website, blog page, or squeeze page. This is an especially good strategy when you are starting out and getting a small number of visitors, say less than 100 visitors for your posts. But if you write for a blogger with many more visitors, say 500 for each blog, you've gotten five times as many visitors for the same amount of work, and you have used your bio to introduce new visitors to your site.

Guest blogging can be an effective way to start your own blog too, such as Jon Morrow did. He found it much more efficient to write for other bloggers as a "guest lecturer," inviting readers to his coming soon page with an invitation to join his mailing list. Then, when he was ready, he sent out a link to his new blog to 13,000 email subscribers to let them know about it. For more information on doing guest blogging, you can find his course at www.guestblogging.com, and Publishers, Agents & Films (www.publishersagentsandfilms.com) can send a query for you to several hundred book bloggers, which include bloggers open to guest blogs.

## How to Find Guest Blogging Opportunities

A good way to get a guest blog is to reach out to other bloggers and individuals in your field with large networks to let them know about your helpful information, so they may share it to their readers. One way to find these contacts is by looking for directories and lists of bloggers on the Internet. For example, Jon Morrow has created *The Big Black Book of Rock-Solid Guest Blogging Targets,* which includes about 100 blogging sites he has found especially receptive in different categories, including business and entrepreneurship, career, freelancing, marketing, news, culture, and entertainment, parenting, self-improvement, social media, and the editors at the *Huffington Post* and *Fast Company*.

When you approach bloggers about being a guest blogger, think broadly about their potential audience, since their interests might not just be confined to a blogger's topic, but to other subjects of interest to their demographic. For instance, take someone is writing about gardening. Beyond just pitching his blog to other gardening blogs, he might broaden his pitch to encompass the wider audience for his blog. In this case, since the majority of gardeners are women with kids, and many are money and health conscious, they are likely to be reading parenting sites or health and self-improvement sites. So he should pitch his guest blog to bloggers with such sites. Likewise, think of bloggers writing for audiences who might be interested in your subject, too.

## Becoming a Blogger for the Huffington Post

If possible, write a guest blog for the *Huffington Post*, which has 95 million visitors a month and thousands of writers. If you can write three blogs for them, you could be invited to be a columnist, so you have a regular link there, such as I have. The post has to be reviewed by an editor, but as long as it meets their guidelines, it is usually posted within a day or so. You won't get paid, but you will gain in credibility as an expert on your subject.

As a *Huffington Post* blogger, you can't write an article that's directly promotional, but you can include information about yourself in your bio, including a link to your blog, company website, squeeze page, or subscription form. Your article should provide the reader with useful information on some subject.

For example, I have written articles on new trends in

science, technology, business and society (which later got turned into a book called *Transformations*), on avoiding consumer and merchant fraud (which later became a book, *Scammed*), protecting oneself from Internet book piracy (later turned into a book, *The Battle Against Internet Book Piracy),* and some self-help topics. After you write the article, you suggest the category for it.

When you write these *Huffington Post* articles, it's best to include several links to related topics or to resources you used in researching your article, since this gives your article more credibility and the editors like having these links. While I originally got connected through a publicist, Jana Collins of Jones & Omalley (www.jonesomalley.com), then got an invitation to become a columnist, and now can post articles myself, Morrison includes a list of editors you can contact directly in his *Big Black Book*.

# CHAPTER 37: CREATING A PODCAST OR RADIO SHOW

Creating a podcast or radio show can be another way to spread the word about what you are doing, increase your credibility, and gain interest in your book and other programs. Having your own podcast or radio show can also help open up doors, where you can get interviews with experts and high-profile people in your field, as well as gain free or reduced admission to events, because you are now considered a member of the press.

There can be money in your broadcasts if you get a large enough audience, such as getting paid by sponsors, or if you create a podcast with more advanced information for those who pay. But initially, think of the broadcast as a way to further promote and sell your book or programs.

The four major elements required for a great podcast or radio show include having great content, presenting it effectively, producing it well, and promoting it so you build an audience.

## Creating Your Content

Your show needs to be something that people want to listen to, so you can build an audience. Think of this as an audio blog, where you are getting people to listen, because you are providing useful or interesting information. As Daniel J. Lewis, an award-winning podcaster who helps others launch and improve their shows, writes in the "4 Cornerstones of a Great Podcast," (http://theaudacitytopodcast.com/the-4-cornerstones-of-a-great-podcast-tap207), the two key reasons that people listen to podcasts is because they want to be helped or entertained. If you are being helpful, you are "educating, equipping, encouraging, or inspiring people." If you are being entertaining, you are "making people laugh, engaging their minds, feeding their passions, or giving them a good time."

Any content can be both helpful and entertaining, and if it's both so much the better, since that helps them want to share it with others, and as more and more people share, that can help it go viral and experience massive growth through word of mouth.

As for what topics to talk about, keep it related to your book or programs, just as you might do you in your blog or articles based on your subject. For example, provide additional how-to tips in your field, comment on trends in the news related to your subject, and interview guests that are in your field.

While podcasts can be any length, radio shows typically follow a 30 minute or 1 hour format, with a few minutes in the beginning, during the show, or at the end, devoted to announcements, pitches for your book or programs, and any messages from your sponsor or advertisers. If you are not following the usual 30 minute or 1 hour format for a radio show, a good time for a podcast is about 5 to 15 minutes, so people can listen to your program in a short segment, which works well given the shorter attention span of people today.

## Presenting Your Content Effectively

To present your content well, to prepare what you are going to say and practice, unless you are good at improvising from guidelines on what to talk about. It's best not to have a written script, which can sound canned – and it can take longer to prepare than talking with authority about a subject you are familiar with. Rather, a good way to put on your show is to have an outline of a list of topics you will be discussing, so you have a general idea in advance of what to say.

If you are going to be interviewing a guest, as I did on my Changemakers program on various stations for three years, it's helpful to create a list of questions you plan to ask and share these with your guest in advance, so he or she can prepare what to say.

In the event you have any advertisers or sponsors, or want to pitch your own book, programs, website, or blog, it helps to write that out. This way you can present this announcement in a short, succinct way – perhaps 10-15 seconds or at most 30 seconds for each pitch – and then back to regular programming.

If you are new to broadcasting or public speaking, practice to smooth out your delivery. For instance, pay attention to when you say speech fillers, such as "uh" and "you know," and strive to get rid of them. Becoming aware is the first step to eliminating any habit, and when you feel a filler word or phrase coming on, don't say it. Instead, focus on saying what you want to say without the filler, which is usually a placeholder for being unsure of what to say next. It's better to simply pause, and after a while, these quiet pauses will become shorter and shorter, as what you say becomes smoother. This process will not only help you speak better on air but in everyday life.

As your speech becomes smoother, you can speak with more enthusiasm and authority, so whatever you say is more convincing and compelling. That can help when you talk about the value of your book or programs, and you will find that more people are interested in them, more likely to buy whatever you are selling, and more apt to spread the word to others.

## Producing Your Program Well

Having good sound quality is another critical component for a podcast or radio program, just as it is critical for a video. If you don't have good sound quality, people will generally tune you out and stop listening -- and you will seem unprofessional and not credible no matter what you say.

While some of the latest smart phones have good microphones as do many laptops, desktop computers, and video cams, an ideal solution is to get a good quality mike. You can get high quality studio or lavalier mikes for as little as $50, such as the Audio Technica 4000, though figure on spending about $100, such as for the Shure 58 series. You can get these at any store that sells audio equipment, such as the Guitar Center (www.guitarcenter.com).

Besides producing a great show, create a great looking website or page on your website featuring your show with attractive cover art, since you can use that image in promoting your show on the social media, on your sales page, and in the flyers you hand out at meetings or other places. As Daniel J. Lewis notes: "Podcast cover art is often a potential subscriber's first impression of your show in many podcast directories. Great website design can enhance your content, calls to action, and make watching or listening to your episodes easier."

## Promoting Your Show

Finally, you have to build your audience, just as you do for your blog, website, squeeze page, sales page, or whatever else you are promoting. In turn, all of these elements contribute to promoting each other, since you can use your blog to promote your show, use your show to promote your blog, and use both to promote your book and programs. In effect, you have multiple doors to enter your house, and individuals can enter any door to learn about and obtain your books and programs.

It can be easy to launch a show when you already have a loyal following, have a large mailing list, or have become a well-known celebrity. When you are just starting out, you have to create all of these things, but as each element grows, that contributes to the growth of everything else.

So wherever you are in the process, start promoting your show, along with your book, programs, blogs and everything else you do to increase your audience and sales.

# CHAPTER 38: SETTING UP YOUR PODCAST OR RADIO SHOW

Once you decide on what your podcast or radio show will be about, the next step is setting it up, so you can start broadcasting. You can readily set up a podcast on your website using audiofiles for each show, or you can set up your podcast on a hosting company. If you create a radio show, it can be turned into a podcast by rebroadcasting the files of your show through your website or podcast hosting program. Alternatively, upload your podcasting file into your radio show. You can use the same content in both formats.

## Creating a Podcast

The simplest way to create a podcast is to set up a page for it on your website or embed the file for each podcast onto an existing page and announce your show. For instance, you can add your podcast to your blog and write about the topics discussed on your show. Or set up a series of podcasts on the same page, much like you might create a page of articles or thumbnail video links with a few lines of introductory copy. This way, a person can choose to read the article, view the video, or listen to the podcast.

Another approach is to use one of the podcast hosting companies, which provide different types of assistance in producing and monetizing your show. You can get started for as little as $5 or $10 a month. The two major hosting companies are Blubrry (https://www.blubrry.com) and LibSyn (https://www.libsyn.com).

- **Using Blubrry**

  With Blubrry, you can host a site starting at $12 a month for 100 MB of monthly storage, and this hosting is seamlessly integrated with WordPress. You can also obtain the #1 podcasting plugin for WordPress at no charge, and set up your podcast on your WordPress website or on your blog on a self-hosted WordPress site (though you can't do this on a free WordPress.com blog). By posting a podcast on your website or blog site, podcasting becomes an extension of blogging. Plus you can get professional media statistics which measure media downloads, including demographics, geographical data, and the devices that downloaded your data, so you know who is listening to your podcast. The costs are as little as $5 a month for a basic plan.

  Blubrry has a podcast directory with over 35,000 podcasts, and you can submit your own. It also has an affiliate program and a Podcasting Manual to help you create and monetize your podcast. You can access this manual for free on the Blubrry site. The manual covers these key topics:
   - starting your show;
   - your goals, content, and format;
   - logos, branding, and theme;
   - your podcast website;
   - creating podcast media;
   - media podcast hosting, syndication and RSS feeds;
   - statistics and analytics;
   - podcast promotion;
   - monetizing your content.

  Besides describing how to plan and produce your show, the Manual recommends using a WordPress site to make podcasting an extension of blogging, so a blog post becomes a podcast episode. To integrate your websites, blog, and podcast, first set up your website. Then set up a hosting service for your podcast, and set up syndication for it, such as by using a PowerPress plugin for

WordPress. If you are using WordPress with PowerPress, that makes the process very easy. You create a new blog post, upload your podcast to your media hosting company, and enter the media URL into the PowerPress episode entry box. If you are using Blubrry's media hosting services, click the Blubrry upload icon, upload the media, and click "Publish."

Then, you can set up Web statistics, such as with Google Analytics, and set up media download statistics. You can download Blubrry Basic Statistics for free and easily add it to your website with the PowerPress broadcasting plugin. Plus you can set up an audience survey, such as with Blubrry's free audience survey, when you use its PowerPress Podcasting plug-in, which enables you to quickly access your Bluburry media download stats from your WordPress dashboard. This plug-in also enables mobile device users to subscribe to your podcasts.

Once you start making these podcasts, as the Blubrry Manual explains, promote them as much as possible. A first step is to add your podcast to as many podcast directories as possible, such as iTunes and Blubrry's Podcast Directory. Other methods include using the social media, such as Twitter and Facebook, and attending conferences and tradeshows that relate to your content and genre. Set up a mailing list and newsletter, too, so you can regularly send news and information to subscribers. Consider using Google AdWords, as well.

- **Using Libsyn**

Libsyn is another big podcasting hosting service that hosts over 10,000 shows, including podcasts from big name producers. The service was the first to host and publish podcasts in 2004, and since then it has become the largest podcast network with over 1.6 billion downloads and over 18 million monthly audience members as of 2011. Now many many more.

The service enables podcasters to put their podcasts on multiple platforms, which include not only WordPress, but Facebook, Twitter, Blogger, and mobile apps for Apple iOS, Android, and Windows. Its smartphone app not only accepts audio podcasts, but video, PDF, and text, so you can easily share your episodes on popular social media outlets and provide downloads for offline listening and viewing.

Its classic plan starts at $5 month, and besides 50mb of storage, the plan includes a podcast RSS feed, Podcast Page, Network App Listing, and Directory Listing. For basic statistics, it's $2 a month. Other plans range from $15 to $75 with increased storage space and other add-ons each month. The Classic 250 plan is designed for podcasters who are becoming more serious and are producing regular audio and video episodes. If you want your podcast to appear on smartphone apps, the costs start at $20 a month and up, depending on how much storage space you need beyond 400 mb.

## Creating a Radio Show or Station

Though you can upload your podcast file into your radio program or save your radio file to create a podcast, a radio show is a more structured format. There are some hosting services that enable you to create your own radio station for free. The most popular radio show site is BlogTalkRadio (www.blogtalkradio.com). Another one that is less well-known is Spreaker (https://www.spreaker.com) which invites people to create podcasts or radio programs. A few sites even invite you to create your own radio station, such as Radionomy (https://www.radionomy.com), which is free.

- **Using BlogTalkRadio**

The long-time radio platform which has been used by over 250,000 people to create an online radio talk show – and the one I have used – is BlogTalkRadio (www.blogtalkradio.com). You can get started for free, where you can host up to one half-hour show a day outside of prime-time, which is from 5-8 p.m. in your broadcasting location.

The advantage of this BlogTalk platform is you can use any phone and web browser to call in at the time you schedule, though it's best to call in 10-15 minutes before your show starts to make sure everything is ready, including any guests you plan to interview. After a 1 minute countdown, the show goes live and is recorded and archived as a podcast which you can download and use anywhere else. In fact, BlogTalkRadio provides unlimited podcast storage, so even though I paused my own show four years ago, the original shows are still there, so I can readily revive the show, as I plan to do, as if nothing happened. Listeners can access any shows in these archives and access particular shows, if you let them know about this. In my experience, most listeners access your show after your live broadcast, so unless you want a longer show and want to go live during prime-time, a free account is a good way to start.

Another feature of this platform is you can have a live chat with listeners – up to 5 simultaneous guests or listeners when you have a free account. They phone in on the access line for guests, and you indicate who has live access, while anyone else can listen. You can readily share the link to the show on social networks, as well as embed it on your blog or on iTunes.

Once you get more serious, the next plan for $39 a month, with the first month free, includes a 2 hour show per day, 50 live callers, and prime time scheduling. You can also record Skype calls and get 1000 promotional impressions. For $99 or $249 a month, you can have shows up to 3 hours a day, and even more callers and promotional impressions. If you want to downgrade your plan, which I did after recording programs less frequently, you can easily do so, and go free again until you are ready to upgrade it again, and you can pause your show indefinitely, while keeping your old programs alive in the archives.

It's easy to set up your show. Just enter your email, confirm it, pick you show URL and title, and describe what your show is about.

- **Using Spreaker**

With Spreaker (http://www.spreaker.com), you can create either a podcast or a radio show, and as a listener, you can tune into a wide variety of podcasts and live broadcasts each day in different categories, including the best of the community, society and culture, information, music trends, lifestyle and health, electronics, fun and entertainment, comedy, and news and politics.

The site, started in 2010, provides website and mobile apps for both Apple and Android platforms with tools which guide you through the creation process, so you can readily create, host, and distribute your podcasts from your desktop or smart phone. You can use Spreaker's recording console, store previously created shows, connect with social networks, and have access to detailed audience analytics.

To get started, you pre-record or broadcast live via the studio console on the web or on a smart phone app, and then distribute your podcast to iTunes, YouTube, and other platforms. You can chat with listeners while you broadcast live and follow their comments on the page for each episode. Later, you can measure the results, such as your program's total plays and the location of your listeners.

Like BlogTalkRadio, Spreaker has a free start-up program, and you can upgrade to get extra features, such as more audio storage space and extra analytics. When you start for free, you get 30 minutes a day for your program, 10 hours of audio storage, and basic analytics. If you upgrade to their Broadcaster plan for $19.95 or $199 a year, you get up to 3 hours a day, 500 hours of audio storage, more advanced audience analytics, and a custom RSS feed. Or for even more program time, their $49 a month or $499 a year Anchorman program provides for 5 hours a day, 1500 hours of audio storage, and even more complete audience analytics.

- **Using Radionomy**

You can produce your own online radio station at no cost, no matter how big your radio gets, through Radionomy (https://www.radionomy.com). The company shares your station with the top radio directories, so you can reach fans around the world. It takes care of all the hosting and streaming for you, using high quality 128K unlimited streams.

If you want to use the show for interviews and talking about anything as on a regular talk show or podcast, you have to select at least two types of music. The company covers the music licensing, and you can use the company's popular music library of thousands of tracks or upload tracks from your own library. You can even incorporate news, weather reports, and other content provided by Radionomy, in addition to your own content, so you sound like a professional radio station.

If you want to prerecord a program for later play, you can use Radionomy's RadioManager and radio scheduler. Or you can go live.

Since Radionomy has partnerships with all of the major online radio directories and devices, you can be heard on iTunes, Tunein, SHOUTcast, Sonos, AppleTV, and many more. You can check on your stat dashboard to see how your audience is doing, where they are listening from, and what directories and players are most popular to them. If you reach a large audience, you can get cash from the company, too.

It's easy to sign up in minutes, and besides describing what your program will be about and selecting up to 5 keywords to describe it, you have to select at least two genres of music from their list of different types. Then, you are good to go.

# CHAPTER 39: MAKING MONEY FROM YOUR PODCAST OR RADIO SHOW

As a general rule, think of your podcast or radio show more as a vehicle to share your message and promote your book and programs, rather than as a source of income, unlike video, where there is more potential to make money, such as in marketing webinars and training videos. With podcasts and radio, the ability to make money, such as through advertising and sponsorships, requires a large audience, which can involve a large time commitment. Thus, generally, focus on creating an entertaining and informative program to attract attention to you, your books, programs, and business, rather than seeking a direct profit from your podcast or radio show. Hosting a program helps to make you more of an authority, so people are more apt to become your customers and clients.

Still, if you can attract a large audience, building on the topics covered in your books and other programs, the potential is there. For example, John Lee Dumas, the author of *Entrepreneur on Fire* and superstar of the podcast world, claims to make more than $150,000 a month from his Entrepreneur on Fire podcast.

Some of the stats on the size of the podcast market is encouraging, since as of 2014, 30% of Internet users listened to podcasts, according to Edison Research, cited by Tony Armstrong in "How to Make Money with Podcasts." (https://www.nerdwallet.com/blog/small-business/money-podcasts). This audience is up from 2013, when 27% of Internet users 18 and up downloaded or listened to podcasts. As another milestone, Apple announced that it had reached one billion podcast subscriptions in its iTunes store this year, according to an article in *The Media Briefing* by Henry Taylor.

One way to create a podcast is to record it as a video, and then separate off the audio to become the podcast. This way, you can get double duty from the same program. For example, *The Economist* produces both, but its core audience listens to its podcast rather than the video. (http://www.themediabriefing.com/articles/podcasts-economist-times-video-guardian-media-talk-economics).

To make money from your podcasts, Dumas suggests eight top ways in his two-hour course: sponsorships, coaching, books, masterminds, joint ventures, affiliate relationships, speaking, and products and services. In his podcasts, he interviews today's most inspiring and successful entrepreneurs five-days a week. For more information on his course, you can visit his website at https://www.udemy.com/monetizeyourpodcast.

The major ways that podcasters make money are the following according to Daniel J. Lewis, an award-winning podcaster who helps others launch and improve their podcasts and has his show at The Audacity to Podcast (http://theaudacitytopodcast.com/how-podcasters-are-making-money-with-podcasting-tap206). All of these methods might apply to your blog, too.

- Creating Products or Courses. This is the best way, according to Lewis, because you make up to 100% of the profits, when you have invested the time and resources to create a product, which is what the most successful podcasters have done. Besides John Lee Dumas, who specializes in podcast training programs, Cliff Ravenscraft provides training on podcasting and other digital products, and Jason and Jeremy have a $7 ebook and Internet Word Mastery coaching program. Lewis recommends starting small for your first product, say charging only a few dollars, since if customers like it, they will want more from you. Moreover, starting small helps to show people the value that you create, and they only have to make a small commitment. A good starting point is an ebook, PDF guide, or short video tutorial. Another strategy of successful podcasters is they give away great content for free, and that helps audience members want more, because they have found that free content so valuable.

- Providing Services or Coaching. As with blogging, you can earn money by offering your expertise through one-on-one coaching and consulting. Podcasting helps to give you more authority and credibility, so people see more value in what you are offering and become more interested in buying your services. For example, podcasting is ideal if you work as a teacher, speaker, coach, or consultant, since you are sharing information which shows what you know, so you can readily offer these services or coaching. If you are a good teacher, you can teach others how to do something. Or you might offer to provide your services to do something in return for a fixed fee or hourly rate, with a special discount for your listeners.

- Premium Content. If you have content that others might find worth paying extra for, offering them access to premium content might work for you. For example, some podcasters with a dramatic series, have offered listeners access to exclusive or previous episodes. Others have provided access to an exclusive community, such as a forum for all those who have taken part in a workshop on blogging, so now they can become part of a community of bloggers to share their experience and provide leads for future opportunities. Another example might be if you are specializing in a real estate market for land sales. You might offer an introductory overview to everyone through your podcast, which could also be offered as a webinar. Then, you offer an exclusive program whereby you provide leads and consulting on how to best negotiate and buy a particular property. Likewise, think about whether you have premium content you might provide to some of your audience members who might be interested.

- Sponsorships.  Getting sponsors is the easiest way, because you simply promote their product and get paid for doing so.  Sponsors are less interested in the actual size of your audience, but how engaged they are and how likely they are to buy the sponsor's products or services.  Commonly sponsors pay based on how many thousand impressions you get (CPMs), how many actions are taken (CPAs), or a flat rate.  While potential sponsors want to see large numbers, what's more important to them is the likelihood that your audience will make a purchase.   But before you approach potential sponsors, you need a great podcast with great content, presentation, and production.  You also need to know your actual numbers, which you can obtain through a service like Blubrry Stats (https://www.blubrry.com) or LibSyn (http://www.libsyn.com), which host podcasts for as little as $5 a month.

- Affiliates.  Selling for affiliates can be a great source of income, though you have to pick products or services that fit well with your books and programs and that you can sincerely recommend to listeners.   For instance, if you are using a web hosting company for your website, squeeze page, and other pages, you might get money from recommending that.   In many cases, you can sign up to make referrals through a company's affiliate program. Or if a company doesn't offer such a program, you might work out a coupon code, so you get a percentage of all orders that come in with that code.  If you approach potential affiliates, explain why there would be a good fit with your show.   If you have different affiliate accounts for different programs, track them separately, so you can tell how well different arrangements are doing.

- Selling Products.  Products can range from physical to digital products, though digital products are much easier to sell, since with physicals products you have to arrange to drop ship products yourself or through a fulfillment house.  But with digital products, like recordings and videos to download or access online, you just have to set up a payment arrangement. For either type of product, however, you may need a reseller's license and in some cities, a business license.

- <u>Donations</u>. Finally, donations are another possibility, though you need a very enthusiastic and loyal fan base to gain success through donations. To get such donations, you need to make the audience members feel they are part of the show, such as by giving them online shoutouts to thank them for their support or presenting them with a special gift. Perhaps give the bigger donors an opportunity to be on your show or even co-host a program with you.

Now think about the possibilities and what might work best for you. It's fine to only use your podcast to promote your book or programs. But you can make additional money in other ways through your podcast.

# CHAPTER 40: CREATING AUDIO RECORDINGS AND PACKAGES

Besides recording your face-to-face speaking, workshops, and seminars, you can create audio recordings which you offer for sale individually or as part of a package. In many cases, individuals use videos to share the same message, but unless you expand on what you are saying with cutaways to dramatize your presentation, an audio recording can convey much the same message, and some customers prefer this, since they can listen to your recording while driving. As with videos, you can combine hearing your message with a workbook with charts, exercises, and other materials. While a video is great to show PowerPoint slides while you talk or to show you giving a workshop to an audience, an audio recording can also be effective. It's a good way to start less expensively due to much lower recording costs.

There are several ways to create an audio recording:

- Set up a recorder at a speaking engagement, workshop, or seminar to record your program. Or record whatever you want to say using your book or a script adapted from your book or your workshop. One excellent recorder is the Zoom H5 or H6 Recorder, which can record on SD cards with up to 32GB memory, and you can operate with a battery or power cord. You can later transfer the recording onto a computer with a USB cable. Many smartphones can capture recordings, and you can send the recording to your computer.

- Put on a webinar or teleseminar and record that. There are various platforms for doing these recordings, such as Go to Meeting (www.gotomeeting.com), which offers a 30 day free trial, and has packages starting at $24 a month if billed annually or $29 per month, where you can have up to 5 participants at the meeting.

Although this basic plan doesn't include recording the meeting, you can set up a recorder on your phone to do this. The next level up, which is the company's most popular format, is $39 per month if billed annually or $49 per month, with up to 25 participants at a meeting and it includes a recording. The same company also has a video package called GotoWebinar, described in the section on creating video recordings and packages. Another company that offers audio programs is Instant Teleseminar 2.0 (http://instantteleseminar.com), which has a 21-day $1 trial; thereafter the basic cost is $47 a month, where you can have up to 20 people on a call.

- Set up a radio talk show, where you can talk directly to listeners or have up to a certain number of people call in as guests. One service is BlogTalkRadio (www.blogtalkradio.com), where you can start your program for free with up to 5 call-in guests, and all your shows are archived as podcasts. The next level up is $39 a month, which includes broadcasting during prime-time (5-8 p.m.), up to 2 shows a day, and up to 50 guests, although I found that most people access the shows in the archives, so free is fine, unless you want these added features. There are additional packages with even more features. However you set up your programs, you can organize your show like a speaking engagement, seminar, or workshop presented in 30 minute or 1 hour segments. After you record a show, you can use it as a podcast or package these shows for sale. While people can find your program online and listen to it at no charge, you can sell recordings of these otherwise free programs if you package them together, and possibly you might add workbooks or other features. You can also use these programs on your website, as well as on the BlogTalkRadio site, to promote other programs you are selling..

Once you have a number of these recordings which feature your workshop or seminar or are based on chapters from your book, you can start marketing them in a number of different packages, from accessing the recording online or downloading it to purchasing a package with CDs, DVDs, or flashsticks.  If appropriate, you can include a workbook as a PDF to accompany the audio recording.

Even if you are only marketing the audio package for online access through streaming or downloading, create an attractive picture for a cover or use photos from a physical workshop or seminar you have given.

However you do it, you need a sales page where you direct people to promote whatever you are selling.  You offer different types of packages with the various combinations of items you are selling.

But before you start promoting your sales page, focus on getting your audio package together if you will be selling that.  You need to be ready to deliver what you have advertised once you start selling anything, since customers who order online normally expect to get what they ordered very quickly – sometimes within hours, although at most 24 or 48 hours.  So get everything ready and then start to sell.  Later, after you set up your sales and distribution channel, you can easily add more and more products, as you do more speaking, seminars and workshops.

# CHAPTER 41: CREATING AUDIO BOOKS

Once you have an ebook or print book, you can increase your income by making an audio book. This can be an important source of income today, because you can attract a new audience, since some people only or primarily listen to audio books, rather than reading print books anymore. The average person now purchases 17 audio books a year, according to ACX, the largest distributor of audiobooks, and audiobooks have become a $1.6 billion industry.

Many people are drawn to audiobooks, because they are not readers in our media driven culture or because they are very busy, so they would rather to listen to a book while driving or doing something else.

The audiobook market is relatively new, so it is less competitive, because there is some barrier to entry. One barrier can be the cost of hiring a professional narrator, which can range from $300 to $2000. Another barrier is you need some equipment, costing about $150-250, to get started if you do the recording yourself, and it takes several hours to produce, edit, and publish an audio book.

Once you learn how to do it yourself, you can keep your costs and time down, and you can outsource some of the routine tasks like editing your final audio file. Another advantage of doing it yourself is that many people like hearing the original author narrate the book, since they feel a deeper connection to the author.

## A New Audio Format for Creating an Immersive Reading Experience

Another new technology allows you to create an immersion reading experience, so a reader of your book on Kindle (and eventually on other devices) can both read your book and hear you speak it at the same time. It's called Whispersynch for Voice and Immersion Reading. The way it works is by synching your spoken words with the words on a page, which are highlighted as you go along.

For this to work, your narration has to perfectly mirror the words on the page, which means your audio book must be edited well to match what you say, and you can't add any other content in the audio version. You can't read any footnotes or describe figures or photos not in the book. Unfortunately, the technology doesn't work if the narrator has a very strong accent, which makes it difficult to match words. You also can't make updates in the book copy, since this will make the book become unsynchable, although you can make cosmetic and sales changes, such as changing the margin size, font color and size, background color, minor punctuation, price, title, author, and book description.

The system is so amazing that a person can click at any time to start the audio version, and switch back and forth between reading and listening without losing his or her place. For instance, a reader might want to do this when they are driving, so they listen to the narration, but back in their living room, they want to read or listen to the narration while they read.

## The Market for Audio Books

Currently, the major distributor of audio books is ACX.com, though another option is AuthorRepublic.com, which has similar royalty rates and non-exclusive distribution. Both companies primarily distribute to Amazon, Audible, and iTunes. As the market grows, there will probably be other distributors and platforms for audio books, so stay tuned.

ACX.com is an Amazon platform, which makes it very easy to turn your book into an audio version and start selling it. You simply put in the name of your book and a search on Amazon reveals books with that title or a similar one. You then indicate which book or books are yours (such as if you have different versions).

ACX.com offers 3 ways to create an audio book.
1) You look for a narrator through ACX.
2) You already have the book in audio and want to sell it.
3) You will narrate your own book and add the audio later.

However you do it, you need an audiobook file ready to upload, much as you would upload a book file to publish your book. The quality of the book must meet the professional standards of ACX and other distributors. Professional narrators and editors will know about this, or you need to learn what to do if you narrate your own book.

With ACX, if you have an exclusive arrangement, you get a 40% royalty; with a non-exclusive arrangement, a 25% royalty for ACX sales, and whatever royalty you arrange with other channels. With AuthorsRepublic you have a non-exclusive arrangement. You receive 25% of what your book is sold for on Audible, iTunes, and Amazon, and up to 35% for sales on other channels.

## Promoting Your Audio Book

You can promote your audio book much like you might promote any book, such as using the social media, on your website, and through emails to prospective customers. In addition, there are audio book reviewers, who you can contact through their websites. You can find a list of them on Good Reads https://www.goodreads.com/topic/show/1421482-audiobook-review-sites.

## Finding a Professional Narrator through ACX

If you decide to hire a professional to narrate and produce your book, you can look for one on ACX. To do so, you agree that you have audio rights to the book, want to add your book to ACX to get it produced, and can meet potential narrators and producers, although you may also be contacted by audiobook publishers who might purchase audio right to your book and produce it off of the ACX system. You further agree that you will distribute the completed audiobook, at a minimum, through ACX's distribution channels at Amazon, Audible, and ITunes, and you can choose to distribute it on an exclusive or non-exclusive basis.

Then, you describe your book – or if there is already a description on Amazon, the ACX form will pick up that description, though you can edit it. You also include the copyright owners name, year, and the Audiobook Copyright Owner, which will be read by the Audiobook's Producer in the credits section of the book. Next, you characterize your book as fiction or nonfiction, indicate the best category for your book, and describe the ideal narrator's voice based on gender, age, language, vocal style, and accent. For example, when I went through this process for the *Researcher's Bible*, I indicated it was nonfiction and I recommended a female adult reader with an authoritative vocal style.

You additionally can provide directions or advice to narrators and producers who want to audition for the book, and include marketing information and selling points. For example, I suggested my *Researcher's Bible* would have a broad appeal to high school and college students and to teachers of research methodology. Use a few pages from your book for an audition script.

Next, indicate the number of words in your book, after which ACX will estimate the book's length (the average is about 9300 words per finished hour), and indicate your territory rights, such as world rights. You then indicate how you would like to pay for the audiobook's production, which can be a straight 50-50 royalty share and exclusive distribution deal through Amazon, Audible, and iTunes, with a 40% royalty. Or you can choose to pay for production, and indicate how much you are willing to pay per finished production hour (ranging from $50-1000, which will affect the number of people auditioning. Additionally you can choose an exclusive 40% option or a non-exclusive arrangement with a 25% royalty, so you can grant rights to other companies in any market or format.

After you fill in all this information, you get a profile about your book and the kind of narrator you are looking for, though before you can post, you have to add in your tax information and the email you have registered for your account. Once your tax form is approved and you get a W-9 form, you can post your request for a narrator, after which ACX seeks to match authors with actors to narrate your book. Once you post this information, it takes about 5-10 minutes to post an additional book.

Of course, whether you find a narrator through ACX depends on the appeal of your book, especially if you are proposing a 50-50 split, rather than offering to pay a fee now. You are also competing with hundreds of other authors who are seeking narrators. So while a partnership could be a great no-cost way to go, if you don't find a narrator this way, paying for a narrator might help if you have the budget for it.

Alternatively, you might find a narrator through other sources. Some possibilities include posting a casting call on a local casting network, such as SF Casting in San Francisco or LA Casting in L.A., where you indicate that you are looking for a voice-over actor for your book. You will get more response if you are willing to pay, though some actors do volunteer projects. Another source of narrators is going to the film and video schools in your area, such as the Academy of Art in San Francisco, or to local film community groups, such as Making Movies throughout the Bay Area (MMTB), where you may find actors willing to volunteer or narrate your project for a low fee.

Or you could narrate your own book, described in the next section.

# CHAPTER 42: NARRATING YOUR OWN AUDIO BOOK

Narrating your own audio book can be a good way to go if you haven't found a professional narrator through ACX or other channels, or if you want to narrate your own book to feel closer to your reader or think it would be fun. Plus you will earn more than if you have to share the royalties with a narrator or pay upfront. In fact, many audio books are read by the author in a casual style rather than by a trained voice actor, which provides a more personal touch.

If you narrate your own book, you can always outsource the more technical audio editing, which is still much less expensive than hiring a professional narrator and editor to put the whole package together for you.

Figure on it taking about three times the length of reading your book to obtain a finished audio recording, especially if you have done some extra takes in reading the book which the editor has to smooth out. After you complete a recording of the full book, you can hire an editor to polish your recording so it is acceptable to distributor. There are a number of outsourcing services, such as Fiverr (www.fiverr.com), Upwork (formerly Elance) (www.upwork.com), and Guru (www.guru.com), where you can advertise for an audio editor.

You want to end up with an mp3 file, the standard audio file format, which can play in a number of devices, from your computer or mobile phone to your car radio.

# The Requirements for Narrating Your Own Book

Your narrated book needs to meet some basic standards to be acceptable to a distributor. According to ACX, the audio submission requirements are these.

- <u>Your audiobook must be consistent in overall sound and formatting and be composed of all mono or all stereo files</u>. This consistency is required because it gives the listener a good experience, since any drastic changes are jarring. Moreover, extreme changes in volume means the listener has to control their listening device, which detracts from the listening experience and may lead to poor reviews and reduced sales. Mono files are recommended, because this results in better audio consistency.

- <u>You have to include opening and closing credits and a retail audio sample that is between one and five minutes long</u>. Minimally, you have to include the name of the audiobook, author or authors, and narrator. Closing credits must at a minimum say "the end." The audio sample should start with narration, not opening credits or music, since it is designed to preview your book and appeal to prospective customers. On iTunes, the preview automatically uses the first five minutes of the book. Also, the audiobook has to be narrated by a real person; you can't use a text-to-speech recording.

- <u>Each uploaded audio file must contain only one chapter or section that's shorter than 120 minutes, and the narrator must read the section header aloud</u>. You need to put the opening credits and closing credits in separate files. The reason for keeping the files for each section separate is so that listeners can easily navigate between sections, and they can skip forward or backwards one section at a time. If a section will run over 120 minutes, find a good break in the narration and split this into two files. Should the second file continue a chapter, you can call it "Chapter X continued," which helps the reader move from section to section.

The reason for the section headers, such as "Prologue," "Chapter 1," "Chapter 2," whether in the beginning of a file or continued in the text, is to help readers know where they are in the book.

- <u>Each file must begin and end with a room tone that only records the ambient sound of the room and has no extraneous sound, such as the sound of mike pops, mouse clicks, and outtakes.</u> The reason for the tone is to give listeners an audio cue that they have reached the beginning or end of a section. The space is also necessary to make sure that titles are successfully encoded in the various formats made available to customers. The reason for no extraneous sounds is these can be distracting to listeners, and outtakes sound unprofessional.

- <u>Each MP3 file must measure between certain frequencies and have a noise level under a certain value.</u> This requirement gets technical, but you can learn the specifics when you set up your recording system. The goal is to keep the files within a specific volume range, so it's not too loud or too soft. This way, you reduce the possibility for distortion if the recording level is set too high, or if it is too low, a high level of extraneous noise makes it difficult for listeners to focus on the material. The MP3 must also meet certain specs, including being 192kbps or higher, since those values are required for encoding the audio file in a variety of formats that customers can download.

- <u>The maximum file size is 170MB; if it runs larger, break it up into smaller files by finding a good break in the narration.</u>

## Getting Prepared to Narrate Your Own Book

In order to meet these exacting audiobook standards, you need to create a home studio set up, where you have a good mike and recorder and a quiet environment. You need audio editing skills to do your own editing, though you can outsource the editing once the editing you have a file of your recording. I'll provide some basic guidelines, and for more technical guidance, you can sign up for a course at a local school that offers this training, or there is a helpful class on "Audiobooks Made Easy" by Derek Doepker (http://audiobooksmadeeasy.com/).

Begin with some pre-production set-up. You should have 2 GB of free space per hour of audiobook, though you need to cut these up in the editing process so they are under 170MB. If you are recording on a hard drive or flash drive with at least 16GB of free memory, that should be fine for most books. Copy anything onto a hard drive or flash drive if you have an outside editor polishing up your material.

You can obtain some software for recording and editing sounds. One free open-source cross-platform software is Audacity 2.1.1 (http://sourceforge.net/projects/audacity). You can get professional recording software from Sound Forge, now owned by Sony http://www.sonycreativesoftware.com/soundforgesoftware, that starts at $59 for the Sound Forge Audio Studio 10. The way these programs work is you plug a microphone into your computer's sound card and you capture the audio. Then, you edit the recording and turn it into a variety of popular formats including MP3. A good mike for this purpose is a dynamic microphone, such as the ATR2100 microphone from Audio Technica, though you can get other recommendations from a store that sells audio equipment, such as the Guitar Center (http://www.guitarcenter.com).

Another approach is using a Zoom Recorder, which comes in a variety of styles, such as the H4N Handy Recorder for about $200 or the H5 Handy Recorder for about $270, where you record on a SD memory card up to 32GB in an MP3 or Wave Format. These are the same kind of recorders that reporters often use for field interviews, so they have excellent quality. I've used them in recording interviews for films, workshops, and seminars. You can find them online or in stores that sell electronic equipment, such as BestBuy.

Some other equipment you need for a home studio includes monitor headphones, microphone stand, and a music stand to place your book. You also need a way to minimize noise, such as setting up heavy blankets or clothes around you and the microphone. If you have a relatively soundproof room in your house or apartment, that will work well.

When you get ready to record, check your sound levels by listening into the headphones. If you are using Audacity or Sound Forge software, you can check the sound levels on your computer. Check that the level doesn't go above the line, which means the sound is too loud or below the line, which means the sound level is too low so you may pick up room noise.

Test out your recording after about 30 seconds or so and play it back to see that you have  good sound quality.   Try recording a section of your book and find a natural break to stop. These could end up being separate sections or you can combine together files in the editing process. Keep all the files together in their own folder on your computer when you record with a mike. If you copy files from sound cards, put them in their own folder, too.

## Recording Your Narration

When you record your narration, record exactly what is in your book, which will also be what you need for the immersion reading experience, where the audio is synchronized to what you have written.

Take about 3-5 seconds of silence before you start narrating, which will help in the editing process. Unless you want to do something different, an ordinary conversational style is fine, and it's a good approach to make you seem closer to your audience.

If you have graphs, footnotes, or links in the text, don't refer to them if you want to synch your audio and written copy. Instead, to make this information available to listeners, you can combine them on a resource page, which listeners can review later on a page on your website with that content. Or advise listeners to download a PDF or refer to your print or ebook for that information.

Include an introduction with credits and a conclusion where you say "the end" as provided in the ACX specs.

Adjust your recording schedule based on the length of your book and the hours needed for a recording, figuring on about 9300 words per hour, which works out to an average speaking rate of 155 words per minute. Since files can be no longer that 170 MB or 120 minutes, cut your sections accordingly. You can record continuously and cut later, although it may facilitate the editing, if you cut the recording session into the sections for each file.

One common recording approach is to record a single chapter or section in its own file and go through the editing process chapter by chapter. Or record the whole book in a single audio file and edit the whole book into sections. Either you or an outsourced editor can organize the files. Label your files in order, starting with 01, 02, 03, etc.

If you make any mistakes during the recording and have to make additional takes, mark the times when the mistake occurred and ended, so that can be cut in the editing and the corrected track used to replace it.

Once you have completed your recording, you can edit it yourself or turn the files over to a professional editor to clean up the recording and finalize it, so you can upload it for distribution. If you hire a professional editor, figure on about $2.00-$2.50 a minute of audio, though you may be able to get a lower price by working with students in a film, multimedia, or music program. If you do the editing yourself, clean up the file by removing noises, retakes, loud breaths, and any reverb or echo, and format the film so it can be uploaded to audiobook distributors.

Often you or an editor will be working with .wav files, which are the highest quality raw audio files. Eventually, you want to convert them into .mp3 files, which the sound software will do. In keeping with the ACX guidelines, create a separate file with a 1-5 minute sample from the book – or in the case of iTunes, use the first 5 minutes. Create separate files for the introductory credits and the close of the book. Then you are done.

## Distributing Your Audio Files

Once your audio recordings are complete, you can upload the files onto ACX, as well as onto AuthorsRepublic, which have similar royalty rates and distribution arrangements with Amazon, Audible, iTunes, and additional services. There is no charge from either service – just money for you when they sell your audiobooks.

With ACX, the basic process is to create a free account on its website (www.acx.com). Then, you search for your book by its title or author's name to find your ebook or print book. Once you find it, claim the book as yours, indicate you have the full rights to it, and that you want to sell it. You can choose an exclusive arrangement in return for a 40% royalty or a non-exclusive arrangement for a 25% royalty, if you plan to sell the book on your own or give it away freely. Next add in your book summary, which may already be imported from your book description on Amazon, upload your audio files, and upload your cover art or import your cover from Amazon. After a few weeks, your book will be available at retailers.

## Recording Your Books through AuthorsRepublic

While AuthorsRepublic is less well-known as ACX, it not only acts as a distributor, but has a special program to help authors record their own books, so you don't have to use expensive equipment or complicated software.

The program is called Recordio, and you can record and publish your audiobook from your smartphone or computer. You start by downloading the app from the App store (http://itunes.apple.com/US/app/id935773584). Currently, you can only use the Google Chrome or Mozilla Firefox browsers.

As Recordio (www.recordioapp.com) describes it, you use the microphone on your iPhone or computer and record as many takes as you need to. Then, you review and select your best takes. After this, you import your ebook, and Recordio's patent-pending technology automatically synchronizes your recordings with your text for each chapter. You read your ebook off your phone or computer, so you don't have any background noise from shuffling papers.

As with any recording, find a quiet place, ideally a small, quiet carpeted room with a lot of soft surfaces. Turn off the air-conditioner or anything making noise in the background. Ideally, record in the same room each time and try to sit in the same position and hold the phone the same way each time. Briefly listen to what you recorded in the last session to keep the tone and pace the same.

The basic steps for recording are:

1) In the app, from the My Books section, choose the book you'd like to work on by clicking on it.

2) Recordio will load your ePub book, divided into sections/chapters, as indicated by your headings. You choose the section/chapter you want to work on by clicking on it.

3) You will see the text broken up into small segments, with the "active" text in black. You can select any text to be active. Then, you hit "Record" and read the text that is active. When you get to the end of the text, click "Stop" to save it, or click/tap on the next segment to activate it, if you want to record continuously. If you are using the web app, you can advance through the segments using the down arrow key.

4) Keep reading until you finish the book or want to take a break. You can hear any segment by pressing "Play" or hear all the segments in that section by pressing "Play All."

Should you make a mistake along the way, you can hit "Stop" and "Discard," which will erase your current take and start again. If you notice a mistake while reviewing your takes, choose that segment/chapter from the list and record a new take. Select the take you want and delete unnecessary takes.

After you finish, you push a button and Recordio puts it all together. It publishes your audiobook in a finished file, which you can then use for self-publishing or share with friends.

If other types of noises, such as clicks occur during a recording, Recordio has a processing method to eliminate them. Once you finish the recording, you email a .zip file of your audiobook records to the company at contact@radioapp.com, and they let you know when the polished version is ready.

The reason the company can use this approach is that cell phone microphones have gotten much better. So the mikes on newer models are up to the standard for recording an audiobook.

For even better quality, you can get a high-quality mike and plug it directly into the phone. Since the company has both an iOS app and a web app, you can access it both on a phone and computer.

To use this approach, however, you have to have your book in an ePub format. If you only have a Word document, you can convert it to ePub by highlighting each section or chapter title and changing these to Heading 1, which is how Recordio knows to separate any sections. If there are any sections you won't include in the audio version, such as the table of contents, copyright information, and other books by this author, remove them. Recordio also breaks up the text within each section into segments, usually containing a paragraph or two, so you can easily review or re-record your audio book in parts. This way if you do multiple takes of a segment, you can choose the one you want. When you finish recording and select the sections you want, save your book and convert it using an ePub conversion tool, such as Calibre, which is free (http://www.fosshub.com/Calibre.html).

Once your file is ready, go to the My Books page on the Recordio website to add your book and follow their import wizard to upload your ePub file. Hit the "Prepare Audiobook" button next to the title you finished recording. Recordio will piece together all the segments and publish it into separate audio files, which is what you need for submitting your files for distribution. Finally, click the download Audio button to export a .zip file of all the mp3 files.

Once you have your completed audio book, you can submit it through AuthorsRepublic. If you don't already have your free account, sign up (https://www.authorsrepublic.com/auth/register) and AuthorsRepublic will take it from there.

# CHAPTER 43: CREATING VIDEOS

You can use videos to both promote your programs and create a video program you can sell.

## Using Videos to Promote Your Programs

When using videos to promote your programs, keep them short – about 1-2 minutes and sometimes as long as 3 minutes – to create a sizzle reel with highlights of your programs. The video might start with you announcing your program and how it will help the prospective client. Then, ideally include some clips from the face-to-face or online program you are promoting. This will give the client an idea of what the full seminar program is like.

Another approach is to offer the first 5-15 minutes of a complete program you are selling, which prospective participants can view online, such as on your website, Facebook fan page, or YouTube channel. Then, promote links to that.

## Creating a Video Program

Many of the same principles apply when you are creating a video program as in creating an audio program. Additionally, you have the added appeal of a visual, which can be as simple as showing PowerPoint slides when you make a presentation to a face-to-face group or online webinar. Alternatively, you can talk to the camera and hold up charts or graphs during your talk, or the video can feature a combination of you talking and cutaways to slides or graphics while you talk.

Besides these mere informal videos you can create yourself,

you can create a more professionally polished video with the help of a videographer or video team. One simple approach is to hire a videographer or find a volunteer videographer to film a face-to-face workshop or seminar. This can be a workshop or seminar for paying participants; or you can put together a program just for the video. In this case, you might invite some volunteer participants to attend a free program in return for being in your video. However you do it, get the participants to sign releases indicting that they agree to be in the video.

While it is best to work with a videographer with a video camera to take the video, as an alternative, you can set up a video camera on a tripod and turn the camera on and off with a remote. Smartphones also can take videos, although the battery power might limit you to breaking down the program into short segments which you film and then replace or recharge the battery. Preferably record your program more professionally if you have the budget for it.

While one videographer can make a single track recording of your program in real time, ideally have a second camera person, so the two cameras can be positioned to shoot from different angles, and one can take close-ups while the other takes long or medium shots. This way you can increase viewer interest by switching between different views in editing. It can further contribute to making professional video when the video team has a crew member to handle lighting and another to record sound.

Another approach to getting a video is to create a webinar by using one of the video conferencing platforms. In a webinar or video conference, you typically are shown on one screen, while attendees view the program or sometimes appear on their own guest screen, so they can interact with you. If you have illustrations, charts, photos, or graphs, you can hold them up, or these might be shown on another screen. The webinar can go back and forth between you, a participating guest, and the visual you are discussing.

The same company that has the GotoTeleseminar package has a video package called GotoWebinar (www.gotowebinar.com or www.gotomeeting.com/webinar/homepage ( $99 a month after a free trial). Other companies that offer video conferencing include Any Meeting at www.anymeeting.com ($78 a month after a free trial), and Cisco's Webex (http://www.webex.com) with plans for $24, 49, and $69 a month for up to 8, 25, or 100 attendees respectively (and a little less for an annual package). With all of these programs you control a full screen or split screen, and you can insert a certain amount of video feeds like a TV director deciding which shots you want to show.

There are dozens of these webinar services. One site that rates the top ten services is the Webinar Services Review (http://webinar-services-review.toptenreviews.com), which can help you in choosing a webinar company.

## Editing Your Video

After you film your program, the next step is usually editing your video, although some informal videos are recorded and posted as is, which can still be effective as part of a series of classes. But ideally, a videographer or video editor should polish up the video by eliminating any technical glitches, mistakes, repetitions, and digressions, so you have a smooth presentation to sell or promote your programs. You can do simple editing with some do-it-yourself programs, such as offered by Real Times (formerly Real Player) at www.real.com and by YouTube's video editor program (https://www.youtube.com/editor). But if your budget can afford this, use a professional editor for a faster and more professional final product.

The editing phase is also when you can incorporate photos, graphics, illustrations, and other videos as cut-aways, which can make your presentation more powerful. For example, if you show these materials in your workshop, the videographer may not be able to capture them, because of the time it takes to shift from a medium or wide shot of you to a close-up of what you are showing. So often, videos of presentation materials are taken separately, before or after your workshop or at another time. Then, too, if you have a JPEG of something (or a Word or PDF document that can be converted into a JPEG), the editor can insert this at the appropriate place.

For example, suppose you are talking about how using a particular sales approach can make someone money, and your chart shows the amount of money earned with a different number of sales. As you hold up the chart, the video can cut away to a close-up of the chart, which can be taken by the videographer separately from your workshop, or the editor can insert a picture of this chart.

In some cases, you can use stock photos or videos, which you can purchase from a stock photo/video house such as Dollar Photo Club (www.dollarphotoclub), 123RF (www.123rf.com), or Fotolia (www.fotolia.com). Then, as you talk about something, the editor can insert this photo or video. For example, if you are talking about how your fitness program improves health, the editor might insert a photo or video of people exercising at a gym or swimming laps in a pool. Aside from the Dollar Photo Club, which has a standard $1 price for each photo, which generally has a 300 dpi resolution, the other services have varying prices, depending on the size or resolution of the photo, the length of the video, and sometimes the price set by the photographer or videographer. Figure on about $3-8 a photo and about $20-60 for each video clip, depending on the size and resolution. Clips range from about 5 to 40 seconds. Sometimes videographers and editors have their own stock footage, or they can take a couple of hours before or after your workshop to shoot additional footage to cut into your workshop.

## Packaging the Promoting Your Program

As with creating audio recordings, once you have a number of videos which feature your workshop or seminar or are based on chapters from your book, you can start marketing the website where you are selling them. As with audio recordings, you can offer the videos in a number of different of packages, from accessing a video program online to downloading it to purchasing a package with DVDs in an attractive case. If appropriate, you can include a workbook as a PDF to accompany the videos.

Creating an attractive cover is important, too, even if you are only marketing the video package for online access through streaming or downloading. Use a cover design that features the theme of your program, or use photos from a physical workshop or seminar you have given.

In some cases, you might offer both videos and audio recordings of the same workshops and seminars. If so, you might price them differently, with a higher price for the video programs. For example, if you sell an audio package of a 6-hour workshop based on your book for $49, price the video package at $69 or $79.

Once your video programs are ready to sell, as with other programs, you need a sales page, or squeeze page, and you want to direct prospects there to excite them about buying your program, which they can obtain online right away.

But first, have your video programs ready to go once you start selling them, so customers can buy and receive what they order right away – generally within 24 to 48 hours, since online customers want to get whatever they order now. After your sales and distribution channels are set up, you can easily add additional products, as you do more speaking, seminars and workshops.

# CHAPTER 44: CREATING A VIDEO PROMOTION CAMPAIGN

In today's world of social media, mobile phones, and website SEO, using a video to promote your book, workshops, seminars, consulting, or other products or services is almost a no-brainer. You can use a video for all kinds of purposes, as well as sell an instructional video or video series.

Using a video or video series can make a big difference in building awareness and getting people to buy your book or other programs, because people are more likely to pay attention if you couch your message in a video, rather than text. Moreover, a video is more memorable than reading or listening to a message.

To make your message even more memorable, include stories or examples to illustrate why something is true or a better way of doing something. Stories are so powerful and memorable because they evoke emotions, and as much as we may want to be logical and rational, humans from time immemorial have been driven by emotional responses. Even judges, who are supposed to be rational in making their judgments based on legal reasoning and legal precedents, commonly have an initial emotional reaction that leads to their judgment. Then, they use rational arguments to justify a decision influenced by their emotional response.

Stories help to express this emotional component, even if you describe a story in just a sentence or two, such as when you describe what inspired you to write your book or how your training has helped participants.

## The Different Ways of Shooting and Creating a Video

There are now all kinds of ways to create a video, and you can decide what's best for you, depending on your strategy and budget. These different ways include:

- Creating one or more short videos of 1-3 minutes with the aid of a professional videographer or video team.

- Using a videocam on your computer monitor to film you at or near your computer.

- Using a smartphone – such as the Apple iPhone 6 or Samsung Galaxy S6 – to record a video wherever you are.

- Recording a video where you are the guest of an interviewer.

- Creating an edited video of 2-5 minutes with short clips from any TV appearances, online video interviews, self-videos, workshops and seminars, presentations to business networking groups, close-ups of your book or other products, or highlights from your other videos.


## Different Purposes for Your Video

There are numerous ways you can use your videos.

- Create your own video channel on YouTube and link these to your website, Facebook page, or other platforms.

- Create a video tips series based on your book or workshops to get viewers to want to learn more by buying your book or signing up for one of your programs.

- Launch your book, program, products, or services, where you introduce something new and perhaps tie this to a bonus or discount for buying now or placing a pre-order.

- Provide video testimonials for people who have read your book or participated in your programs.

- Conduct interviews or panels on the subject of your book or programs.

- Use the video as an ad to offer your book for sale or registration for your programs.

- Personalize who you are to help sell your book or get

sign-ups for your programs.

      - Invite viewers to let you know what they want by going to a link featured in the video.

      - Supplement a pitch for your book to a publisher, agent, or film producer, so you stand out and show how you can help promote your book.

      - And more…based on your own ideas of how a video might help you.

## Posting Your Videos and Beginning Your Campaign

Whatever you create, you can post it on your website, Facebook, and other sites. Ideally, post your videos on YouTube, which has far more viewers than any other video platform. You can embed the link to your video on your website and other sites, so you don't have upload it each time. Even if you already have a YouTube channel, unless it is dedicated to promoting you and your book, create a separate channel to feature these promotional videos. Then, promote your links to that channel, such as in your press releases, on Twitter, Facebook, and LinkedIn.

I have used most of these approaches myself, starting with a video about 10 years ago with assorted clips and me speaking to the camera. Now I am planning a video series, starting with more informal videos from my iPhone and webcam, and guest appearances on other programs. You can similarly incorporate different formats in creating your own video series.

## Planning Out Your Video or Video Series

Whether you are working with a videographer, taking your own videos, or being interviewed by a program host, plan what you want to say on your video. While it's great to be spontaneous and speak from the heart, design your video so you stay on message, succinctly tell a story, and focus on your end goal in creating or participating in the video.

A good way to stay on message is to write out a series of questions which the videographer or program host can ask you or you can ask yourself. Keep in mind the length of the video in preparing these questions, so you can answer them in the time allotted. When you make a series of videos, you can say whatever you want without a time limit, since you can later cut each video to a shorter time, say 2-3 minutes. But if you record a series of videos at the same time, stay on topic, so you can readily cut up the video for each subject, rather than shifting from subject to subject.

Some common questions might be:
1) What is your book about? (And who is the publisher, when did it come out, and where is it available)
2) What inspired you to write it?
3) Who is the main audience for the book?
4) What has been the response to your book so far?
5) What are some of the main things readers can learn from your book?
6) Did you have any memorable experiences in writing your book?
7) How did you find your publisher?
8) What kind of programs are you doing based on your book?
9) Are you involved in any upcoming events?
10) And so on....

Figure out what you want to most talk about and in what order and put them in question form. If you are working with a videographer or video host, provide the questions a day or two in advance, so the videographer or host can prepare. Often these questions will be edited out if you have a video editor, but not always, such as if the host wants to be a presence in any interview. If you ask yourself these questions using a webcam, you can post them on the monitor or wall behind your computer, so you can readily see them an in front of you. If you are using a smartphone, hold the questions down, so they don't appear on the paper you are holding. Then, glance at each question, and once you know what to say in response, hit the record button and start talking.

In creating the final video, especially if it is part of a series, it's best to create a 3-4 second opening, where you start with an introductory title, video or photo clip, and some music, to start each program. This provides a more professional introduction to your video, rather than if you simply start talking. Be sure to include your name in the beginning, if it is not already part of the title. For example, if you are doing a series of videos about trends in the film industry, you might create your video opening like this:

1) As the title scrolls across the screen, you walk out from a dark place into the light, as if you are coming onto a stage; then you turn to the audience and say hello.

2) The title might say something like: "Inside the Latest News from Hollywood," or "How to Make a Great Film as an Indie Filmmaker."

3) The subtitle might add in: "Conversations with (YOUR NAME): An inside look at the movie business today."

Preferably design these videos, so you don't have to do much editing, aside from taking out glitches. This way the video is quick to create, and it's less expensive than if you work with a video editor.

# CHAPTER 45: CREATING YOUR OWN VIDEOS

Consider creating your own videos to be like posting a regular blog or broadcasting a radio blog or podcast. But now you are sharing your thoughts on video on a regular basis.

If you can afford it, starting with a professionally created video or video series can be a good way to launch your video blogs, since you start off with a professional look before you go more spontaneous and home-style. Or start creating and posting your videos, and if you have a mobile device, you can live-stream your videos as well, using an app like Periscope.

If you start without a professionally created video, begin with some videos to introduce yourself, your book, and what else you are doing (such as if you are doing speaking, workshops, and seminars). After you have introduced the basics, you can create videos that expand upon your introduction, bring up other topics, or find new material or angles to keep your video posts interesting.

## Setting Up Your Video Recorder

The two main ways that people record their own videos are using a video cam on their desktop or laptop or by using a smartphone, like an Apple iPhone 6 or Samsung S6, though the iPhone seems to be winning the mobile device wars, since it has more apps.

In either case, set up the video cam or smartphone so you are positioned from about the waist up in a close-in medium shot or a close-up. Be sure to use the horizontal or landscape mode for video framing.  If you hold the phone in a vertical position, you will get a picture that looks like it was taken through a door with black walls on either side.

Set up the shot so you have an attractive background that contributes to your professional image.  For example, feature a bookshelf with your books, a stylish living room, or a room where you do your writing, if you are limited to the room where your computer is located.  If you have a laptop or smartphone, you can take your video anywhere, and you can vary the location to add to your message.  For example, one client who has traveled around the country speaking to different groups about how youths can stay off drugs does short videos at coffee shop meetings, in front of landmarks in different cities, and at workshops with kids.  In many of these videos, he holds up his book.

Take some time to frame the shot, so you are centered in it, and avoid a cluttered background, if possible.  If your room is filled with all kinds of equipment and papers so it is overly busy, position your webcam or smartphone to take in a different view.

Before you start recording, check your sound to make sure it is clear.  Modern webcams and smartphones have a built in microphone, so generally you don't need an external mike.  As long as you are close enough to the webcam or phone, it will successfully pick up your voice.  However, if there are nearby sounds, such as an air conditioner, kids playing, or construction, the mike will pick up the sounds.  Thus, you need to be in a relatively quiet area or need to be closer to the mike to get good sound quality.  If you can, reduce the background noise, such as by turning off the air conditioner or moving away from the sounds on the street.  In any case, do a test recording to see if the sound quality is good.  If not, make any necessary adjustments, and try again until the sound is clear, because viewers will typically stop listening if the sound is bad, though they may continue viewing, despite problems with the picture, such as poor lighting.

Since a webcam is stationery, there's no problem with a shaking camera. But if you are using a smartphone, hold it still and avoid any shaking if possible. One way to do so is to place the camera on a stationery object, such as a high shelf or table, and click a remote on and off to start and turn off the video. Or try using a "selfie stick," in which you attach the phone to a holder at the end of a stick which is about 12" to 24"long, and shoot from there. If you can, rest the selfie-stick on something stationery to help you hold the phone steady.

## Recording Your Video

Once everything is set, start talking. Use your list of questions to help you know what to say. If necessary, use notes indicating what you will talk about, such as bullet-points which you can easily read. If you set up your video for a medium or close-in shot, you will cut off the picture at your waist or chest, so no one will see your notes.

Keep whatever you say conversational, as if you are talking one-on-one to each person who is listening. Avoid comments like "hello, everyone" or "hi to everybody watching this," since that sounds like you are addressing a large group. You want to make your video sound more personal, since people typically watch videos one person at a time.

So talk as you normally would to another person, as if you were at a coffee shop or at your home. Be your authentic self, so you come across as real and sincere. Include stories and examples to illustrate your experiences and make them memorable, though keep your stories and examples short. Don't go into extensive detail, or you may lose your audience.

Generally, figure on each video being 1 to 3 minutes,

though you can go longer if you necessary to explain an idea. You can divide up longer videos in the editing process or cut out mistakes and glitches, though generally figure on these informal videos being complete or nearly so after they are recorded. Perhaps do a simple edit to incorporate a 3-4 second intro you have pre-recorded. You can remove any glitches if important enough in a simple editing program, such as on YouTube or Real Player. Using these programs, you indicate where you want to begin and end the cut, clip, and you've eliminated that section. You can create separate segments by making a copy of the original and cutting out a section in the beginning or at the end to create the shorter video.

Ideally, record a few videos at the same time, since this is more efficient, and you can readily post individual videos every few days or once a week, much like you might post a regular blog or podcast.

Once completed, you can post these videos on your website, Facebook, YouTube, and other sites. After you post your video on YouTube, you can embed the link on other sites. Preferably create a separate channel for your videos on a particular topic, book, or program, so your channel features a certain theme, like a TV series. This channel might include posts, using any professionally made videos. Later, if you develop other books and programs on other topics, you can create a separate channel for them, much like this is another TV show, although you might create another channel for your professionally made videos.

# CHAPTER 46: USING A PROFESSIONAL FOR YOUR VIDEOS

## The Advantages of Using a Professional Videographer

If you have the budget for it, a good way to start is with a video or short series made by a professional videographer, preferably using a small team to assist with lighting and sound. The sound quality is particularly important, because viewers generally expect clear sound, and they will often stop viewing your video or judge it as unprofessional because of poor sound. But when you work with a professional, he or she will make sure the sound quality is good, and can usually tell by listening with headphones, or a separate sound person will do this.

While you should prepare a list of questions in advance, as you talk, the videographer may come up with other questions, so you can further explain something or probe more deeply. This is one advantage of working with another person to shoot the video – having someone to ask you the questions like you are having a regular conversation. What you say in the video may seem more natural, like you are really talking to another person, and you may feel more at ease than when you are both talking to the viewer and shooting the video at the same time.

Another advantage of working with a professional is that he or she can take different shots of you from different angles or distances, so this can vary your image on camera, which helps to maintain viewer interest, as compared to a single talking head, unless you later edit in graphics. The videographer might also be able to use cutaways, as appropriate, such as of you walking to your house, holding up your book (difficult to do when you are holding a camera), demonstrating a technique described in your book, and the like. Good videographers will be able to see what will make interesting shots to incorporate with you talking. Having the questions to ask in advance will help the videographer in previsualizing potential shots.

Working with a videographer can help with editing the video afterwards, since he or she will already have an idea of what to include and how this will all go together in editing. Certainly, you can hire an editor to edit any video you take yourself, but a good professional videographer will have an ability to pre-see the completed video. And if the videographer isn't doing the editing, he or she can work with the editor to realize this vision.

Finally, a professional videographer can help you design and film an initial 4-5 seconds intro for the video or each video in the series. Many videographers can further help in selecting the music that might go in this opening section, and they may have a library of royalty free music you can select from.

## How to Work with a Professional Videographer

A good way to work with a professional is to start your campaign with one or a few professionally done videos to contribute to your credibility and authority, before you create more spontaneous-style videos using a video cam or smartphone to take your own pictures, which is what I decided to do.

Before the shoot, decide what you want to film and in what locations. Preferably, limit any shooting to a single central location, such as your house. Though separate rooms may be technically considered separate locations by filmmakers, a videographer with a handheld camera or easily movable tripod can go from room to room with minimal set-up, especially if he or she is using sound on the camera or has a sound person following with a recorder.

While shooting, make each segment, such as a response to a question, as smooth as possible. You can do retakes to better express yourself, though keep such retakes to a minimum to keep down the time for the shoot and the costs. As necessary, the videographer or editor can take out any errors in the final edit.

Generally, during editing, the videographer or editor will take out the questions to you, though you can keep the questions if you prefer. When you plan to drop out the questions, answer them so you incorporate the question into your answer. For example, if the question is "How did you get inspired to write your book?" you would answer: "I was inspired to write my book because," rather than only saying why you were inspired.

After the shoot, the videographer can show you the rough footage, so you can choose what you want to include. Or the videographer can do a rough edit, which involves taking out obvious glitches, such as mistakes you made during the shooting. In either case you indicate what changes to make, what responses to include, and what to delete. You can also determine how you want to cut up these videos into segments in a series.

Finally, the videographer can add the introductory section with the title, any subtitle, and music to each video.

# CHAPTER 47: WHAT TO TALK ABOUT IN YOUR PROMOTIONAL VIDEOS

Your promotional videos are different from the videos of programs you are trying to sell. Those videos will typically be about 20-90 minutes and feature your workshops or show a series of PowerPoint slides as you talk about the topic.

By contrast, the promotional videos to promote your programs or build a relationship a prospective customer are short, generally 1-3 minutes, though sometimes they run up to 5 or 6 minutes. Another approach is creating an introductory free video to present the highlights of your program and book, and invite the person to sign up to learn more. As an incentive, you can include a low-price offer if they sign up or buy your book now.

## Creating an Introductory Overview Video

Whether you use a videographer or do it yourself, this introductory overview video is designed to highlight the major ways you help others and the benefits of getting your book or signing up for your workshop, seminar, or other programs.

It is important to plan what you are going to say in this video to reduce any mistakes and the need to edit them out.

Ideally, include a close-up of your book or of you holding it, along with clips from any of your talks, workshops, or seminars. Also, describe the highlights of what the person will learn from reading your book or attending any of your programs. You might include your experiences or insights that led you to create the book and these programs. If you have any success stories or testimonials, you might mention them, too.

Conclude with a call to action, such as a place where people can buy your book or sign up for your workshop or seminar. If you are offering a discount, include a promotional code people can use when they sign up, though don't include a termination date, since this overview video is designed to be featured on your website, Facebook page, YouTube channel, or on other sites on a long-term basis. It is like a brochure featuring the highlights and benefits you are offering.

## Creating an Ongoing Videos Series

Consider creating a video series as a way to build a story about you that reinforces you, your book, your brand, and any programs you have created, whether you work with a videographer or do some or all of the videos yourself.

In your first videos, introduce yourself, your book, and your programs. If you already have an introductory overview video, refer to that in these videos, which people can check out for more information, and include the highlights. You don't have to go over what you have already described in more detail in your overview video.

Then, build on that initial introduction. One way is to include highlights or tips from your book or program to help people in their everyday life or work. Feature a different highlight or tip in each video. Perhaps go chapter by chapter in your book, and pull out one or two highlights from a chapter for each video. Conclude by inviting people to learn more by getting your book or participating in your workshop or seminar at a designated location, online, or both.

You might also include activities you do each day, particularly if they relate to the subject of your book or workshop. For example, if you have a meeting with someone in your field, create a video where you discuss a key topic for a few minutes and conclude with a link to your website for more information. If you are doing a talk to a group or leading a workshop, include a few minutes from that. Or perhaps describe your plans for a follow-up book or workshop/seminar program, and invite people to comment on what they think of your plans. Another possibility is to comment on something in the news that relates to your topic. In short, think of new ways to attract interest in the topic of your book and what you are doing, and conclude with some comments or a website link for more information, including how to order your book or sign up for a workshop.

## Creating an Introductory Free Video about Your Program

The introductory free video is a way to combine an introduction to your program with a pitch to learn more. After viewing a few of these pitches for webinar and training programs and signing up for some of them, I've drawn up these general guidelines for creating this video.

First, you need to already have a program, such as a webinar, workshop, or sales page for your book set up, so viewers who are interested can immediately go there to place their order.

Second, you need to set up in advance a special offer or coupon offer section, where people can place their order by a certain date or enter a promotional code to get the lower price.

Load up any slide show information to use as you talk. If you have a PDF a person can download, many platforms have a place to upload that.

Then, you are ready to set up your free video webinar. Use one of the platforms which enable viewers to call in and listen on their phone or use their audio on their computer or smartphone. These platforms generally have a window where participants can type in questions, and sometimes participants can call in questions. Some of these platforms, as noted, are www.gotomeeting.com and www.instantteleseminar.com.

Start with a welcome to let people know they have joined the online program successfully and are about to learn some important information that will help them that is related to your book or workshop program.

Include some description about how and why this video will help with some techniques, tools, or valuable information, so you get them to continue to listen. For example, if appropriate, include some stats about the topic, such as the number of people writing reviews for Amazon or writing blogs with book reviews.

Additionally, provide information about what your program will tell viewers to help them achieve what they want, such as attaining financial success by understanding the different methods for investing. Or to take another example, in one of the introductory video webinars I attended for a program called the 30-DayVideoChallenge, led by Felicia Slattery and Lou Bortone, http://www.30-dayvideochallenge.com, the goal was to get us to sign up for a program on using storytelling to create promotional videos. So after a introduction to the importance of using video today, the seminar leaders described the evolution and history of storying. Then, they provided some keys to creating an effective video, followed by a discussion of how much more we would learn from their intensive seminar program.

One way to organize these videos is to begin with about 10-15 minutes of informative content followed by directions on how to join the program or get your book for more information. Then, participants can follow a link to a sign up page, where they can place their order and get any early-bird special for signing up now.

Another approach is to include a description of how much more viewers will learn in the more in-depth program or in your book, so they can sign up right now, even before the end of the seminar to get an early-bird special. As such, the promotional video serves much like a squeeze or landing page which features the benefits of the product, service, or program and highlights what it offers, followed by buy buttons. Likewise, the introductory free video features a series of highlights, benefits, and opportunities to buy, often with a time limit of 5-15 minutes after the seminar to sign up for the early-bird price.

To further promote buying now, you might add an extra bonus or two for those listening to the webinar. For instance, since the program I was viewing was all about creating a story-telling video, the special bonus was a training on how to use Periscope, a popular new format for streaming live videos worldwide. Likewise, in your promotion to join the webinar, you might offer a bonus for those who view the video live, rather than viewing a later replay.

Include some time at the end for questions, which people can write on a side panel, so you can pick the questions you want to answer. Or create some of your own questions to use if you don't get enough questions or don't like the questions you have gotten.

Finally, end the question session with more information about how people can contact you or sign up to participate in your program or get your book.

In sum, these free videos can be a very effective way to introduce a training program you have created, as well as sell your book. But you still have to advertise the invitation to view this video so people know about it. If you have created an effective promotional video with the links to sign up for your program, that can help you both get sign-ups and sell your book.

# CHAPTER 48: STREAMING A LIVE SHOW

A new video and podcast technology has been developed, where you can record live on a smartphone. For the last decade it has been possible to record low and no-budget videos on webcams, and recently recordings have been possible on smartphones through YouTubeLive, Google+ Hangouts on the Air. Now you can do more immediate live streaming and post your live shows on some websites that provide a forum for these shows.

This live streaming may work well for building an audience for certain types of books and programs, where informality and spontaneity provide a personal and authentic touch. However, if you want a more a more professional, polished look, this is probably not the right approach.

If creating a live show sounds appealing, the new technologies include Periscope, Blab, and Meerkat, These are live-streaming platforms developed as apps for the iPhone, and some websites have been developed to show off the live shows. While the apps take video as well as audio, you can use only the audio in a podcast.

Since this technology is still very new, other apps are likely to be developed for Android smart phones, and there will be other improvements to make a more professional show. Here are some basics about how this works.

## How and When to Stream a Live Show

Live streaming might be good for certain types of shows, where you want to capture live action or interaction. Some possibilities might be:

- Interviewing someone at an event;
- Providing commentary before, during, or after an event;
- Reacting quickly to some issue in the news that is related to your book or programs;
- Getting feedback from people you encounter on the street;
- Bringing a few people together to discuss a topic.

While the technology allows you to reach an audience while you are recording, you can save the video on your website or on sites like Meerkat Streams (www.meerkatscreams.com). A great many of these videos are short, personal posings. However, you can create a more polished video, and in time, it seems likely that more professional sites will develop to show off the better quality videos. In the meantime, you can post these live shows on your blog, website, or make them available as a guest contribution to receptive bloggers.

## Creating a High Quality Show

As a first step, make sure you have good quality audio and good lighting, which can be more difficult when you are shooting these videos in an everyday setting with everyday noises. To reduce extraneous sounds, get the mike as close as possible to whoever is speaking. For even better sound quality, use a plug-in mike on a cord, rather than your smartphone mike. Check with a retailer of electronic or audio equipment to get a good mike.

Pay attention to the available lighting, since normally you won't use a lighting kit. For example, position yourself so the sun is behind you or to your side, not in front of you, so the faces of others in the shot are not in the shade. If you are indoors, be sure that the people you are filming are lit up by the lamps or overhead lighting.

As long as you have good quality sound on your smartphone or can plug in a good mike, you should be able to produce a high quality show, if you keep in mind these other elements:

- Stay focused on the subject.

- Clearly state what the show will be about in the outset, if it's to share information, let the viewer know what he or she will learn and why it is important to know this.

- When you have more than one other person involved in the conversation, guide the discussion so people don't talk over each other or go off topic.

- Invite people to give you comments or simple reactions, such as "likes" and "hearts," which others can send to you by clicking on the menu in the app.

- If you plan to use the live stream to create a podcast, which is shared or replayed through audio only, describe things that are visual in addition to showing them, so your listening audience can imagine what they are like.

- Stay in control of any live audience, whether people are sending in comments that appear as bubbles on the screen or are present with you. Should the onscreen comments be distracting, you can turn them off, and you can politely stop a person at the recording if they are disruptive or overly dominate the conversation. Practice some ways of dealing with a crowd at your live streaming recording.

Before or after your recording session, consider ways to repurpose the material as a video or as audio only. For example, you might post the full version on one of the live streaming sites or on YouTube, while you might post the audio track on one of the podcast hosting sites. Also consider if the videos or audio recordings might be developed into a series that could sell as a training or as a source of valuable information, which only a certain number of people can access. This repurposing is much like what you might do for other types of videos and podcasts.

Finally, for audience members who might view this recording live, mention in the beginning and from time to time where you will later post the video or audio, so if viewers drop out, they can still access this and other videos you have done. Preferably, refer them to your website or blog, since that platform will be more permanent, and they will more easily find other material by you, rather than looking for you on a live stream website that has numerous videos from others.

# CHAPTER 49: LIVE STREAMING YOUR VIDEOS

Live streaming videos are now available on mobile platforms, where you can stream your video live around the world and later save and download it before it disappears. If others like your video, they can forward it on, and you can become part of a growing community of people using these apps. People may even send you likes in the form of a burst of hearts on your smartphone.

The two major platforms for live streaming are Periscope and Meerkat, and they ideal for a video series which you create on your smartphone. For example, use them to offer your latest tips based on your books or programs, or share your inspirational thought for the day. While Meerkat was the first out of the box and took an early lead, Periscope seems to be winning the wars for viewers, especially since it has been bought by Twitter. Both apps have been designed for the iPhone, though versions for the Android platform are being developed but may not have the full version.

Another recent entry is Blab, where up to four people can chat at the same time. Since these platforms are designed for live streaming, there is a cut-off time for how long the video lasts, though a new app called Katch.me, enables you to save these live feeds into a file for later use. Some websites offer a place to feature these live streams. Here's how these platforms work and how to use them in your video promotion campaign.

You can use these apps like other social media to expand your reach and make people aware of other ways to get in touch with you. Plus when you save the recordings, you can use them to provide trainings, as materials for giveaways, in paid workshops, or in other ways.

# Periscope

Periscope is an app available through Apple's App Store or Google Play (https://www.periscope.tv). Using Periscope, you can broadcast live video worldwide. It was created by Twitter, initially for the iPhone, but may be available for other operating systems. In the App Store, you can download it through iTunes: https://itunes.apple.com/app/id972909677. Once you go live, you can instantly notify your followers, who can "join, comment and send you hearts in real time." The more hearts you get, the higher they flutter on the screen. Also, viewers can comment on what they are seeing, and their comments will appear on the screen.

I saw a demonstration of the app when I was interviewing a media savvy client who was promoting his book and public appearances around the U.S. After he sent out a video describing how we had done an interview for his book, several dozen hearts erupted on his screen from a dozen or so of his followers who were online, so they could follow his video feed. Some shared their reactions with comments like: "Sounds like you are having a great time there," "Way to go," and "Can't wait to read your book."

The way Periscope works is you click on the app and while it is running, you broadcast whatever you want into your phone for up to 7 minutes, though it works best to keep the video to about 1-2 minutes, because people have short attention spans and like short videos. You can readily share your broadcasts on Twitter by tapping its icon before you start broadcasting. Once you go live, tweet a link, so your Twitter followers can watch. Periscope keeps track of how many hearts you get from viewers, and the more hearts you get, the higher you go on the "Most Loved" list. The app has a fairly easy to use interface, since the most used functions, such as switching from a back-facing to a front-facing camera, or ending the broadcast, are easily accessible. You just tap or swipe anywhere on the screen, and you can clearly see everything you are filming.

After your live broadcast is over, you can make it available for replay, so viewers can watch later. When they do, they will see any comments and hearts you have gotten while broadcasting, so they can relive the full experience. The replays last 24 hours, though you can delete the replay at any time.

You can use a MAPS feature to see who is tuning into your broadcast around the world, and my client showed how he had viewers in major cities on almost every continent. To make your broadcast private, press a "Private" option before you go live and choose who you want to invite.

One way that people who don't know you can find your streams is that Periscope has screens where people can browse live feeds or they can check out the "Most Loved" list to find broadcasts getting lots of hearts and join those.

If you can tie your book or programs into a news event, that would be ideal, since Periscope has become a way to immediately access events as they occur. It is like Twitter with video, and it is rapidly spreading to the general public.

While many users have used Periscope to show what's going on in their daily life, much like using tweets with visuals and audio, it has been picked up by many radio presenters, producers, and personalities as another channel to stay in touch with their listeners and friends. You can use Periscope in a similar way for creating podcasts and videologs. As described in an iTunes pitch: "Periscope lets you broadcast live video to the world," and once you go live, you will "instantly notify your followers, who can join, comment, and send you hearts in real time. The more hearts you get, the higher they flutter on the screen". Should someone take a screenshot during a broadcast, a screenshot icon will appear on the screen alongside the hearts in the broadcast, and you can share the screenshot on Twitter.

# Meerkat

Meerkat (http://meerkatstreams.com or http://meerkatapp.co) similarly streams your video live, and it is available from iTunes and Google. It also features live streams on Twitter and indicates how many people are watching in different cities. Once you download the app onto your smartphone, press "Stream" to instantly send out the live stream everywhere. When you do, friends with the app will be notified and can watch, comment, and interact with your live stream. You can include a photo from your camera, so this can be an ideal way to show a photo of your book. Later, you can save your streams to your Meerkat library, where viewers can restream any stream to their own followers in real time, while everyone can watch on the web.

One advantage of Meerkat is that if viewers make comments, they don't appear across your video feed as with Periscope. Instead they appear near the bottom of the feed, and other options are at the top. So the center of the screen is clear, making Meerkat a much less cluttered experience, especially if a lot of people are making comments. But unlike Periscope, the camera operations isn't designed as well, since the buttons to operate the camera block portions of the screen.

## The Periscope-Meerkat Battle

Regardless of which platform you prefer – Periscope or Meerkat, Periscope seems to be winning, according to some recent articles about the battle of the apps, including "New Data Suggests Periscope Is Wining the Social Live-Streaming Race" by Janko Roettgers, in *Variety* in July 15, 2015 (http://variety.com/2015/digital/news/periscope-meerkat-twitter-social-live-streaming-1201540620). The evidence is that Periscope's live streams are getting more mention on the social networks than Meerkat's. Perhaps a big reason for the difference is that Twitter has bought Periscope, which seems like a natural brand extension, in that Periscope is like a Twitter feed with video. So if you choose one platform, it's probably better to choose Periscope, though many live streamers are choosing both for now.

## Meerkat Streams

Meerkat Streams (http://www.meerkatstreams.com) is a site that aggregates live and scheduled streams into one central location. It was developed by a New York digital and social agency, GLOW (http://www.weareglow.com) The site also has a LVR (Live Video Recorder) feature which allows people to record upcoming scheduled streams and store them in their own video library. The LVR feature allows for unlimited recordings with up to 60 minutes of recordings per video, while it is still in Beta. Plus you can get full chat transcripts of recorded videos. Anyone can visit the site and view live or scheduled streams, while those who log in can record scheduled streams and store them in their LVR library.

## Katch

Katch (http://katch.me) is a program that works with Meerkat or Periscope and saves your replays to the cloud. Within seconds after you finish streaming, you can replay the recording to watch or download. You can also share and embed your replays in other sites. You simply add #katch to the title of your video and tweet it. You don't even have to download an app to do this. Just add the hashtag -- #katch -- and tap the Twitter icon, so Katch can see your stream. The app records your stream and collects any comments and hearts, and after you finish recording, @KatchHQ sends a link to Twitter. You tap on the link to play, fast forward, or rewind, as well as view and scroll through your comments.

You can choose for your video to be public or private, and can delete any videos after uploading them. To archive your posts, sign up on the Katch website, and it will archive your posts automatically.

The platform also provides the ability to download your videos, so you can later upload them anywhere, as well as automatically create a YouTube video. Thus, besides live streaming your videos, you can later use them in a video series to promote your videos, provide tips based on your book or programs, or otherwise use them like regular videos. So this can be a good platform to create advanced programs which are only available to members, who can access your privately stored videos.

## Blab

Blab (www.blab.im) is a video chat app in which four people can have a video chat simultaneously, as an audience watches, comments, and can switch places with one of the four chatters. To use it, you sign in with your Twitter credentials, and when someone clicks on your name in Blab they can see your Twitter handle and bio. If a new video chatter attempts to join a chat, the creator of a Blab can accept or deny that person from joining, as well as decide who stays or leaves, since a chat is limited to four people. After the chat is completed, the moderator can let it disappear or hit record to save it for others to view later.

Blab also provides an ability to like someone's video chat box by "feels" which show the "praise" emoji of two hands in the air. They appear on the screen much like the hearts in Periscope and suggest who is the most popular of the four chatters.

The app also allows the moderator to mute any or all of the four video chatters, such as if you or another chatter are interviewing someone. You can mute the three interviewers and just listen to the answers from the person being interviewed. This feature provides a big potential for using Blab for public conversations about important topics, such as if you create a video show featuring video chat guests, while commentators on the right side of the screen add commentary, questions, and "feels." You can schedule Blabs for a later day, such as if you use them for a regular video show or podcast. Because the app is closely tied to Twitter, you can easily share links on Twitter to a selected video chat.

While group video chats are already possible through video chats services like Google Hangouts and Skype's group video call feature, Blab adds the social networking feature. So you can quickly share your Blab chats with the world, as well as post them on topic channels.

## The Future of Live Streaming

In short, these live streaming video products and services can provide you with an additional vehicle for creating programs and promoting them. Since the live streaming industry is just in its infancy, there will probably be many more products and sites devoted to this industry, along with improvements in the quality and length of the live stream videos you can record.

# PART IV: ADVERTISING, PR, AND THE SOCIAL MEDIA

# CHAPTER 50: ORGANIZING YOUR SALES AND MARKETING CAMPAIGN

In order to better market one or more books or programs, organize your campaign and marketing materials, so you can more quickly publish your book on multiple platforms and use multiple marketing techniques. An organized system can also help you track your sales on different platforms and what approaches are producing what results. This way, you can improve what you are doing in the future to increase your sales.

## Information about Your Book

Put your information about your book and programs in a readily available spot so you can easily use this for posting on other websites or responding to media requests for information. This includes basic information on your title and other materials you have created, such as catalog sheets, one-sheets about your book, descriptions of your workshops, list of tropics to your talks, and press releases. Create a folder on your computer for all of your books and programs, and subfolders for each one of them. Each subfolder should contain the following information:

- Basic Book Information. This is where you include the type of information about your book which you will commonly be asked to include when you publish your book on different platforms. This information is the following:
- Title
- Subtitle
- Author's (or Authors') Name
- Book Description
- Keywords (select 7, though some platforms limit you to 5 keywords)

- Category (this is the Basis listing, where you select certain established categories that describe your book)
- Number of Pages

Although not all publishing platforms ask for this information, publishing is faster if you have this information readily available, so you can readily copy and paste it into the form you get for details on your book.

- Files for Publishing Your Book. This is where to collect the files you need to publish your book on different platforms, depending on what files are requested.

- A Word file (usually of the interior only)
- A PDF file (usually of the interior only)
- An ePub file (of the whole book)
- Cover of your book in a JPEG and PDF

Commonly, publishing platforms want your interior and cover in separate files, but sometimes they may want them together, so if needed, add your cover image to your Word, PDF, or ePub file. Conversely, if you have included your cover with your book interior, delete it from the file if requested to do so.

- Marketing and PR Materials for Individual Books and Programs. Here's where to keep your files for the different ways you market and promote your materials.

- Press releases
- Query Letters
- One-sheets with book descriptions
- Catalog sheets with price information
- Descriptions of workshops and topics for talks
- List of questions for interviews
- Catalog sheets with price information for multiple books or books of a certain type
- Bio and promotional information about you
- Information about your company

# Information about Your Campaign

The other type of information to keep track of is about what you are doing to sell and promote each book and program with what results. To this end, create a spread sheet with the relevant categories and post this information by week or month. You can either create a single spread sheet with all of the information, or if there are too many categories, create different spread sheets to track these key types of information. If you have multiple books and programs, include each one separately on the same spread sheet or different spread sheets, and create a spreadsheet that consolidates all of this information.

- Press release titles, date released, and responses
- Query letter titles, date released, and responses
- Book sales, what type (ie: paperback or ebook), income, number sold, price, type of sale (ie: credit card, PayPal), where sold (ie: Kindle, Smashwords, Apple iBook).

A spread sheet might look something like this, using a press release or query letter as an example.

| Results for Press Releases and Query Letters | | | | |
|---|---|---|---|---|
| PR Release/Letter | Target Market | Sent | Number Sent | Responses |
| Release #1 Success Secrets | Newspapers, Internet | 9/1/15 | 800 | 200 Pickups |
| Release #2 Worldwide Fans | Newspapers, Internet | 9/8/15 | 2000 | 350 Pickups |
| Letter #1 Getting Reviews | Writers | 9/1/15 | 750 | 50 Replies 30 Orders |
| Letter #2 Mistakes to Avoid | Bureaus, Mtg. Planners | 9/15/15 | 1500 | 135 Replies 20 Invites |

Likewise, put in the information you want to track on your spread sheet, and look at the results for different approaches to see what's working or what isn't. Then, you can better decide what strategies to continue and how you might change any copy for future marketing pitches and promotions.

# CHAPTER 51: SETTING UP YOUR SQUEEZE PAGE FOR YOUR AD OR PR CAMPAIGN

Having a website or squeeze page is an essential part of any advertising and promotion campaign. Consider creating a series of website pages or free standing squeeze pages for different campaigns, each with a different message. Following are suggestions on different services to consider, whether or not you already have a website.

## Setting Up Your Website for Your Squeeze Page

Once you choose a domain name, the next step is determining where to host your page. There are two basic approaches:

- You can create a page on your current website, and point your domain name for the page directly to that page.

- You can create a free-standing website which is devoted to hosting your squeeze page, sales page, and related pages, such as for your free gift, report, and materials for sale or workshops to sign up for.

I recommend a free-standing website for your campaign, since you have more control over the look and the connections with related pages. You can keep this separate from your own website, that has more information about you and your books, though you can readily link these sites to each other. It is preferable to use a WordPress site for your squeeze page, since there are various tools you can use to create sales and promotional copy, such as Instabuilder, discussed *Monetizing your Book: Part II*, on creating an online sales campaign. It is also preferable to give your squeeze page and other related pages their own look and feel. In fact, if you develop squeeze pages and programs for different books and programs, consider creating a separate free-standing website for each one, though you may be able to include all of these pages as part of a hosting package on a website hosting service.

## Selecting a Webhosting Service

There are dozens of webhosting services, and some services which sell domains, such as Dotster (www.dotster.com) and GoDaddy(www.godaddy.com ), offer hosting services for a few dollars a month. For example, at Dotster, which I have used, after you purchase a domain for about $15 a year, the monthly basic hosting charge is $3.75 for a single domain, $6.75 for multiple domains, and you get more email address. At GoDaddy, the first year price is about $3, then $15 a year afterwards, while the cost of hosting a basic WordPress site is $1 a month for a yearly commitment, otherwise $4 a month, with other hosting with more features of up to $15.

These plans can get complicated, so do some comparison shopping to decide on what you want to do. If you plan to create more than one website, it may be worth getting a more expensive monthly plan where you can host multiple domains. In general, hosting plans range from $2.00 to $3.50 a month, and most provide you with a domain name free for the first year, though you may have to pay to renew it afterwards. If you already have a name from a different source, you may still be able to get a free name, but that's for another website you host there in the future. In some cases, it may make sense to get the name first to be sure you get it, before you decide on the hosting service, which is what I did for www.monetizingyourbook.com. I obtained it through Dotster, where I have about 50 other names, to keep them all together. But then I looked for another hosting service, which had an easy to use WordPress platform already integrated into the website, which would make setting up WordPress on the site easier to do myself, rather than use a webdesigner as in the past.

Which hosting service should you choose? There are a number of web host rating services that list the best, so I have combined the ratings from all of them to pick out the most commonly high ranked sites. These ranking sites include: The Ten Best Web Hosting Sites 2015 (http://www.webhostingbest10.com), 2015 Top 15 Web Hosting from Editors Review (http://hosting.editorsreview.org/top15us.html), Our Best Web Hosting Picks 2015 from Consumer-Rankings (http://www.consumer-rankings.com/hosting), and Top 10 Best Website Hosting (http://www.top10webbuilders.com/best-web-hosting).

The sites are ranked slightly differently on the different review services, but the sites that got repeated rankings on at least 2 review services in the top ten were:

eHost – www.ehost.com
iPage – www.ipage.com
BlueHost – www.bluehost.com
HostClear – www.hostclear.com
IdeaHost – www.ideahost.com
JustHost – www.justhost.com
SiteBuilder – www.sitebuilder.com
WebsiteBuilder – www.websitebuilder.com
HostGator – www.hostgator.com
GoDaddy – www.godaddy.com

You can install WordPress on any of these websites, but a few sites make it easier to do this automatically, such as BlueHost, which has a one-click WordPress install feature. A few sites offer their own drag and drop website builder, such as EHost, IPage, JustHost, and IdeaHost. I ended up choosing BlueHost, because of its close integration with WordPress, and because my web designer recommended it as the one he uses with most of his clients.

# CHAPTER 52: CREATING A FACEBOOK AD AND VIDEO CAMPAIGN

Facebook offers an ad platform from promoting your book, besides your social media efforts. There are several ways to do this, which include promoting your page or posts, and placing sponsored ads which appear in a news feed.

## Boosting Your Photo or Video Post or Promoting Your Fan or Company Page

An inexpensive way to spread the word is to expand the reach of a post about your book or programs for as little as $5 for a one-day post campaign. Or you can promote your fan page or company page for as little as $5 a day for a 7-day campaign. The basic process is the same for both. You can use a link in your post to get people to visit your squeeze page, website or sales page.

One way to use this approach is to post the ad you want to promote as a regular posting in your news feed or on your fan or company page. You include some basic copy and a photo or video. If you post the ad in your newsfeed, it will zip by along with posts by others. If you post it in on your fan or company page, you can expand your reach when you "Boost" a post or "Promote" a page.

For example, I created an announcement: "Latest book. Be the first to review it on Amazon," along with a link to the book for sale (*Turn Your Dreams into Reality*). An image of the book showed up, along with its full title and a 2-line description on Amazon, *Turn Your Dreams Into Reality: Simple Techniques to Get What You Want*). Empower yourself to get what you want, feel more satisfaction at work and in your personal life, and prospect in all that you do. Filled with easy-to-learn yet powerful techniques...." Users could click on the book or link in the copy to learn more.

In another case, I uploaded a video trailer for my film *Suicide Party #SaveDave* in MP4 format. After about 3 minutes, the video was processed and it appeared like a regular post with a video, after which I could boost the post, just as I could boost a regular post with or without a photo.

Once you click on "Boost" for a post, you have a number of options. It can go to an audience of people who like your page, people who like your page and their friends, or you can select people through targeting based on their location, age, gender, and interests. You give your audience a name, so you can select that audience again in the future. Additionally, you can select your total budget and indicate whether the ad lasts for 1, 7 or 14 days, and Facebook gives you an estimate of the number of people who will be reached, such as 490-1300 people with a $5 budget. Once that's done, you submit your ad for a review which takes about 20 to 60 minutes, so the Facebook staff can make sure this is an acceptable post. Once your ad is approved, you get a notice, and the clock starts running down on how much money you have left from your budget.

In the case of a video, you similarly write up your announcement and upload the video, using the "Photo/Video" option. It takes a few minutes to upload it, and you get a notice when its ready to view. You can then edit the video or post it. If you post it in a news feed, it will zip by like other news feed posts. But if you put this announcement on your fan page or company page, you can boost the post, as above.

Finally, you can promote a fan page or company page on Facebook. In this case, you can create a replica with the same information as on your squeeze page or website site, and include as much of the most important information as possible. Plus you can include a link to your squeeze page, sales page, or website.

To promote your page, the targeting menu is much the same, whereby you select the location and the major interests, age, and gender of your target audience. Finally, you select the budget and duration, although in this case, the minimum is $5 for 7 days, or you can select a higher budget (ie: $10, 15, 20, 25, 30) or duration (ie: 14 days, 1 month).

The boosts could be an ideal way of supplementing a social media campaign by selecting certain posts or pages on Facebook to promote to a larger audience. Then, those who are interested will find their way to your squeeze page, sales page, or website.

## Creating a Targeted Ad Campaign with Photos or Videos

The other advertising approach on Facebook is creating a targeted ad campaign, using a photo or video to promote your book or programs. You can similarly target your campaign based on location, demographics, interests, whether customers buy online or offline, and other categories. You will also get updates from Facebook on how your ads perform – including how many people saw each ad and how many engaged with it.

These ads are basically designed to appear in the News Feed. The photo ads feature 2 lines of copy of up to 90 characters above the photo, followed by a caption and "learn more" button, which can provide more information and link to your squeeze page, sales page, or website.

The video also includes 2 lines of copy up to 90 characters, and a video a person can click. You can include a thumbnail image which users see before they click on your video. Videos can be up to 45 minutes with a file size of up to 1.75GB, with an mp4 format preferred. You can use these videos to show behind-the-scenes footage, stories of people featured in your book, tips drawn from your programs, and more. If the ad is to get people to go to your squeeze page, sales page, or website for more information, keep it short – up to 40 seconds. If you want, you can add a call-to-action button to tell people what to do now, such as shop now, learn more, sign up, download, or watch more. You will probably want to use the "Learn More" button, since your goal is to get people to go to your squeeze page, sales page, or website.

Once your ad is ready to go, set your budget, which is the total amount you want to spend on the ad. Then, as with Google AdWords, you participate in an ad auction, where you can pay a specific amount per day, such as a $5 maximum or a lifetime budget. Facebook will then run your ad continuously until your budget is reached or your ad date arrives. By default, your ad is automatically optimized to reach people within your chosen audience who are likely to click on your ad or watch your video. However, Facebook doesn't use the CPC (Cost-Per-Click) or CPV (Cost-Per-View) approach for ads on Google or YouTube, which depend on people clicking or spending a certain amount of time on a video for you to be charged per click or view. Instead, Facebook uses a more general exposure measure, based on how many people are exposed to your ad. It's not as precise as the AdWords approach, but it could be less expensive if more people respond to your ad.

## Deciding Where to Advertise

The key about where to advertise and how much to spend depends on what works best for you. To determine the best approach, try different types of ads on Facebook, as well as compare your results on Facebook with your AdWords results.

# CHAPTER 53: CREATING VIDEOS FOR YOUR CAMPAIGN

There are multiple ways to create your video for your campaign.

1) Do it yourself, such as by setting up a videocam or using a smartphone to record your video.

2) Hire a professional team to shoot and edit your video.

3) Use a video template service, such as VeeRoll (www.veeroll.com) to inexpensively create a video, where you combine your ad copy with video templates.

Whichever approach you use, start with a clear idea of what you want to say and prepare a short script, which you can say on camera, turn into a voice over, or turn into text to appear with the images in the video. Generally, create a video ad of up to 40 seconds, though, a video can be much longer for a more narrative to promote your book or programs featuring highlights or tips from them or creating a documentary style video.

## Creating Your Own Video

In DIY – do it yourself approach -- is the simplest and least expensive way to create a promotional video, although more commonly, these DIY videos are part of an ongoing instructional or training program or provide a live action commentary on what the person is doing now. They may not be as effective as a promotional message of how a book or program can help others. Then, too, as an initial introduction to your book and programs, they could come across as unprofessional, so others may feel less impressed with what you are doing. It is different when you use these videos for further instruction or post them as a video blog, where informality can work well. But initially, making a more professional appearance, using a professional videographer or a template might make a better first impression.

If you do go the DIY route, there are a few ways to do this by yourself.

1) <u>Use a videocam,</u> which you can set up on your computer and position to show you talking. Preferably talk against a solid or uncluttered background, or at least a background that reflects the work you do. Set the videocam up for a medium shot, about waist high. If you want to show any images or stats on a bulletin board, blackboard, or poster, hold them up, so the camera can capture them. Generally, don't move the camera, unless you plan on some editing. If you stop the videocam, change to another angle or change the focal length, crop out extraneous footage, and edit the pieces together. But usually, it easier if you don't move the videocam. Just start the recording, talk, hold up any charts, or turn to a blackboard or poster behind you, and continue talking. Today videocams have built in mikes, so you don't need an external mike, though a good mike will give you even better sound quality. Generally, this videocam approach is good for the training or educational videos for a class, but they don't make very persuasive promotional videos, because they are so low tech.

2) <u>Use a smartphone,</u> which you can set up almost anywhere to take a video of yourself speaking. You can get a "selfie-stick" to hold the camera further away from you at varying distances for different types of shots. You can include charts, writing on a blackboard, or posters you want to show off. A smartphone is also ideal if you want someone else to join you to share ideas. Since you can use a smartphone to move around and have different backgrounds, this is a step up from sitting in front of a stationery webcam, so it looks a bit more professional. Since smartphones like videocams have built in mikes, you don't need an external one, unless you want even better sound quality.

3) <u>Put a video camera or SLR camera on a tripod</u>. Video cameras that are fine for postings on Facebook or Youtube have come down in price, so they are very affordable at about $300 to $900. Also you can get SLR cameras that both take still photos and videos for $300-1000. You can use these cameras to set up an even more professional looking shoot by yourself, since you have the mobility of a smartphone and the stationery feel of a videocam. You can easily move the tripod and camera to another location or focus it on your charts and graphics, while you are beside them or provide a voice-over. Using a camera lends itself well to an online workshop series, where you film all or some of the videos in different settings and include you and includes you and cutaways to graphics, photos, and videos of whatever you are talking about.

## Hiring a Professional Team to Shoot and Edit Your Video

Going pro can be a good approach to give you a very professional video or several videos which you can use for your initial promotions to get prospect to your squeeze page, sales page, or website. But because of the cost, it may be best to keep these videos to opening promos, and use the DYI approach for additional content, such as for creating training or educational videos.

Typically, a video producer will work out a script and shooting plan with you, so you know what you will be filming when and where. Then, a production team of two to three people, which may include the video producer, but not always, if the video producer acts more like a consultant or sales agent for the group. Whoever does the filming, there will minimally be a videographer, who takes the picture and a sound person who records the sound off camera for a better sound quality, though the videographer will often turn on the camera mike for a back-up copy if needed. Plus there may be a third person who handles the lighting and sometimes provides a second camera to take different angles and

B-roll, which are shots of different scenes to add later in editing the video.

During filming, give your pitch or talk as you would in other videos, though you have more freedom, since you are not tied to a single camera and built in mike, as in the DIY model. Also, the video team will more carefully check sound levels, and they can do more extensive editing, so you can film multiple takes if needed to say what you want even more smoothly. A video team will also have more flexibility on filming you in different settings, as well as zooming in on your charts, graphs, or posters.

One way to keep down costs is to contact a local film school or college with a film department, since you may be able to find a video team for a much lower price than hiring a professional, although the final quality may be less certain – and the students may delay completing your video project, because they have school commitments. Otherwise, this could be a good way to go on a limited budget.

If you go with a professional team, figure on costs of about $2000-5000 for one to a few videos, with lower costs if you can do all of the filming on the same day. The cost of filming is about $500-1000 a day, depending on the size of the video team, and the other costs are for editing your final videos.

## Use a Video Template Service

In this video template approach, instead of you talking, you use a few short lines of copy to let prospects know why they need your book or programs, how they will gain the benefits, and how they can get more information by clicking on the video to go to your squeeze page, sales page, or website to learn more.

With a video template service, you don't even need your own video cam, smartphone, or camera, since you just write the lines of text that will go in the video. The service does the rest by adding each line of text to each video screen. In the simplest type of video, you might see a hand going across the screen writing your first text message, writing youe second text message on another screen, and so on. But with more premium packages, your text appears against a series of photo or video clips that illustrate your message. You can then download the completed video and upload it to Facebook or Google for your ad campaign. Or the service might also post the videos on Google or Facebook or both for you.

Commonly, these services have a free trial, so you can see how this approach works for you by creating a few videos. If you decide to continue, the company will have a monthly or yearly plan, so you can create a series of messages with different looks.

# CHAPTER 54: CREATING A PROMOTIONAL VIDEO THROUGH VEEROLL

One excellent program for creating a promotional video using a video template is Veeroll (www.veeroll.com). It is designed to create a 40 second video, based on your writing five lines of a script to convey a strong message of why people in your target audience will benefit from and want your book and program. Thus, it shows them they can get more information by clicking now – which takes them to your squeeze page or website. After you enter your 5 lines of text, Veeroll does all the rest to create your video that is designed to be placed on YouTube or Facebook. You can upload the video through the service, which may be easier than using the AdWords interface yourself.

Your script is based on dividing the 40 seconds into 8 3-5-seconds blocks. You enter your five lines of copy, one on each block, with a few extra seconds to start and conclude the video. The company developed its formula for making an effective promotional video based on nine years of market researching different video ads.

The formula is based on what they call the AIDCA model, where A stands for Attention, I for Interest, D for Desire, C for Conviction, and A for Action. For anyone in sales, this will be familiar as the basic way in which a salesperson appeals to a customer, builds to a close, and gets the person to buy.

## The Seven Step Process for Preparing to Write Your Script

Before you apply the formula to writing your script, you

follow a 7-step process in which you do the following:
1) Define your target audience.
2) Get clear on the problem of your target audience.
3) Find out where your target audience hangs out.
4) Define your solution that solves their problem.
5) Get clear on your unique selling proposition.
6) Define where you want to send traffic.
7) Write your script based on the AIDCA formula.

Regardless of what approach you use for creating any video ad – or any ad for that matter, defining your target audience is critical, since you will direct your ad to that market. That's where defining the characteristics of this audience is crucial, since this helps you narrow your audience to those most likely to buy. For example, these characteristics are used by Facebook users in the targeting their ads, based on location, demographics such as age and gender or interests. In addition, consider where your audience hangs out online, such as types of videos they watch on YouTube or what groups they belong to on Facebook.

Then, think about why your book or program might appeal to them, and in particular what problem they might have that your book or program might help them with. While a group's members may be concerned about multiple problems or issues, you want to prioritize which is the most important to the group, next most important, and so on. Then, focus on a single issue in each video.

Next, consider the kinds of videos or key words with the most appeal to this audience. This is what Gideon Shalwick, the Co-Founder of Veeroll, suggests in the Veeroll Scriptwriting Guide to quickly create powerful scripts for your video ads. For example, if you are using Facebook ads, consider which other business pages they have liked or what their interests are. Or if posting your ad on YouTube, consider what a viewer might type into the YouTube search engine.

Then, rather than describing your book or program, focus on the solution that this brings to your target customer and emphasize the emotional benefits rather than features. For example, if your book is about losing weight through good nutrition, highlight how a person will enjoy a healthier lifestyle as a result of this diet.

Next, think about how your book or program is unique, which salespeople call the Unique Selling Proposition or USP. This is the quality you offer that makes your book or program stand out in a crowded marketplace.

Then, decide on where you want to send traffic after seeing your video. This might be your squeeze page, sales page, or website, or you can target a selected YouTube video or channel, Facebook page for your company or book, or wherever else you want.

Finally, taking these points into consideration, write up your script for an up to 40 second video using the AIDCA formula.

## Writing Your 5-Line Script

Write the first line to grab the viewer's <u>attention</u> in the first five seconds. According to Gideon, the best way to do this is to focus in on the exact pain or problem that the target audience is experiencing. If you do this right, you have an "Audience to Problem Match," where you have selected the right problem for the right audience.

Write the next 5 seconds line to keep the viewer's <u>interest</u>. One of the best ways to do this, according to Gideon, is to hint at your practical solution to their problem, so the viewer wants to keep watching to find out what it is.

For the next 5 seconds, highlight the benefits you are offering to show why your solution is so good, compared to what else is out there. This is where you highlight your Unique Selling Proposition or USP to create desire.

In the next 5 seconds, to inspire conviction, to use a psychological trigger to influence people to take action in response to your call to action or CTA. The six basic triggers are reciprocity, commitment (and consistency), social proof, liking, authority, and scarcity. In reciprocity, you give someone something, so people feel a sense of obligation to give you something back, although this doesn't fit, because you haven't given them a free gift yet.

- Commitment or consistency comes into play when you appeal to someone based on them being committed to something else to act, because it is consistent with what they have done before.

- For social proof, you show people that many of their peers have already taken action, or you use testimonials from a customer that is representative of your target audience.

- Liking is important trigger, because people like to do business with people they like and trust, but there is no time to really establish this in a short time – about 20 seconds at this point in the script.

- Authority can be an important influence, if you can get an endorsement from a recognized authority, expert, or celebrity, since people naturally trust others in a position of authority or expertise.

- Scarcity occurs when you create a perceived lack of a

desired resource, such as by suggesting that there is a limited time to get the offered discount or that there are only a small number of slots available, so people will miss out if they don't respond immediately—though only use this if the scarcity is real; if not, you will quickly lose trust.

While there are these six triggers, you can only use one in your ad. Gideon suggests using social proof or scarcity. If it doesn't make sense to use a trigger in your ad, mention another strong benefit or expand on your unique selling proposition.

Finally, end your video ad with a call to action -- to click on your ad, which is the link at the end of the video.

You can choose from a selection of music to add to your video, although often it is better to not use music, especially on Facebook, since viewers can find this annoying.

In applying this formula, I came up with the following lines, each limited to 40 characters, for my ad for *Monetizing Your Book:*
- Difficult making money from your book?
- A new method makes it easy to do.
- This free report shows you exactly how.
- Hundreds of writers now do this.
- Click the button for your free report.
- www.monetizingyourbook.com

## The Advantages and Costs of Using a Video Ad Program

One of the big advantages of using a video ad program is its simplicity. You don't have to spend time taking the videos, editing them, and uploading them, since the program takes care of that for you. Also, the program uses a time-tested formula, and it can look more professional with the company's templates than a video of you talking to a videocam or smartphone. The cost is much less than hiring a professional video service to create the videos for you   And the company helps with targeting and training in how to create a good video script.

After a free trial, the starter plan which includes 4 videos a month is $35 a month paid annually; $47 if paid each month, with other plans if you want to make more videos. You might also get an offer to create double as many videos each month if you act now, which would be an advantage if you want to make additional video for your campaign.

I was impressed enough by their presentation to try out their program once I am ready to start advertising this book on YouTube and Facebook.

# CHAPTER 55: OTHER WAYS TO BUILD TRAFFIC

Besides using video ads on Facebook and YouTube to build traffic to your squeeze page or website, other techniques include:
- Using SEO so people find you on the Internet
- Postings on social media sites
- Creating flyers, postcards, and business cards to hand out
- Attending local networking and referral groups
- Going to special events in your community or industry

While you may already be using some of these activities to promote yourself and your business, now your goal is to use these techniques to get people to go to your squeeze page or website to learn more about your book and any programs based on it.

## Using SEO So People Find You on the Internet

SEO – or search engine optimization – helps people find you, when they are searching for something by bringing people to your site through increasing your search engine ranking. With a high ranking, the link to your squeeze page or website comes up higher on the pages people see when they do a search by keyword on Google, Yahoo, or other search engine. The sweet spot is the first three rankings, or at least showing up on the first page, because that's where most people stop their search.

You can increase your SEO ranking by knowing what keywords to use, so that you use them throughout your squeeze page or website copy -- and it helps if you continue to add new content with those words to increase your rank. You can continue to add content with additional pages or blogs on your squeeze page, sales page, or website, though sprinkle those keywords every 100 words or so, or in every paragraph or two, though don't overuse these words too much – or the search engine wizards who create the formulas in algorithms for ranking websites will penalize you.

For example, don't mention your book title or program title just once, Rather, incorporate it, every paragraph or two as noted above. Plus put in your city, nearby city, or county, so potential customers or press people in your area are likely to find you. Also, since search engines are constantly looking for new information, every week or so add new content or edit what's there to update the page, such as adding another free gift to your offer or adding a few lines about how your program is coming soon and inviting people to sign up now for an extra discount or extra free report on a subject of interest.

## Postings on Social Media Sites

Another way to draw interest to your site is by regularly posting in the updates or status section of the social media, such as Facebook and LinkedIn, or sending out tweets through Twitter. In creating your posts, provide an insight or something newsworthy related to your book or programs, and include a link. With Twitter, include a hashtag (#) such as #yourbooktitle (or a shortened version if this is too long), so all of your posts and any responses go there. Ideally, send out a post every day or two, and if you have photos, you can add them. You can similarly add posts with images to Pinterest, and you can add links at Reddit.

For example, I have a client who has been putting on various events where he helps young people stay off drugs, and after each event, he has someone take a picture of himself with the group. Typically, he holds up a copy of his book, and adds a short description of what happened at the event. Generally, he posts these on Facebook once or twice a day, and he sends out tweets about his appearances as well.

These posts whiz by because so many people are posting in the general news feeds. However, you can also join groups of people who might share an interest in the subject of your book or programs, and put your posts there, too. However, don't just start by pushing information and links, since you might turn off group members who might consider your post spam. Instead, take some time to get familiar with what people are talking about, then join the conversation with relevant and helpful information related to your book or programs. For example, answer questions others ask or share advice based on your insights in writing your book or conducting your programs. This input will help to establish you as a go-to expert and increase your authority and credibility, so people will be more receptive and interested in learning more about your book and programs.

The way to find groups to join is to indicate the topics of interest in the site's search engine. For instance, if your book is about improving your health, put in words like "health," "wellness," "diet," "nutrition," and "medical." Then, you will see a list of possible groups to join. Just click on those groups and indicate your interest in joining. With some groups you will become a member automatically; in other cases, you have to wait to be approved by the moderator. Once you are in the group, introduce yourself, get a sense of what others in the group are posting and talking about, and as it feels right, add your advice, opinions, and information about your book and programs, along with your squeeze page or website.

# Creating Flyers, Postcards, and Business Cards

Flyers, postcards, and business cards with your squeeze page and website or both can be another way to get people to your site. While going to networking events and giving out business cards can help you make contact with people who might be interested themselves or might tell others about your book and programs, you also need the collateral material, so people remember you. Plus, you can leave this information in a prominent place with other literature or in other places where people are likely to see it – such as the table by the entrance where people sign in or by the food buffet, if you are allowed to leave it there.

This way, even if you don't meet someone personally, they may see your information. If you have a compelling headline about what you are offering, that might lead them pick up your flyer for more information – and perhaps go to the link provided on your material. Perhaps mention you are offering a free gift in your flyer or postcard as an incentive to go to your page. Then, they have to provide their email to get your gift.

In making these flyers and postcards, have a strong headline, much as in writing a video ad script, that gets attention. Then, use a subhead to generate more interest, and follow with a short paragraph or a few bullet-points to highlight how you can help them with whatever you are offering. Next, inspire conviction with one of the triggers, such as the peer support appeal where you include a few testimonials by people who have read your book or participated in your program. Then, list the link to your website, squeeze page, or sales page. For a local pitch, include your email and phone number, too. Lastly, invite people to go to your squeeze page, sales page, or website to take advantage of your offer. Perhaps even announce a limited time period to get a benefit, such as a discount.

# Attending Local Networking and Referral Groups

Attending local networking and referral groups and other events is a great way to meet people or talk to a group where some people might be interested in your book or offer. There may also be special events where you can attend or volunteer to help out in the booth of an organization you belong to, like your local chamber of commerce. Whenever possible, bring along your sales material to hand out or display.

Look into what groups you might join or attend as a guest in your area, such as Business Networking International, BNI (www.bni.com), LeTip (http://letip.com), and the Successful Thinkers Network (www.successfulthinkersnetwork.com, which have chapters in some cities. There are also some business referral networks in certain regions, such as GoRampUp (www.goramp.up) and the B2B Gathering (http://b2bgathering.com) in the East Bay. You can find the groups in your area by putting in key words such as "business referral groups" or "business networking groups" and your area in a search engine. Some Chambers of Commerce also have business partners or leads groups.

The groups have various formats, but generally meet for 1 to 1 ½ hours once or twice a month or once a week. Typically they meet in the morning starting at 7 to 9:30 or they have lunch time meetings starting at 11:30 or 12. While some groups have lunch or dinner, with additional costs to pay the restaurant for the food, others don't have any food at the meetings. Usually you can go once or twice as a guest to check out the group and then have to join. Membership are generally for 6 months to a year, and some have an initiation fee when a new member joins, though some have no membership or have a month to month arrangement, which you can stop at any time.

At a typical meeting, everyone gets to give a 30 second to 1 minute introduction, or in some cases, the person who invited you give a 15-30 second intro to tell the group some key things about you – your name, business, how you can help others with what you do, your best referrals, and your power partners – people in related fields. While most of these groups only have one person per industry, some groups like GoRampUp are open to everyone. After introductions, people commonly pass around business cards and sales materials, and sometimes one to three group members give a more extended 7 to 15 minute presentations, followed by a short time for questions. Uniquely, in the case of GoRampUp, members spend about 20 minutes discussing some theme related to being successful in business and professional development.

Usually these groups emphasize people in the group getting together on a one-on-one basis or in a small group of 3 or 4 people for coffee, so everyone in the group gets to know each other better and feels more comfortable making referrals to one another. After a while, some of these groups build up a kind of family feeling.

I have found some of these groups especially helpful for finding clients and getting leads. But the response is different for everyone. It depends on where you are, the mix of businesses in the group, and how well your book and programs fit with the interest of group members or their contacts. So check out the groups in your area to see how well these groups work for you.


## Going to Special Events in Your Community or Industry

Going to special events, such as trade shows, conferences, conventions, festivals, and street fairs in your community or industry is still another way to spread the word about your books and programs.

Sometimes you can prepare in advance by signing up, so

you get information about the attendees or can become a member of this group, such as if you attend the American Film Market ([www.americanfilmmarket.com](www.americanfilmmarket.com)), which is the big film event with several hundred exhibitors from around the world, held each November in Santa Monica. Another big industry event is the Book Expo of America ([www.bookexpoamerica.com](www.bookexpoamerica.com)) held year is at different venues around the country, such as New York, Chicago, and L.A.

You will also find special events in your industry or the industries of potential clients, such as conferences and trade shows for the health, travel, insurance, and other industries. You name it, and there will usually be an industry show somewhere. If it's convenient and related to your book or programs, you might find good connections for pitching clients or finding partners. So check out what industries or organizations have meetings in your area and the costs and arrangements for attending. If you go, bring along your flyers, postcards, and business cards, and get the cards with emails of the vendors and other contacts you meet for follow-up later.

Finally, you may find local fairs and festivals a place to meet people interested in your book or programs. Walk up and down the booths, and if you see people in the same or related fields, talk to them about what you do. If they are interested, leave some materials and follow up later. Then, too, you might meet attendees who are interested in what you are doing. These events are unpredictable, and they can just be fun or be great for business.

# CHAPTER 56: GETTING REVIEWS FROM NEWSPAPERS AND MAGAZINES

Getting good book reviews can a major contributor to the success of your book, as well as the programs based on it. It's ideal if you can get reviews in newspapers and magazines both print and online.

Traditional publishers typically send out review copies two or three months before publication, but many smaller publishers don't do this at all or send to only a limited number of reviewers. If you have a traditional publisher, you can supplement what they are doing, or do this yourself if your publisher isn't doing any PR for you.

If you self-publish your book or send information after your book's publication or with an insufficient lead time before publication, some newspapers and magazines won't review your book. So get an early start on contacting prospective reviewers. If you have self-published your book, you might still try for reviews if you have your own imprint or ISBN number on it. Just don't list CreateSpace or one of the print-on-demand companies as the publisher – a clear give-away that this is a self-published book and generally the kiss-of-death for getting a newspaper or magazine review.

The traditional approach has been to seek reviews from reviewers in newspapers and news magazines, as well as a few publications for librarians. According to Adelle Waldman'a *Slate* article: "Book Report: How Four Magazines You've Probably Never Read Help Determine What Books You Buy," the four big book review publications are *Publishers Weekly, Kirkus Reviews, Library Journal*, and *Booklist.*

The biggest of these is *Publishers Weekly* or PW, published by Reed Business Information, which is sold on New York newsstands as well as by subscription, for $200 a year. Each issue contains a few hundred reviews of most types of books, from fiction to self-help and children's books. Over a year, in both the printed editions and on the magazine's website, there are about 10,000 reviews, which are written anonymously and primarily by freelancers, who include published authors, academics, schoolteachers, and librarians, with a knowledge of the subject area. While the magazine only has about 25,000 subscribers, it is read by almost everyone in publishing.

Perhaps the next most influential of the publications with reviews is *Kirkus Reviews*, which only includes reviews by anonymous freelancers. It is published biweekly and has about 5000 subscribers, primarily librarians, for a cost of about $450 a year.

Another book review source aimed primarily at librarians is *Booklist*, published by the American Library Association on a biweekly basis through the school year. A subscription is about $80 a year.

Finally, the big four includes *Library Journal*, also published by Reed Business Information, with a section of reviews written and signed by librarians. It costs about $135 a year.

While the influence of the big four has been waning, according to Waldman, due to the increased visibility of trade reviews on the Internet and the increased ease of communication among booksellers, the big four still have tremendous clout. A starred review in PW "still increases a book's chances of getting media coverage and showing up in your neighborhood bookstore."

Even so, there are a growing number of other sources of early information, especially *Book Sense 76,* a monthly list of books recommended by independent book stores and published by the American Bookseller's Association since 1999. Now known just as *Book Sense*, the publication got its name because 1000 independent booksellers used to vote on their 76 favorites from current, forthcoming, and backlist titles within thirteen major categories, including fiction, history, biography, general interest, and children's books. Now each month, the independent booksellers recommend their 20 top favorites called *Book Sense Picks*, followed by the *20 Book Sense Notables*. Plus *Book Sense* includes online listings of additional titles nominated by independent booksellers.

Besides these major players, if you do an online search, you will discover dozens of other book review magazine editors and reviewers. These include *The New York Times Sunday Book Review* section, *BookForum*, a quarterly book review publication focusing on literary fiction, serious nonfiction, and photo art books, *The Bloomsbury Review*, a bimonthly book review magazine, and the *New York Review of Books*, published 20 times a year.

How do you get reviews in these books? It's best to write to the overall editor of the publication or the editor handling your type of book about two to four months before your book is published, since some publications want to do prepublication reviews and need the time to submit the book to reviewers and get their reviews. However, some publications will do reviews after the date, and some consider self-published books differently from those published by traditional publishers. For example, *Kirkus Reviews* asks for a payment for self-published books and already published books.

In your letter, include the following information: the author, title, the name of the publisher, address, phone number, email; date of publication, price, number of pages, and an ISBN or LC (Library of Congress) number if you have this. Include a brief description of the book, its intended audience, and a short bio about the author. Indicate if you will be including any illustrations, an index, or a bibliography.

You can send in galleys, page proofs, or manuscripts. If you only have finished books, send them as early as possible and note "in lieu of galleys" with the publication date on the cover.

You will find the names of the editors and websites or contact information for these books online, such as one published by BookMarket (www.bookmarket.com/magazines-books.htm). In addition, you can contact newspaper book review editors. A list of these is published by Book Market (www.bookmarket.com/newspapers-wz.htm). However, since contact information often changes, check for each publication for the current listing.

Alternatively, you can use a query service, which has already created a current listing of book reviewers and will do a query for your book to newspapers and magazines which appears to come from your own email. For a query service, you can contact Publishers, Agents & Films (www.publishersagentsandfilms.com), a company I work with that has just launched a query to book reviewers.

Additionally, you can contact freelance reviewers on Amazon to get reviews of your book, as discussed in the next section.

# CHAPTER 57: GETTING REVIEWS ON AMAZON

Since Amazon is the biggest seller of books, getting good book reviews on Amazon is another key to your book's success, as are the other independent book reviewers and book bloggers. This section will focus on how to get good review on Amazon.

Getting good reviews is important to help your book stand out from the millions of books on Amazon. By some estimates about 3500 new books are published every day, about 1.3 million books a year. So you have to do something to get known – which will not only help you sell more books when readers buy books on Amazon, but you can use these reviews in your promotional material to sell your book and programs in other ways.

The more good reviews you can get, the better, because this will give you a higher ranking in Amazon's search algorithm, making your book more likely to show up on the various lists Amazon creates, such as "more items to consider." Also, as you get more reviews, your book might be featured in Amazon's spotlight reviews, which are based on the number of people who find reviews of your book helpful. Generally, you need at least 10 reviews for these Amazon features to appear. These are featured first under the title: "Most Helpful Customer Reviews," and in some other categories, most notably the Best Books of the Month and the "Editor's Picks by Category." While most of the books selected are from traditional mainstream publishers, some are from small publishers (and possibly some self-publishers). The more reviews you get, the better your chances of being included as one of these picks on Amazon.

# The Major Ways to Find Amazon Reviewers

There are two major ways to find Amazon reviewers, which you can do yourself. To contact reviewers, do the following or use a service to help you find these reviewers and contact them:

1) Look for reviewers who have reviewed books that are similar to yours. To do so, put in the keywords associated with your book, click on the other books that turn up, and scroll down to see the list of reviews and reviewers. You can click on each reviewer's name to see what else they have written and view their profile and reviewer rank. Later you can find their contact information if they are listed as top Amazon reviewers.

2) Check out Amazon's list of their top 10,000 reviewers https://www.amazon.com/review/top-reviewers, which includes reviewers of both books and other products. About half of these book reviewers have email contact information. This list is based not only on the number of reviews but on the ratings of others on Amazon, so there is no one to one relationship between the ranking and number of reviews. For example, while the number one reviewer Ali Julia published 3618 reviews as of this writing, the number 2 reviewer, J Chambers published 3892 reviews, and the number 3 reviewer JJCEO published 4774 reviews. There is even more divergence in rankings and reviews for the number 9 and 10 reviewers. While the number 9 reviewer Jackie Cooper published 664 reviews, that is far less than the number 10 reviewer Mandy Payne, with 3345 reviews. Since many of these reviewers review products in addition to books or don't review books at all, check out who are doing book reviews, if your book falls into the types of books they review, and if they have emails or other contact information. Also, since the total number of top reviewers may seem daunting – though less so when you consider there are about 14 million Amazon reviewers, start by contacting the first 200, 500, or 1000 reviewers.

All of this research to find Amazon reviewers can be very time-consuming. But there are alternatives. One is to use a book review broker, such as Book Review Broker (http://bookreviewbroker.com), who has gone through the list of the top 10,000 reviewers and have extracted the 1000 best profiles. You select the genre you are interested in and create a small pitch on the site using the guidelines for writing the review. Then, you offer to send a hardcover or paperback, gift the reviewer a copy from your book's page on Amazon, or email a digital copy. Depending on the genre you choose, your cost is $14 to $116. The average response is 9% and the agreement to review rate is 6%

Another approach is to use an email query service, such as Publishers, Agents & Films (www.publishersagentsandfilms.com) which has a list of 250 reviewers who review books and have listed their emails drawn from the top 2500 Amazon reviewers. The service sends a personalized email to all of the reviewers, and those interested in reviewing your book respond directly to you.

Though these services can't guarantee a response or reviews, they facilitate the process which otherwise might take you 30 or 40 hours to identify the Amazon reviewers to contact and individually email them.

## What to Say in Contacting a Reviewer

When you contact a reviewer, personalize your email if possible to show you are aware of the other books the reviewer has reviewed, although you can skip this personalization if you are contacting a number of reviewers at the same time with a single personalized letter. A review letter might read something like this:

Dear *********

I saw you listed as a reviewer on Amazon. (IF YOU ARE PERSONALIZING THIS, YOU MIGHT ADD THE FOLLOWING. I saw your review for (NAME OF BOOK) which you posted on (DATE).

I have recently written a book on a similar topic appealing to the same audience: (NAME OF YOUR BOOK). The book is about (DESCRIBE IT IN UP TO 50-60 WORDS) You can find it on Amazon at (INDICATE SALES PAGE LIST).

I hope you will be interested in reviewing this, and I can send you a free review copy if you send me your email address.

Sincerely,

YOUR NAME
ADDRESS
CITY, STATE
EMAIL
PHONE

If the reviewer is interested, he or she will contact you to request the book. If not interested, most reviewers don't respond, though some may reply with a thanks but no thanks letter.

Generally, you can respond with a PDF copy of your book, though some reviewers prefer an ePUB or ePUB3 file, which they can read on a Kindle.

# Dealing with Negative Reviews

While you can hope for a good review, most top reviews seek to offer a fair review, based on their opinion of their book. If they like it, great; you will get a good review. On the other hand, they could post a negative review if they don't like it or not post any review at all. While you can ask reviewers to not to post a review if they don't like your book, you can't stop them, and it might be awkward to request that they don't post a negative review. By asking this you are already putting them in the frame of mind to think they might not like your book, so they might be more critical or not review your book at all. It is probably best to just hope for the best. However, if you see that a reviewer has posted a great many negative reviews of other books, it might be best not to request a review of that reviewer to reduce your own chances of getting a negative review.

Normally, once a review is there, it's there forever, though Amazon will review negative reviews under certain circumstances, such as if a review includes personal information, defamatory or insulting remarks, or if you have received a request for payment to get a good review. As Dana Lynn Smith points out in The Savvy Book Marketer : "What Should I Do About a Bad Review on Amazon," Amazon will remove any book that violates its terms of service, which includes obscene or distasteful content, profanity or spiteful remarks, promotional materials, personal material about other people, feedback on the seller, or details on the availability or alternative ordering and shipping information. Other inappropriate reviews are those which are an invasion of privacy, violate intellectual property rights, or are commercial or political postings.

If you feel a review is unjustified and seems to fit Amazon's criteria for inappropriate reviews, send an email to Amazon's community help desk (community-help@amazon.com) and ask them to remove the negative review about your book and explain why. Include the book's title and ISBN, along with the reviewer's name, date of the review, and the first sentence, so the Amazon team can find it. If the team member reviewing your complaint agrees the review is unjustified, Amazon will remove it. But if the reviewer simply didn't like your book and criticized it harshly, you are out of luck.

Yet, even if a negative review remains up, you can respond in a few ways to lessen the impact of such a review. If the review has factual errors, such as stating that the book was missing certain information, you can click on the "comment" button and leave a response. If you do respond, don't be defensive. Just state the facts, such as pointing out that the reviewer might have missed a chapter which included this information. You can also click the "no' button next to the "Was this review helpful" question. A good solution which many writers use is to look for good reviews to offset bad ones, such as by contacting friends, business associates, and family members and asking them to buy a book so they can review it.

## Posting Reviews from Major Publications and Adding Author Information

If you get reviews from newspapers and magazines, you can add them to your book's detail page on Amazon through your AuthorCentral.com account, where you add any books you have written.

To add these reviews, click on that book, which will indicate the book's ASIN and ISBN numbers, along with the average reviews and current sales rack. Additionally, you will see a "review section" where you can add in any reviews and include the text, source of the review, and a brief quote of up to 1-2 sentences, with a limit of 600 characters. This is also a place where you can add in a short product description, book flap or back cover copy, and an author's bio. You can further add your comments about the book as the author, such as your inspiration in writing it.

This information will be added to your book's detail page. You can add other details to your author page, including your biography, blogs, upcoming speaking engages, URL with a link to your author's page, up to 8 photos of yourself, video interviews, book trailers or book signing videos, and your latest tweets.

Providing updated information, in addition to Amazon reviews, can help readers decide to buy your book or be interested in learning about other programs you have developed.

# CHAPTER 58: GETTING REVIEWS FROM INDEPENDENT REVIEWERS AND BLOGGERS

Besides the reviewers on Amazon and in newspapers and magazines, many independent reviewers and bloggers do book reviews that can help you promote your book and get sales. If the reviews include a link to your website on their blog or review, you can direct it to a sales page for your book and other programs.

There are several ways to find independent reviewers and book bloggers, as well as sell your book through independent book sales sites. Besides posting your book for sale there, independent reviewers and book bloggers might discover your book there and review it. Some of the book sites feature books that are free or discounted, which can be a way to get your book noticed initially, though after a few weeks or once your book starts to sell, you can stop the free giveaway or discounting.

Since it may be time-consuming to contact many sites to list your book, consider hiring a low-cost assistant through various freelance services, such as Fiverr (www.fiverr.com), Upwork (www.upwork.com), or Guru (www.guru.com) to create these listings for you.

## Promotional Book Sites

A number of a promotional book sites feature reviews and blogs about books. In some cases, these feature free or discounted books, or books sold on Kindle for $2.99 or less. Another approach which some authors use is promoting their Kindle book by enrolling in Amazon's KDP select program where you have 5 days in a 90 day period to give your book away for free. This can be a way to kickstart the sales of your Kindle book, though you have to advertise your free days to get prospective readers to know about your book. But be aware that your ebook isn't supposed to be available anywhere else while it is in the KDP select program, though you can list it elsewhere when the program ends. Once you decide you want to drop out of the program, you have to remove your book so it won't renew for another 90 days.

Some of these promotional sites are featured in Martin Crosbie's book *How I Sold 30,000 EBooks on Amazon's Kindle*. Some of these sites are free; others have free and paid services. You can find an extensive listing of promotional sites for free and discounted books at www.indiesunlimited.com/book-promo-sites, and each listing includes a link to that site. For example, some of the listings include The E-Reader Café (www.theereadercafe.com/p/authors.html), E-Reader Utopia (http://ereaderutopia.com), the eBook Lister (www.ebooklister.net), BookBub (www.bookbub.com),The Choosy Bookworm (http://choosybookworm.com), Reading Deals.com (http://readingdeals.com), and many others.

Another source of listings is Authorpreneur Magazine (www.authorpreneurmagazine.com), which features 72 sites where you can submit your book.

A site which features both book reviews and listings of bargain books is Books on the Knob (http://blog.booksontheknob.org). It offers daily deals, bargain books, new releases, and starred reviews. It also has a feature called "Hot New Releases on Kindle."

# Independent Book Sales Sites

Then independent book sales sites are sites where authors can post information about their book to encourage sales at other sites, such as Amazon. One popular site is Goodreads (www.goodreads.com), where authors can post their books, as well as join groups, such as the History: Actual, Fictional or Legendary group with 846 members or the Support for Indie Authors Group with 3057 member. The site also includes local groups, such as the Women of the World (WOW) Book Club based in San Francisco with 158 members. Before joining these groups and posting information about your book, check how recently active the group was. For instance, when I checked on these groups, the Support for Indie Authors group was last active 5 minutes ago and the History: Actual, Fictional or Legendary group was active 9 hours ago, so these would be good places to participate. However, the Women of the World (WOW) Book Club only had some activity 6 months ago.

Another independent book site is LibraryThing (www.librarything.com), a community of 1.9 million booklovers, where people catalog, review, and discuss books. You can catalog your books there from Amazon, the Library of Congress, and 700 other world libraries, and you can enter 200 books for free, and as many as you like for $10 a year. The LibraryThing is also a place where you can find reviewers. One of the site's features is a member giveaway, where you can give out your own ebooks or printed books. You set up a number of available books to offer and people enter a drawing to win them. While those who receive your books are not required to review them, you can indicate that you hope they do. The reviewers later post any reviews on LibraryThing, and some often post reviews on other sites, such as Amazon.com or Goodreads. LibraryThing also has a number of groups where you can join the conversation. It lists the groups which are most active, such as Books Challenge for 2015, and the ones with the most members, such as Librarians Who, Non-Fiction Readers, Science Fiction Fans, Historical Fiction, and a Crime,

Thriller, and Mystery Group,

Another indie book site is Scribd (www.scribd.com) which offers readers the opportunity to read all kinds of books in different categories for $8.99 a month for a premium membership, and it offers a 14 day free trial for prospective members. Authors with a premium membership can share their work and offer it for free, charge for it, or link to a sales site such as Amazon or your own squeeze or sales page. When an author's work is part of the premium membership service, authors are paid the full price of their work every time a reader reads a work in the program, and Scribd uses money from the members' monthly fees to pay publishers. As the Scribd FAQ describes it: "Being in the program grants all our authors a large audience of avid readers like yourself. They place their work on Scribd, and instantly millions of people have the opportunity to read it. Everyone with a membership to the site can seamlessly go from book to book with no need to go through the process of 'check-out' every time they want a new book to read. This means, every author now has a greater chance of their work being read while still being fully compensated for their work!" Meanwhile, readers gain an unlimited access to all of these titles.

You can also sell your book through the Scribd store. Though the store no longer works with individual authors, it represents authors who have their books on various digital platforms, including Smashwords (www.smashwords.com), Inscribe Digital (www.inscribedigitial.com), BookBaby (www.bookbaby.com), and Draft2Digital (www.draft2digital.com). The typical arrangement is that the author gets 80% of the sales.

In the past there has been some concern about individuals uploading pirated books to Scribd, but now Scribed has a 'verified' account program in which a check next to the author's name on a title or author's profile shows that the book has the author's stamp of approval, so it has been published with the author's permission. Scribd also has much self-published work in the library's Document section, which have been uploaded with the author's permission. Scribd additionally has a BookID copyright protection system which checks content uploaded by members for possible copyright infringement, and the company seeks to keep any material that violates copyright off the site. If Scribd discovers any individuals who fail to follow copyright laws, they will be dropped from membership.

## Indie Reviewers and Book Bloggers

Indie reviewers and book bloggers, who sometimes have their own websites are still another way to get your book noticed. They often look for books in a certain category, though some will review anything that interests them. Besides finding them through groups and forums that discuss books, such as on LinkedIn or Facebook, you can obtain lists and directories with the most prolific reviewers and bloggers.

One such list is the Indie Reviewers List (www.theindieview.com/indie-reviewers), which provides links to sites that review indie books. It includes about 275 reviewers who are actively posting reviews, review ebooks, don't charge for their reviews, and aren't affiliated with a publisher. The reviewers commonly have submission guidelines for an indie author to submit an ebook. Some of the most prolific indie reviewers include: A. Fae, with the Truth About Books website, who reviews fiction; The Snarky Bibliophiles, who review all types of books; The Paperback Pursuer, who reviews all genres; and hundreds more. The site also lists the most Prolific Indie Reviewers, who post a review at least weekly.

Another source of book reviewers is the Book Reviewer Yellow Pages (www.bookrevieweryellowpages.com), which has an extensive list of about 300 book reviewers, who are listed alphabetically by their websites or blog sites. The list indicates what types of books the reviewer is most interested in. The Book Reviewer Yellow Pages has been helping authors get reviews since 2009, and it has a free book reviewer list, which includes basic information about many of its reviewers (www.bookrevieweryellowpages.com/book-reviewer-list.html. You can also get the sites annual directory, updated each year, for $7.99, which includes email contact information for hundreds of reviewers (www.bookrevieweryellowpages.com/book-reviewer-list.html).

The Book Blogger Directory (https://bookbloggerdirectory.wordpress.com), lists hundreds of book blogs, divided into genres and listed alphabetically. The directory requires that bloggers primarily talk about books on their blog, with at least 8 out of 10 blogs being book related, and the bloggers must provide a link back to the directory. For instance, some non-fiction book blogs that feature general interest books are The Book Garden (http://the-book-garden.blogspot.com), the Beck Valley Books Blog (http://beckvalleybooks.blogspot.com), and Tomes of the Soul (http://tomesofthesoul.blogspot.com).

Blogrank (www.blogmetrics.org/books) lists the top 50 books blogs in various categories: the ultimate rank, RSS membership, unique monthly visitors, Google indexed pages, number of incoming links, Google PR, the Alexa site rank, and Complete rank. Commonly, the top blogs are found on the different ranking sites. For example, the top five ultimate blogs include Paulo Coelhos Blog, OUPblog, Books on the Knob, the Book Smugglers, and Joe Wikerts Publishing 2020 Blog. You'll find links to all of these blogs if you go to the site.

The Book Blogger List (www.bookbloggerlist.com), is a database of book bloggers organized by genre of interest, and bloggers with multiple interests are listed in each category. To find bloggers interested in your type of book, go to the link for their site and follow the instructions. You can add your name and email to be

348

notified when new bloggers are added; then, you'll get a weekly email indicating the latest additions.

Another way to obtain still more reviewers is to use a Google search to find bloggers and independent reviewers who review books in your genre. Try various combinations of searches with the name of your genre (such as history, business, inspiration, self-help, personal development, or YA) plus your target audience (such as book blog, book blogger, book review blogger, book review blog, book reviews, and book reviewer). Try different combinations and add in your own relevant terms. Then, visit the websites and pull out the contact information for the new contacts.

## Services Which Connect Authors and Reviewers

If contacting all of these sources for reviewers and bloggers sounds daunting, there are services which will let reviewers know about your book. Some of these include the following:

The Bookbag (www.thebookbag.co.uk) is a UK based site which features reviews of self-published books, reviewed by one of their panel of 50 reviewers. There are no guarantees, but the site covers a large proportion of the books sent in – about 11,600 reviews so far. You need a listing on Amazon to submit it, and the site prefers to obtain books at least a month in advance of publication. You just need an image of the book on Amazon, a clear synopsis, and a link to the book (which could be a link for pre-ordering the book). The reviewers choose the books they review via a link on Amazon, and the site covers the expense of producing and uploading the books for review, and seeks to cover those expenses through affiliate book sales from its site. The reviewers choose which books they want to review, but if no one decides to review a book after a month, the site withdraws it from the shelves and it won't be covered. It helps to have a press sheet which you can send with the book, along with indicating if you are available for an interview or to write a feature article. Additional information on how to send your book is on their site.

The Author Marketing Club (http://authormarketingclub.com) has free core training and tools, which include a series of video courses on "How to Upload a Book on Amazon," "Selling Your First 100 Copies," "Running Your First Book Ad Campaign," "Building Your Author Platform," "The Ultimate Guide to Launching a New Book" and "How to Sell Beyond Amazon: Finding Readers on Kobo, Apple, Google, and Nook." For a premium member, currently $149 a year or $24.95 a month, the service has other benefits, which includes a premade book cover, where you add your title and name, and various marketing tools, such as guidelines to create a compelling book description, help in displaying books on your website, and tools to easily locate book reviewers for your book. Plus the Author Marketing Club offers advanced courses on how to write, market, and sell more books

Finally, Publishers, Agents & Films (www.publishersagentsandfilms.com) has an email query service that connects writers directly with book bloggers and reviewers. The company created a databased of 250 of the top 2500 Amazon reviewers who both review books and have emails, and it sends a personalized email to all of them. In addition, the company has compiled a list of the top independent reviewers from all the resources listed in this guide, and it has created a database of about 2000 book reviewers through a search using Cision, the PR industry Bible. The service can help you write your letter with their guidelines or can write it for you. Then, a query goes out under your email and is personalized for each reviewers or book blogger, and those interested in your book respond directly to you. Though the service can't guarantee a response or reviews, it can facilitate the process which otherwise might take you 30 or 40 hours to identify Amazon reviewers or independent reviewers and bloggers to contact and individually email them.

# CHAPTER 59: WHAT TO SAY TO A REVIEWER

## Making Individual Contacts

If you are going to contact reviewers individually, rather than using one of the connection or email query services, cut down your research efforts by only contacting reviewers interested in your type of book. Additionally, read the review policy on their website, or listing to determine if they are reviewing e-books, printed books, or both. Check the genres they want to read and if they are accepting new books for review. Some reviewers will indicate a preferred time for sending in review copies – such as one to four months before publication, and what type of submission is acceptable – such as an epub, PDF, galleys, or printed book. If you are doing a blast through a query service, after briefly introducing your book, ask interested reviewers for their guidelines for submitting your book.

## Sending a Targeted Individualized Query

When you do individualized queries, personalize your email with a salutation and their name, rather than writing "Dear Reviewer." Preferably use their first and last name, or first name alone if you don't know both. If you can't obtain their personal name from their website or profile, use their user name.

If you know this, indicate how you found the reviewer and how your book will fit in the category of books they review – even mention a book or two by name. If you don't know this, tell the reviewer about your book, when it will be published, and a little about yourself. In either case, indicate that you will be glad to send a copy if they are interested, and indicate the book's format, such as if it's a PDF or epub file or a printed book, or ask which format they would prefer. Indicate that you look forward to hearing from them and sign your email with your full name. While some people like to thank the reviewer in advance for their time and consideration, I don't like to include that in an initial query letter, since it sounds like you are asking them for a favor, and I feel you are offering them an opportunity to read an interesting book.

## How to Write a Good Email Query

Begin with a captivating subject line, which is short, direct, and highlights what the book is about or makes it especially interesting. For example, you might start with the words, "Review Inquiry" or "Review Request" and in about 10-15 words give your pitch, such as: "Nonfiction Self-Help Book about Breakthrough Techniques that Make You Smarter," or "Historical Literary Fiction about Jefferson's Secret Affair."

While personalizing an email query to show you are aware of some other books the reviewer has reviewed can be helpful for an individualized query, you can't use this approach to contact a number of reviewers at the same time with a single personalized letter, such as when using a query service, since only the name is personalized.

A review letter might read something like this:

Subject Line: Review Request: (GENRE OF BOOK AND 10-15 WORDS TO DESCRIBE THE BOOK AND GAIN INTEREST)

Dear (NAME)

I saw you listed as a reviewer on Amazon.

(IF YOU ARE PERSONALIZING THIS LETTER, YOU MIGHT ADD THE FOLLOWING. I saw your review for (NAME OF BOOK) which you posted on (DATE). I have recently written a book on a similar topic appealing to the same audience: (NAME OF YOUR BOOK).

(IF A GENERAL LETTER) Since you review books in a wide variety of genres, I thought you might be interested in (NAME OF BOOK). The book is about (DESCRIBE IT IN UP TO 50-60 WORDS) You can find it on Amazon at (INDICATE SALES PAGE LIST). The publication date will be (DATE).

I hope you will be interested in reviewing this, and I can send you a free review copy if you send me your contact information and let me your preferred format for receiving the book. I can most quickly send you an epub or PDF file, though I can send a printed copy if desired.

Sincerely,

YOUR NAME
ADDRESS
CITY, STATE
EMAIL

PHONE

If the reviewer is interested, he or she will contact you to request the book. If not, most will not respond, though some may reply with a "thanks but no thanks" letter.

Generally, you can respond with a PDF of your book, or some may prefer an ePUB or ePUB3 format, which they can read on a Kindle. Occasionally some may ask for a printed copy though this is increasingly rare – as well as expensive, so decide if it's worth the cost of printing and mailing a book.


## What to Expect and Not to Do in Seeking Reviews

Following are some tips on what to expect and do or not do, based on "10 Places to Find Reviewers for Your Self-Published Book" by Denise Enck in the *Empty Mirror* , an online literary and arts magazines, which focuses on poetry, essays, reviews, interviews, literary fiction, and art books.

- If a reviewer asks for a book, the reviewer will generally review it, but there are no guarantees. Sometimes a reviewer will not review a book if he or she doesn't like it rather than posting a negative review, or a reviewer may get caught up with other deadlines and is unable to read and review your book.

- There are no guarantees that a reviewer will post a good review, and you shouldn't ask for or expect a positive review. Any good reviewer will post an honest review and indicate how much he or she likes your book – say from one to five stars. You may not agree, but that's the breaks of the game.

- You take your chances about when the review will be

published, which is the reason for sending in a book up to three or four months before it's actual pub date. While you can indicate when the book will be published, you can't ask the reviewer to promise to review the book on or near a requested date.

- Understand that most or almost all reviewers are doing it because they really love books so they want to take the time to give the books they read a careful review, which commonly takes several hours – and most get no pay, apart from those on assignment with mainstream newspapers and magazines. But though the reviewers get little or no pay, don't try to grease the wheels to getting review by offering payment. That's like a bribe, and reputable websites that feature reviewers do not allow a payment. Conversely, if a reviewer asks you for a payment, that's a no-no, and if the word gets around that a site or reviewer is doing paid reviews, that will undermine the value of the review. In fact, a reviewer who asks for or accepts payment can soon lose his or her credibility and may be banned from review websites.

- If you send a query letter to a reviewer, most reviewers only reply if interested. While some may answer to say the book isn't for them, those who aren't interested commonly don't reply, so don't expect a response to your query. In fact, some of the most popular and high-ranked reviewers get so many queries from authors, publishers, and publicists that they don't have the time to reply to everyone who writes – just to those with a book they want to request.

- If a reviewer doesn't respond or indicates a lack of interest in reviewing your book, accept that and focus on communicating with those who do express interest. Don't follow-up by asking why or sending more information in the hopes the reviewer will finally review your book. Just send such reviewers a thank you for their reply, and when you have another book, you can always contact them again.

- After your review is published, don't comment on it, even

if you disagree with it, and even if you find some factual mistakes. That's because, as Enck notes: "Commenting can make you look petty, overbearing or argumentative, and can turn potential readers against you, ensuring they never read your book. " So don't do it.

## Posting Reviews from Major Publications and Adding Author Information

If you get reviews from newspapers and magazines, you can add them to your book's detail page on Amazon through your AuthorCentral.com account, which lists the books you have written. You can also add these reviews to your website, as well to future press releases. You can do this.

Once you list a book on your Amazon AuthorCentral account, when you click on that book, it will indicate the ASIN and ISBN number, the average reviews and current sales, and a "review section" where you can add in any reviews. In adding reviews, include the text, source of the review, and a brief quote of up to 1-2 sentences, with a limit of 600 characters. AuthorCentral is also a place where you can add a short description and your comment about the book, such as your inspiration to write it, book flap or back cover copy, and your author's bio.

Besides adding this information to your book's detail page, you can add details to your author page, including your biography, blogs, upcoming speaking engages, URL with a link to your author's page, up to 8 photos of yourself, video interviews, book trailers, book signing videos, and your latest tweets.

This information, in addition to reviews on Amazon, can help readers decide where to buy your book or learn more about related programs you have developed.

# CHAPTER 60: USING THE TRADITIONAL MEDIA FOR PR

The traditional media can be a major factor in the success of some books, though the media is very selective in picking books to feature. Usually you need to already have a media presence, have a big publishing company and PR push behind your book, or have a subject that is especially newsworthy for the TV and daily newspapers to be interested, though you can still get pick-ups by some of the news services and some radio talk shows that are interested in authors as guests. So you have to be realistic in assessing your book's chances for success in a traditional media campaign. Sometimes starting with a local campaign may be the way to go.

While getting on top TV programs may be the pinnacle of success, unless your book deals with a very timely topic in the news, this is an unlikely goal, so think in terms of what is realistic, what you might do yourself, and when it might be best to work with a professional publicist or PR professional to create a campaign for you.

Since this topic merits more detailed coverage in a book, and there are many books on doing PR, including one I wrote, *The Complete Guide to Doing Your Own PR* from Changemakers Publishing, I will just provide an overview to get you started in thinking about what to do.

## Developing a Strategy for Your Campaign

In creating a traditional media campaign for your book, a first consideration is whether your book or programs are suitable for such a campaign, the appropriate scope of this campaign, and how to position your book and yourself.

In some cases, your book and programs may be more suited to a local campaign, because the local press might be interested in what you are doing since you live in the area. But this local angle usually only works if you are in a small town or community which features local success stories or articles about local residents doing unusual things. If you are in a major metro area, like L.A., San Francisco, or New York, a local angle is unlikely to get much attention, except at some neighborhood newspapers, which usually are weeklies. Or sometimes your program may be best pitched to book reviewers and bloggers, where you develop a list or use a service that has already developed a database of over 2000 reviewers and bloggers, such as Publishers, Agents & Films (www.publishersagentsandfilms.com).

By contrast, if your approach might to appeal to the national media, think of how to position your book and programs to gain media interest. One way is to tie what your book is about to something timely and newsworthy, where you promote yourself as an expert who can comment on this topic because of your book. If you are selected as an expert, you can mention your book and company name, and sometimes your website. In this case, focus on the daily newspapers, news syndicates, the Internet media, and possibly radio, though skip magazines, because they have a longer publication cycle, and many focus on a particular subject area.

Another approach if your book and programs offer helpful advice or deal with trends in some area of interest or industry is to send a press release or letter offering an article on a topic of interest to readers. In this case, focus on contacting the editors of special sections of the newspaper, Internet media that deals with this subject, and magazines in this area. If this type of advice would have broad appeal, radio hosts might be another good target.

Thus, any PR campaign for the traditional media takes some planning, so you can work out the best approach and the best contacts for your topic.

## Getting Your Message Out to the Media

One way to get news coverage is to send a press release directly to the editors at different publications and news bureaus, using a publicist or one of the services that do press blasts to editors. Among these are Publishers, Agents & Films (www.publishersagentsandfilms.com), PRWire (www.prwire.com) and PRWeb (www.prweb.com). Some services will include your press release with others they send to the media each day, such as PRBuzz (www.prbuzz.com).

Another strategy in doing a blast to the media is to offer an article they can publish. Begin with a brief letter describing the highpoints of your article and invite the media to use it in return for letting you know when and where the article appears by a link to it. Then, send your query letter with a copy of your article at the end in the body of the email, not in an attachment, since many people are reluctant to open one from someone they don't know. You can also use this letter to let the editors know you have other articles and are available for interviews, should they want to write up a story.

An advantage of using a publicist or PR company, if you can afford it, is that a publicist can not only help you create your press release or letter and can send out a press blast, but a publicist or PR company can directly contact key editors and radio/TV show producers. Generally, the publicist will already know many of these contacts, and so can help to get your pitch reviewed and given more consideration more quickly than a release or letter that comes in over the email transom. If you have a publicist, figure on $1500 to $3000 a month for a few months to build up the momentum of a campaign. Besides sending out press blasts through Publishers, Agents, and Films, a PR company we have worked with for several years for some projects is Jones & O'Malley (www.jonesomalley.com), based in Los Angeles.

Another approach is to sign up for a service that connects reports looking for stories to authorities and experts with this information, such as Help a Reporter Out or HARO (www.helpareporter.com), Media Diplomat (www.mediadiplomat.com), and Source Bottle (www.sourcebottle.com). These are free to be listed as an expert, and they will send you announcements about reporters looking for experts in the areas listed. Some of these sites, like Source Bottle, have an additional service, where they send information about you to reporters interested in your topic. Also, some services provide a directory of individuals and companies and post your releases in return for a monthly or annual payment, such as Expert Click (www.expertclick.com), one of the services I use.

## Creating Your Press Materials

Whether you do your own PR campaign or work with a publicist or PR company, you need certain materials that you or a publicist can prepare for you. The basic materials include the following, adapted to your particular book.

- A news release about the book or program, or a release showing how your book or program is related to what's going on in the news. The release should have a strong headline and make the major points in a page – about 250-400 words.
- A pitch letter offering an article on the subject to newspapers, magazines, or Internet publishers

360

- A one-sheet bio of you, including a photo
- A one-sheet about your book and programs, including one or two photos
  - Photos in a JPEG format that can be reproduced in print. These photos should include a photo of you and ideally some action shots, where you are doing something featured in the book (such as treating a patient, if the book deals with a medical or health topic)
  - A page of short comments and testimonials, especially from well-known people
  - A pitch letter explaining why you will make a good interview subject for the radio or TV media
  - A list of questions for interviewers, if you are going to be a guest on a radio or TV show
  - An audio or videotape of you speaking or being interviewed, if you hope to be a radio or TV guest.

## Deciding on the Best Approach for You

In reviewing your options, decide whether a campaign to interest the traditional media is the best approach for you. Sometimes it's not the right fit, such as if you are promoting a self-help or popular business book, since these are already heavily competitive fields, and media people tend to want to feature someone who is already well-known and famous. Then, too, they may think you should get an ad, rather than trying to get free publicity.

If you do think the subject of your book and programs might have broad appeal, consider the different options noted above to decide what's right for you. You can check out the websites listed above to learn more about what each service does. If you want to work with a publicist or PR firm, interview the person or persons there who will guide your campaign to learn what strategies they suggest, the costs, whether their proposed program is a good fit, and if you feel comfortable working with the publicist or PR team. If you are considering hiring a publicist or PR firm, ask for a proposal outlining what they will do, the timeline, and the cost. Some companies will already have a description of different PR packages and costs.

Whatever approach you choose, you can't expect any guarantees, since it's up to the media people who are contacted to decide if they want to use the information, write a story about you, or interview you for their publication or show. As you go along, keep track of who you have contacted with what results. As appropriate, adapt your campaign and build on what has gone before.

Don't expect everything to happen right away. Commonly, you need to conduct a campaign over several months to be successful. During this time, add to your story or build on some smaller media coverage you have gotten to expand to a larger audience (such as if you get a local article and use a clip to show that others have been interested in your story; then other media may pick that up). So often a one-shot release or a one month campaign by a publicist or PR firm will only start the process, but won't be enough by itself. So generally, figure on at least 3 months for a PR campaign, although sometimes you may be successful right out of the box, since you may quickly appeal to some media people. Any media campaign is unpredictable, but you can increase your chances by effectively positioning and implementing your campaign. Then, hope for the best.

# CHAPTER 61: CREATING AND SENDING OUT YOUR PRESS RELEASE OR LETTER

When you first contact the media, it's usually best to initially send out a press release or query letter and then follow up. If your news is especially timely, such as if your book is linked to something in the news, you can call first, but be ready to follow up with a release or a letter. Also, you will often want to have a press kit with more detailed information, such as questions an interviewer might ask you, bio information, a photo, or one-sheet about your book.

## Sending Out a Press Release or Letter to the Media

Whether you send out your press release or query letter to the media first or after an initial call to see if there is interest, you can include a link to your website or social media page. But don't send your release or letter as an attachment unless requested, since people are suspicious of getting viruses, trojans, and malware from unknown senders.

A press release and letter to the media is normally 1 or at most 2 single-spaced pages – about 300-500 words. Write it like a news article, featuring the who, what, where, when, and how elements in the first paragraph, so recipients quickly know what the release is about. A press release commonly includes these elements:
- headline in the subject line
- "for immediate release" line or name of the recipient in a personalized email
- body copy
- contact information (at the end in an email release)

# Writing a Headline or Subject Line

Your headline or subject line is critical. It entices recipients to want to read the rest of your release. Keep it short and catchy, with a maximum of 20-25 words, and ideally 10-15 words. Use Upper and Lower Title Case, not ALL CAPS, which comes across as screaming.

Make your headline very specific to what you're doing. Don't be vague or write a headline that reads like promotional or sales copy, such as "Exciting new book that will change America." Instead, write your subject line like a headline for a news story. If there's a tie-in to something in the news include that, such as: "New book on identity theft helps police break an identity theft ring." If there is a dated special event, include the date when it is happening in the headline to make it compelling for the recipient to open the email right away, such as writing, "Author invited to present findings about cults to a Congressional hearing on Sept. 20." But the event has to be really newsworthy to get press coverage, beyond a local calendar listing.

Make your headline very clear, specific, and compelling, because many media people get hundreds and thousands of emails a day, and your headline or subject line can determine whether they open your e-mail or not. If you're sending out a press release by email, put the headline both in the subject line and in the body copy, because once the press release is printed out, it may not have the subject line on it.

Using a subhead is optional if your headline contains all the information you want to convey. Or use a subhead to clarify or explain your subject

Start off with a "For Immediate Release" line or personalized introduction at the beginning of your press release. It can go before or after you repeat the headline and subhead in the body of your copy.

## Writing Your Release like a News Story

In the body of your copy, write your press release like a news story, where you start with a strong opening sentence or two that conveys the essence of the story. Essentially, you are beginning with the what, when, where, why, and how elements in the first few sentences.

The reason for this short intro is that you quickly summarize the story, and this approach enables any media outlet picking up your story to cut from the bottom up as necessary, leaving the most important points of your story in the remaining text.

Using this news story approach also makes it possible for some publications, especially the smaller ones, to pick up your story as is, because they don't have the time and the staff to write their own articles, apart from a few assignments. In other cases, your release may inspire other editors and writers to write their own story, usually by contacting you for more information or conducting an interview with you.

Conclude with your contact information. In a traditional release, the contact information should go in the top left or right hand corner. In emails, it is better to put this contact information in the end at the bottom left, because that way you get people right into the story when they look at it online.

## The Difference Between a Press Release and Letter

An alternative to writing a press release that begins "For Immediate Release," is to write up your information as a query letter directed to the media contact by name. The main difference between the release and the letter is that a query letter is personalized, though you can include the same information in both. You can even write it the same way.

The big difference is that the media contact knows the "For Immediate Release" email is being sent to multiple people at the same time, while the personalized query letter is directed towards that media contact personally. Though media people recognize that software can readily personalize mass mailings, a letter directed to an individual still has a more personal feel, as if it is going to a particular person.

## Finding Contacts to Send Your Release or Letter

When you are doing local PR, you can build your media list by looking at the masthead of local publications or going online to get contact information for local radio or TV stations. To create your list of contacts, look for the editor or producer who handles your type of story, such as a business editor, entertainment editor, or features editor. Or call the media sources to ask for the names and emails of the appropriate contact.

For large scale PR, you can create your own database or use a service that can send your release or letter to hundreds or thousands of media contacts. Cision is the largest of these services, with a database of about 300,000 media contacts in the U.S., including newspapers, magazines, radio, TV, and now Internet media and blogs. You can target your contacts based on geographic area, type of media, beat, circulation, and topics or specific areas of interest. It costs about $4000 to $5,000 a year for a

Cision account , depending on the size of your organization, and a lot of publicists and big corporations have an account with them.

You can use these services to find particular contacts, as many publicists do. They selectively pick out people to contact and contact them individually. Or you can do a category or power search, where you select the type of media beats, and other characteristics, and do a broad search, generating a large number of contacts. In Cision, you can find up to 5000 contacts in one search and export them in a .cvs or Excel file. You can then do a bulk mailing, once you have your contact information in a .cvs or Excel format.

There are a number of bulk mailing platforms, like Constant Contact, or software programs you can buy, such as Group Mail, which I use for sending out mailings. Plus with some programs you need your own email server or a subscription to an SMTP service, such as SMTP2Go (www.smtp2go.com), AuthorSMTP (www.authorsmtp.com), or SendGrid (www.sendgrid.com) to send out your emails. Or you can use a service like Publishers, Agents & Films (www.publishersagentsandfilms.com) to send out the mailing for you to the contacts obtained from a search of a media database.

Either way, whether you send the emails yourself or use one of these services, the software can personalize your release or letter to the particular individuals at the selected media if this information available, or it can send your release or letter to whoever is at that particular email as an "Immediate Release."

## Creating and Sending Out Your Press Kit

Generally, you use a press kit after you have gotten interest from a phone call, press release, or query letter and the media contact wants more information. Typically, to recap the previous description of a press kit, it contains a selection of the following materials. While the starred items will almost always be included, you can choose the others as appropriate for your media contact.

- your press release or query letter *(even if you have sent this out, include it, as a summary and reminder of what your story is about).
- an optional cover letter than summarizes the story and introduces what's in the press kit
- a one-sheet overview of your book, programs, or yourself *
- an individual or company bio*
- a list of questions to ask you
- one or more photos
- testimonials

The advantage of having a variety of items to select from in your press kit is that you can choose what's appropriate to include for each media contact. Some people will want just the basics – the press release and a one-sheet or bio for example, while others will want additional items, such as a list of questions and photos. By selectively deciding what to send and in what format, you cater to what the media contact wants, which increases your chances of getting featured.

For instance, if your press kit is going to the radio, besides the release and one sheet, you might have a list of questions that the host might ask, such as: "How did you happen to write this book or develop this program" A good way to create this list of questions is to note what questions people repeatedly ask you about your book or programs and put those down.

Sometimes if appropriate send the book, CD or DVD with photos, videos, or testimonials, though today, it is common to send the book as a PDF and use links to a website for accessing photos or streaming videos. Photos should be in jpeg format – 72 dpi for the online media; 300 dpi (or as close to that as possible) for print.

If you have testimonials that can really help, particularly if these are from well-known people or people with a high status position. If you only have one or two testimonials, you might include them on the one-sheet overview of your book or programs. If you have a substantial number of testimonials, you might include a separate sheet of testimonials.

Whenever you list testimonials, put the most important ones first, based on the person's name or title, or by the company where he or she works.

When sending your press materials by email, you can send separate attachments for each item. Or to make your material easier to review, combine everything together into a single attachment which you can send by email or provide a link to access this information on a website. The most common format now is the PDF, since anyone can read it on any type of computer or open it in a browser online.

If you have your documents in several PDF fi les, you can consolidate them into a single PDF, which many media people prefer because this keeps everything together. If you aren't sure, ask whether your media contact wants everything in one attachment or link or prefers separate attachments and links for each document.

In either case, send any photographs in separate attachments, so they can be printed. Check on the resolution desired. The typical website format is 72 dpi (which refers to the number of pixels per inch). But often if a photograph is going to be printed in a newspaper or magazine, a high resolution format is preferred, preferably a 300 dpi format.

## Adapting Your Releases to Different PR Services

When you use different PR services, such as PRWeb, PRBuzz, PRWire, BusinessWire, and Expert Click, you will find they have varying formats for setting up a release. For example, one service may ask for a summary paragraph before you start the body of the release, while others may have no specific requirement. Some will invite you to submit multiple photos with captions, while others may limit you to one or two captioned photos. Some also have certain requirements for the size of the photos, such as no more than 399 pixels high or wide for Expert Click.

There also may be certain limitations in sending out the release, such as selecting certain targets and geographic areas for PR Web. While some services send out your release individually, others include along with multiple releases, which each begins with the opening lines of the release and a link to the full release, such as PRBuzz. Others, like ExpertClick, post your release for pickup by journalists and news services.

So be ready to adapt your release according to the specs of different services, and consider the different costs and approaches in deciding if you want to use a PR service and which one to use.

## Some Examples of Press Releases and Query Letters

Following are examples of successful press releases and query letters.

### A Press Release Sent as a Query Letter

The following was a release sent as a personalized query letter to invite the print media to pick up the article with bio information. It resulted in about 40 pick-ups and this media interest eventually led to a sale of the full book to a publisher, Nortia Press.

Subject Line: Article on How Inequality in America Leading to New Middle Ages; Offered at No Charge Due to Importance of Subject

Dear *********:

Because this issue is so important today, this article: "The New Middle Ages" is offered to you at no charge. The full article is 1000 words, but you can cut this down to a shorter article if you wish. Following is the opening paragraph that introduces the article. The complete article is included at the end of this letter.

"Today, as the rich get richer and the poor get poorer, it seems we are approach a new Middle Ages in America, as inequality increasingly spreads through the land. It is as if the superrich are like the new royalty and the top 1% living in mansions like the old castles of kings in the kingdoms that eventually melded into Europe and the U.K. Meanwhile, the media wields the power of the medieval church, placing its blessing on those with wealth and celebrity, who are protected by their retinue of publicists, handlers, lawyers, chauffeurs, and servants, much like the landed nobility who were part of the king's court created a protected and privileged enclave far removed from the much larger class of peasants who worked their land and paid their taxes, which supported the royalty and monarchy in their grand style."

If you wish to publish this article, we ask that you include the author's bio and website, and let us know where and when the article appears with a link to it. I can send you the author's photo in a JPEG if you want to include it with the article.

The author, Gini Graham Scott, based in San Francisco, brings to this topic an extensive background as a social commentator who writes about current trends, social issues, and everyday life as the author of 50+ books with major publishers and a Ph.D. in sociology. Should you be interested in other articles by her I can send you more information. These deal with the battle against Internet book pirates, the new developments in science, technology, business, and society that are changing everyone's life, and insights from everyday experiences.

I hope you will be interested in publishing this article which is designed to draw attention to what is becoming a crisis for American society.

Sincerely,

And here's the complete article: (Then followed a copy of the article from *The Huffington Post*).

**Release to the Media after the Book's Publication**

The following was sent to the media after the book was published to tie the book to a newsworthy topic, resulting in a half-dozen requests for review copies and interviews with a few major publications. It could have been sent as a personalized query as here or marked "For Immediate Release."

Subject Line: Trump's View: "We're Living in Medieval Times," Supported by New Middle Ages Book: Features Parallels Between Middle Ages and Life Today

372

Dear *********:

In CNN's "State of the Union" Talk show on October 25, Donald Trump made the comment that "We're living in Medieval times...We're living in an unbelievably dangerous and horrible world." Those statements are echoed in a recent book: *The New Middle Ages* from Nortia Press by sociologist Gini Graham Scott, Ph.D., who discusses how inequality today has led to parallels between modern life and society in the Middle Ages. Back then, the vast divide between the royalty, nobility, and rich merchants versus the peasants and artisans not only led to increasingly devastating conditions for the lower classes but inspired a series of peasant revolts – much like the growing waves of protests and attacks by terrorists today.

As Scott points out, such revolts are increasingly likely now and are already reflected in the protests of various groups like the Occupy Movement, the racial protests against police violence against lower income blacks, and the strikes by low wage workers at Walmart. Even terrorism has its roots in inequality and social injustice around the world.

A reason for the popularity of Donald Trump and Bernie Sanders is they have tapped into a growing resentment of politics as usual, such as described by Robert Reich, a U.C. economist and professor of public policy, in an article, "Revolt Against Ruling Class Elevates Trump, Sanders."

So yes, as Trump suggests, we are living in Medieval times, as Scott details in her book, which was inspired by the article: "The New Middle Ages," originally written for the Huffington Post and spread around the Internet by several dozen ezines and magazine publishers. As Scott illustrates, there are multiple parallels between now and then, such as the battles between the high tech titans much like medieval nobles fought for territory, the growing division of labor and income, the divergent lifestyles of the very rich and very poor, and the increasingly restive peasantry in the face of higher taxes to pay for the lifestyles and wars of the wealthy. It concludes with recommendations on what to do about the problem of inequality, which a growing number of billionaires, like Warren Buffet, are concerned about. For instance, Kenneth Langone, Home Depot founder and longtime GOP donor, describes inequality as his biggest fear in an article: "Why Conservative Billionaires Have Started Talking Like Bernie Sanders," because, "We are creating a caste system from which it's almost impossible to escape."

Reflecting Trump's comments, the book's comparison with medieval times presents a graphic image of the modern crisis and shows the need to inspire action to reduce inequality before it undermines the social order.

Gini Graham Scott has a PhD in Sociology from U.C. Berkeley, MAs in Anthropology and Pop Culture and Lifestyles from Cal State, East Bay, and is getting an additional MA there in Communications. She writes frequently on social trends and is the author of several dozen books with major publishers, including two books on current social themes and history: *The Very Next New Thing* and *Playing the Lying Game* with ABC-Clio. Her forthcoming books include: *Lies and Liars: How and Why Sociopaths Lie And How To Detect And Deal With Them* (Skyhorse Publishing 2016), *Internet Book Piracy* (Allworth Press 2016), and *Scammed* (Allworth Press 2017). She is the CEO of Changemakers Publishing and Writing (www.changemakerspublishingandwriting.com) and has a website at www.ginigrahamscott.com.

Please contact me for more information, setting up interviews, and a copy of the book.

# CHAPTER 62: USING THE SOCIAL MEDIA FOR PR

Using the social media has become one of the most important vehicles for promoting your books and programs, although I will only touch on it briefly, since it can be the subject of a book itself. I'll briefly note the best ways to work with these sites and list some of the major sites. For more information, check out the different sites to decide which work best for you, and look at some of the books about using that site.

## Working with the Major Social Media Sites

It's important to have a presence on at least some of the major social media. Aside from the big three – Facebook, Twitter, and LinkedIn, other social media sites include Pinterest, YouTube, Instagram, Tumblr, Reddit, and Google Plus, and others on the list below. It may be overwhelming to work with all of them, so pick out the half-dozen or so that are the best fit for your type of book or programs.

A good way to start is to choose two or three of the big three, and two or three of the other social media sites, and create an account in each of these. You can also create fan pages and company pages, or join groups on many of these sites. In selecting the groups to join, pick those with an interest related to the subject of your book or with the demographics that your book appeals to. For example, if your book is about food and nutrition, this would be a good fit with a group of moms with young kids.

Once your accounts are set up, plan to regularly post on these sites, and where you can include photos and videos, as well as links to your website, squeeze page, or sales page. On Twitter, you can create a central place for all your posts, called "tweets," by using the hashtag (#) sign and a short memorable name, such as #loveandlossbook.

Plan to post at least once a day and ideally two or three times a day, since these posts go by very quickly, because of the many people posting information. Vary your posts, including the pictures you use, so you are continually sharing something new. Don't only post promotional announcements about your books or programs, though you can do so occasionally. When you first join a group, don't start off with a promotional pitch, since people can think of this as spam. Rather, take some time to learn what people are talking about and join the conversation, such as by providing advice based on your expertise. This way you build a relationship and trust with others in the group, so they will be more receptive to your posts about your book and programs. Plus when you offer advice, the group members can come to regard you as an authority in the topic, which can help to interest them in your book and programs.

If you find the time commitment to the social media daunting, which many do, hire an assistant to post for you and engage in conversations with people who respond. A good source of help with these postings might be local high schools and colleges, neighborhood bulletin boards, or Craigslist. Or if you want to hire someone with social media experience, there are people all over the country who work in or own social media companies or are social media consultants and coaches. They can help you set up your social media campaign, as well as arrange to do the everyday postings for you. Still another source of help might be outsourcing these posts through a company like Fiverr (www.fiverr.com ), Upwork (www.upwork.com), or Guru (ww.guru.com), where you provide the copy, but the person you hire posts your announcement all over the social media sites you select on a regular time schedule.

After you select the particular social media to use, monitor the results to see which posts are turning into customers and clients. Continue to post on those sites that work for you, drop the others, and try out new social media networks.

## The Top Social Media Sites

Following are the top social media sites, according to some of the websites that do these rankings. I've listed the top 15 or 21, which are drawn from the following three sources:

- EbizMBA "Top 15 Most Popular Social Networking Sites: September 2015. (www.ebizmba.com/articles/social-networking-websites). This listing is based on each website's *Alexa* Global Traffic Rank and the U.S. Traffic Rank derived from both *Compete* and *Quantcast*, which includes the number of estimated monthly visitors.

- WebTrends, "Top 15 Social Networking Sites You Should Be Using" by Elise Moreau, a trends expert (http://webtrends.about.com/od/socialnetworkingreviews/tp/Social-Networking-Sites.htm)

- Social Media Today. The World's 21 Most Important Social Media Sites and Apps in 2015 by Randy Milanovic (www.socialmediatoday.com/social-networks/205-4-14/worlds-21-most-important-social-media-sites-and -apps-2015).

The top sites, which include the number of estimated monthly visitors, according to EbizMBA, are:

1) Facebook – 900,000,000. As the top social networking site, this is one you should be on. You can use it to share updates with photos, videos, create and join groups and set up fan pages where you can get unlimited fans, unlike the 5000 friends limit on your homepage.

2) Twitter – 310,000,000. This has become especially popular for real-time news sharing, and it is an ideal platform for mobile users. It has recently added some livestream video apps like Periscope.

3) LinkedIn – 255,000,000. The focus here is on business, careers, and linking people looking for job and business opportunities. It is an ideal site to make connections with other professionals and interact in group discussions, if you have a book or programs that would appeal to these groups.

4) Pinterest – 250,000,000. The way to connect on this site is by having images you can post, which can include covers of your book, photos from your workshops, and illustrations. Currently, the demographic is about 75% female, since Pinterest started off as a board for sharing beautiful images, art works, crafts, and food photos. But increasingly, it is appealing to a broader audience and becoming more business savvy.

5) Google Plus+ - 120,000,000. Gradually this site has started to take off, despite a slow start after it was launched in 2011. Plus there is growing excitement about other Google programs, such as Google Hangouts.

6) Tumblr – 110,000,000. This is a very popular social blogging platform and popular for sharing visual content, though it is heavily used by teens and younger users.

7) Instagram – 100,000,000. This app, which is only available to mobile users, enables users to post photos from their smartphone and pass them on to their connections on Twitter and Facebook. Should you have good photos to share from your book or programs, this could be a good promotional site.

8) VK – 80,000,000. This is Europe's largest social media site, which is set up like Facebook, with the same sort of profiles, messaging, and games. Users can enter both personal and professional information about themselves and follow or show support for organizations and businesses. If your book or programs can span the global community, this might be a good site to check out.

9) Flickr – 65,000,000. This is a site where you can upload, access, organize, edit, and share your photos from any device from anywhere in the world. This was one of the first networks for sharing images, before Pinterest and Instagram came on the scene. It is still a good place to upload photos and create albums, which might be a good fit if you have some strong images you use with your book or programs. It includes a weekly Flickr blog, where users can post photos along with copy about that photo.

10) Vine – 42,000,000. This is a mobile video-sharing app owned by Twitter. Its videos can be embedded on Twitter when shared through a tweet, and you can embed them on a website. The videos are limited to 6 seconds, but they can play on an autoloop which repeats again and again. It has become a major social network, and if you can convey your message about your book and programs with strong graphics, this could work for you.

11) Meetup – 40,000,000. This is a great network for organizing local groups around specific interests, and it features face-to-face get-togethers for group members. It's ideal for someone who is just developing an interest in something and wants to learn more, as well as for those who want to meet others socially or professionally with a shared interest. Besides joining groups, you can start groups around the subject of your book or programs, and you can earn money by inviting people to pay to attend workshops, seminars, and special events. I've used it for over a dozen groups myself, 6 of them still running that deal with learning

about and making connections in the publishing and film industries.

Some of the other sites listed on Webtrends are these:

YouTube – the second largest search engine. Although owned by Google and at one time tied into Google+ accounts, it is a separate social network that is focused around video production, vlogging (video blogs), movie-making, and music sharing.

Snapchat – This is a mobile-only social network which is based on instant messaging and "snaps" consisting of photos or short videos which automatically delete after viewing. As long as someone sees the photo or video, that can be enough to share your message.

Reddit – Reddit features submitted links to content which gets voted up or down by users. The links with the most upvotes get published to the page of their subreddits and recognized for having the best content. You can click on the subreddit you feel best fits your link. The site has generated some big hits that have gotten front page news coverage, such as supporting a fundraising campaign for a school bus driver who was humiliated by kids for being fat in a video that went viral. The campaign raised over $100,000 for her. So there is always the potential that a link to a video about your book or program could go viral, too.

Swarm (by Foursqure) – This app is used for seeing where your friends are, telling them where you are, and arranging to chat and meet at a specific location later. This might be a good tool to let people know if you are having an event somewhere, such as a book signing or workshop.

# ABOUT THE AUTHOR

Gini Graham Scott has published over 50 books with mainstream publishers, focusing on social trends, work and business relationships, and personal and professional development. Some of these books include *The Very Next New Thing, The Talk Show Revolution*, and *The Battle for Personal Privacy.*

She has gained extensive media interest for previous books, including appearances on *Good Morning America, Oprah, Montel Williams, CNN,* and hundreds of radio shows. She is often quoted by the media and has websites at www.ginigrahamscott.com and www.changemakerspublishingandwriting.com. She has about 60,000 listings in Google Search Results.

She has been a regular Huffington Post blogger since December 2012 and has a Facebook page for her books and films at www.facebook.com/changemakerspublishing.

She has written, produced, and sometimes directed over 60 short videos, which are featured on her Changemakers Productions website at www.changemakersproductions.com and on YouTube at www.youtube.com/changemakersprod.

Her screenplays, mostly in the drama, crime, legal thriller, and sci-fi genres, include several dealing with changes in science, technology, business, and society, including *The New Child, New Identity,* and *Dead No More.* These are in development with trailers, business plans, and interested directors and talent.

She has a PhD in sociology from U.C. Berkeley and MAs in anthropology, pop culture and lifestyles, recreation and tourism, and organizational/consumer/audience behavior from Cal State, East Bay. She is getting an MA in communications in 2017.

She is also the Creative Director of Publishers, Agents and Films (www.publishersagentsandfilms.com), a service which connects writers to publishers, agents, and the film industry.

Her feature, *Suicide Party #Save Dave*, which she wrote and executive produced, will be released by RSquared Films, in early 2016. Details: www.suicidepartyfilm.com.

# CHANGEMAKERS PUBLISHING
### 3527 Mt. Diablo Blvd., #273
### Lafayette, CA 94549
### changemakers@pacbell.net . (925) 385-0608
### www.changemakerspublishingandwriting.com